C000145524

Why Do Monsters Come Out at Night?

Why Do Monsters Come Out at Night?

Christine Fieldhouse

HAY HOUSE

Australia • Canada • Hong Kong
South Africa • United Kingdom • United States

First published and distributed in the United Kingdom by:
Hay House UK Ltd, 292B Kensal Rd, London W10 5BE. Tel.: (44) 20 8962 1230;
Fax: (44) 20 8962 1239. www.hayhouse.co.uk

Published and distributed in the United States of America by:
Hay House, Inc., PO Box 5100, Carlsbad, CA 92018-5100. Tel.: (1) 760 431 7695
or (800) 654 5126; Fax: (1) 760 431 6948 or (800) 650 5115. www.hayhouse.com

Published and distributed in Australia by:
Hay House Australia Ltd, 18/36 Ralph St, Alexandria NSW 2015. Tel.: (61) 2 9669
4299; Fax: (61) 2 9669 4144. www.hayhouse.com.au

Published and distributed in the Republic of South Africa by:
Hay House SA (Pty), Ltd, PO Box 990, Witkoppen 2068. Tel./Fax: (27) 11 706
6612. orders@psdprom.co.za

Published and distributed in India by:
Hay House Publishers India, Muskaan Complex, Plot No.3, B-2, Vasant Kunj, New
Delhi - 110 070. Tel.: (91) 11 41761620; Fax: (91) 11 41761630.
www.hayhouse.co.in

Distributed in Canada by:
Raincoast, 9050 Shaughnessy St, Vancouver, BC V6P 6E5. Tel.: (1) 604 323 7100;
Fax: (1) 604 323 2600

© Christine Fieldhouse, 2007

The moral rights of the author have been asserted.

All rights reserved. No part of this book may be reproduced by any mechanical,
photographic or electronic process, or in the form of a phonographic recording; nor
may it be stored in a retrieval system, transmitted or otherwise be copied for public
or private use, other than for 'fair use' as brief quotations embodied in articles and
reviews, without prior written permission of the publisher.

The author of this book does not dispense medical advice or prescribe the use of
any technique as a form of treatment for physical or medical problems without the
advice of a physician, either directly or indirectly. The intent of the author is only
to offer information of a general nature to help you in your quest for emotional and
spiritual wellbeing. In the event you use any of the information in this book for
yourself, which is your constitutional right, the author and the publisher assume no
responsibility for your actions.

A catalogue record for this book is available from the British Library.

ISBN 978-1-4019-1544-5

Printed and bound in Great Britain by TJ International, Padstow, Cornwall.

Dedication

In memory of my mum, Margaret Ellen Fieldhouse.

Contents

Acknowledgements

My special thanks go to my husband Ian Cross and our son Jack, for their love, laughter, fun and friendship, and to my brother Chris and his wife Eva for being there in good times and bad. I'd also like to pay tribute to my late uncle, John Shackleton, a good friend to us all.

Thanks to my agent, Jacqueline Burns, for spotting potential in that very first draft, Phil Olley for his Focus Group seminars and regular coaching, and the team at Hay House for being so lovely to work with. Finally, thank you to my good friends – for their wise words, for reading manuscripts and for their excitement and enthusiasm while I've been writing this book.

Preface

Over the years I have marvelled, laughed and sobbed my way through the classics, to chick lit, mum-lit, and then the misery book genre. As I read the latter, and lived through the sexual and physical abuse children and young people have suffered, I have been horrified by their harrowing experiences.

Jane Elliott's *The Little Prisoner* is still half-read by my bed because the sexual abuse scenes were so shocking, they gave me terrible, vivid nightmares for weeks. Yet I was also uplifted that people like Jane Elliott had survived the most awful childhoods and lived to write these books.

On one level, I feel fortunate that the abuse I suffered as a child and teenager was primarily mental – but I know from experience how harrowing, terrifying and hurtful this kind of cruelty can be. The old saying, 'Sticks and stones may break my bones, but words will never hurt me,' is so untrue.

Having shelved my baggage in the past, I was chugging along quite nicely until 2000, when my own life changed drastically. Our son was born, then, four months later, my beloved mum died, and I was catapulted through a range of emotions that included grief, regret, joy, gratitude and sadness. As I grew into my role as a mother, I started to think about the kind of mum I am and the mum I had lost and I realised what a hard job being a mum is.

I searched my mum's home for notes which she may have hidden away for me to read after she had gone, for clues about her life and snippets of information I hadn't known, but I searched in vain. I couldn't get enough information about her-life, her loves, her childhood, her marriage, her parenting style (though I'm sure parenting styles didn't exist in my mum's down-to-earth, non-analytical world) and her adulthood. When she was here, I thought I knew it all, but after she had gone her death left so many questions unanswered for me.

It must have been part of the healing process, but the more I bonded with our son and mourned the loss of my ally, my mum, the more I questioned how my father could treat us, his family, the way he had. How could my life be devoted to making my son as happy, confident and cheerful as possible while my dad's was geared towards making us miserable, insecure, nervous and terrified? What had made him like that, I wondered. How could he live with himself, I asked.

At the start of 2005 I decided to write about my childhood in the hope that, whatever happens in the future, I leave no questions unanswered for our own son. But I didn't want it to be a story of total misery. My life as a mum, a wife and a journalist is happy, exciting and fulfilling. I wanted our son to see how happy, angry, delighted and frustrated he has made me, how scary my past was, yet how enlightening it has been to try to make sense of it. I would like my son to see how I have striven to become a good enough mum for him, in a desperate attempt to ensure that history doesn't repeat itself in my generation.

I hope this is more than a story of mere survival, though survival in itself is laudable. I hope my readers experience the real excitement and pain I have felt in understanding the past and coming to terms with it. I hope it's a book of contrasts which reflect the rollercoaster of emotions that families put you through.

I know some readers will find it shocking while others may label me a drama queen for exposing the past to public scrutiny.

Even within families there are different memories of the same event, so what to me constitutes abuse may be viewed as discipline by another. On occasions, even my brother and I had very different reactions to our father's drunken outbursts – while I was afraid and nervous, my brother seemed more accepting and tolerant.

But if just one person reads this book, having suffered some form of abuse themselves, and feels empowered by the book, so much the better. If, back in 1966, I had had a crystal ball to 2007, I would have felt so much stronger and so much more capable of dealing with what was then to me, a frightened child, a living hell.

CHAPTER 1

Why Do Monsters Come Out at Night?

I'm lying in bed. I'm four, with bandy little legs, and short, dark hair. I wear a coloured ribbon in my hair when we go out so people know I'm a girl, but my mum has already taken it out for bed. The mattress is lumpy and bumpy, but I'm small and thin so I can snuggle down between the ridges if I lie slightly angled on my side.

Like the rest of our house, my bedroom's cold. We have two coal fires downstairs, so if you sit right on top of them, in the living room or dining room, you're warm. But go through the door between the living room and the staircase to come upstairs, and the cold air hits you like a smack in the face. The tip of my nose is freezing, and when I breathe out lying in bed, little whirls of steam float off into the semi-darkness.

I'm surrounded by dark, old-fashioned, heavy furniture – a big wardrobe, a sideboard and a huge blanket box – not the bright white units my friends have in their bedrooms. My dolls, just two of them, Jane and Babykins, sit on the blanket box. My brother's old teddy, Fred, looks out quietly from the corner, still loved but not needed as much these days.

Our house creaks all the time. I used to think the creaks came from monsters in the airing cupboard, which is also in my room. I slept on my left side for ages with a watchful eye on the airing cupboard door, but nothing ever came out.

1

I'm sure my brother Chris told me once there were monsters in our house – well, maybe just the one. When I asked him again what he said, he looked away from me quickly and said: 'Nothing, I was joking.' But he put the idea of monsters firmly in my mind, and the airing cupboard is the only place I can think of for them to hide. My brother must know. He's nine years older than me and he knows absolutely everything.

As well as the creaks, I can hear the people next door in their kitchen. Every little noise carries in our semi-detached houses. I can even hear them run their tap to fill their kettle. Then I hear Mrs Stanger ask her son Malcolm if he wants a cup of tea. I was right, she was filling the kettle.

They're nice, gentle people, an old mum and her son. He's grown-up, not a little boy. They go to church every Sunday and they always say hello to me when I'm playing out. They say it gently, as though I need to be taken care of, not confidently and loud, the way they talk to some of the kids round here, especially when their footballs have gone in their garden. It feels like they're protecting me in a way, but I don't know what from or why.

I can't hear my mum pottering around downstairs. She's probably having a snooze in the armchair by the fire.

I wriggle around and my feet find a hot water bottle. My bed is full of them. One's a proper one, a blue one, but it's wearing a bit thin now with age. The ribbing has all gone. My mum has started filling old bleach bottles with boiling water for me and wrapping them in old towels or socks. She puts them in bed about an hour before I come upstairs, and they warm it a little and she usually takes them out before I get into bed. Sometimes if it's really cold she leaves them near my feet while I get off to sleep. But by morning all but the proper one are gone.

2

Tonight, as usual, she had read me a story, then come back upstairs and kissed me good night for a second time. She chatted while she put the ironing away in the airing cupboard. As she opened the door I craned my neck to see inside, but all that was there was a huge pile of towels and bedding. I don't mind her opening the airing cupboard door, but I'd never open it myself if I were alone.

I love it when my mum does jobs in my room while I doze off. I feel so secure. I know she'll look out for me, keep those monsters away and fight them if they appear. She might be smaller than a lot of people, my mum, but I think of her as tough, and I feel safe to close my eyes and drift off to sleep while she quietly folds bedding in the background. Every now and then I hear a little sigh as she tries to cram even more things into drawers, or the sound of a wardrobe door clicking shut. Sometimes she says to herself quietly: 'Another job done.'

◆◆◆◆◆

I've just started school and my teachers are Mrs Alderson and Mrs Sykes. I love telling my mum things about school. I just have to tell her something Mrs Sykes or Mrs Alderson said and she remembers it for ever. She doesn't even get muddled and say the wrong teacher said it. It's brilliant talking to her. She looks at me and listens as though every single word I say is important to her. Even when I told her about Richard, a boy in my class, weeing in a grate, she asked me if he got told off and which grate it was. She seems to have a mind for detail.

Once my mum has kissed me good night, I know I have just a few hours to get some sleep. Then Chris tucks me in.

Chris has been into my room already so it must be after 10pm now. He comes to my room every night before he goes to

3

bed and pulls my sheets and blankets back to tidy them. The lilac candlewick eiderdown with the cream fringe round is the last to go over me.

I start to wake when Chris does this. Sometimes the dust from the covers makes me sneeze. Sometimes I just feel a draught. In summer it's nice to have that nightly breeze, but in winter in our house, where there is no central heating, I wish he wouldn't bother. Tonight it's freezing.

It takes me ages of zig-zagging my legs round the bed like windscreen wipers to get warm again. I try lying on my front. That seems to warm up the bed. Then I turn over, but I don't go back to sleep. I lie there waiting for the car to come.

Last night I heard my mum and Chris talking really quietly outside my room. There's something about the car coming home that worries them. I could tell from their voices. My mum's voice sounded wobbly, as though she might cry, but she didn't. Chris's voice sounded scared. He said, 'Oh God, no' a lot.

The only other time I heard my mum's voice nervous like that was the other day when she talked to my granddad. We were all in the dining room and the fire was roaring up the chimney. Outside it had just started to snow.

'He's getting worse, Ike,' she said. 'I know you're his father, but I can't help it. I just don't know what's got into him. It's all the time.'

My granddad said somebody was a fool, but I couldn't make out who he meant.

We live in Yorkshire and my granddad always calls me and my mum 'lass' instead of our names. With some people it sounds as though they're angry, but when my granddad says it, it's full of love. He also calls her Nellie. It's shortened from her name, Margaret Ellen.

◆◆◆◆◆

I love my mum so much, but I'm sometimes so ashamed of her in that old brown raggy coat she takes me to school in. It hangs in the kitchen so it reeks of cooking, too.

This morning, on the way to school, I asked: 'Mum, could you wash this coat?'

'It needs dry cleaning,' she explained, 'and that would cost too much.'

I know there isn't much money for us kids and my mum, and if Chris comes home from school needing money for school, I can see from her face she's worried. It's as though she's really concentrating, as my teachers tell me I have to at school. She always finds the money from somewhere, though.

Sometimes, when my mum talks about Chris's childhood, her whole face lights up. Her hazel eyes seem to sparkle and look more green than brown when she's happy. She says what a gorgeous little lad he was and how they even went on holiday to Filey and to our great-uncle's farm in Wales.

'He had great big laughing eyes, and such long eyelashes,' she tells us. 'Everyone used to stop and say: "What a gorgeous-looking little boy."' Then she starts to reminisce.

My mum laughs for ages at her cheeky son and her eyes shine. I love hearing about times when she was happy, when she wore nice suits and weighed 8st 3lb, not 6st like now.

I've never heard her say anything like that about when I was a baby. It's not that she didn't love me, I know she did and still does. It's just that Chris laughed and giggled and had loads of fun and made everyone happy. My mum often sits me on her knee and tells me: 'I love you so much. Thank God I have you, my little Chrissie.'

When my granddad sees her looking at me, he says: 'She'll

be a big help to you one day, lass. Mark my words.'

My mum smiles back.

'These kids are the best thing I ever did, Ike,' she says, focusing on a spot beyond my granddad so she doesn't cry.

◆◆◆◆◆

I seem to have been dozing lightly for just a few minutes when I hear the sound of the car arriving. I listen carefully, my head slightly lifted from the pillow so no sound goes unheard. I can't hear as well when my ear is squashed against a pillow.

The car engine stops just before the garage. I listen for footsteps. They're fairly even. Any shouting or swearing around the garage lock and I know he's in a bad mood. I can't hear anything. He's obviously got his key in. I hear the roll of the garage doors. They slide round on little castors. I hear the engine start up, the car goes in, the car door closes and the doors slide back. Then I listen to footsteps up the drive. Night after night it's the same.

I lie there alert, listening for every small sound. My body is rigid. Seconds are vital to me. Even the squeak of the bedsprings could mask a much more important sound. I will our dog Dinky not to bark. I need to hear every step, every word. I need to be prepared. Whatever happens, I must be prepared. My heart is thumping.

I hear him come through the back door into the kitchen. He's talking to my mum, that's a good sign. I can't make out the words, but the tone is even. I strain to hear exact words. He even laughs. It's an odd exaggerated laugh, as though he might be choking. Any longer and you'd start to wonder if he was OK. It's a bit manic, but at least he's happy if he's laughing. He doesn't seem angry tonight.

I hear him come slowly upstairs. He's careful about every

one of our 14 steps. There's the creak of floorboards at the top of the landing that tells me he's turning to the bathroom. He pees for a very long time, as he always does when he gets in at night. Then he walks along the landing and puts his head round my brother's door. My door is ajar, so I can hear clearly.

'Good night, Topher,' he says. Sometimes he calls my brother Topher Bill. None of us knows why and none of us asks. His name isn't Christopher William or anything. It's John Christopher, but my mum chose to call him Christopher when people started calling him Little John. We have an Uncle John, you see. My mum couldn't hack Big John and Little John.

'Sounds like bloody Robin Hood,' she'd said long before I was born. 'From now on he'll be Christopher.'

Nobody questioned that, apparently. They just accepted it, and started calling the baby Christopher, and later Chris. When I was born, there were serious problems with my blood, and I was christened Christine very quickly in hospital in Bradford. No one ever questioned them calling their children Christopher and Christine. Anyway, we always knew which one of us people were talking to.

He's finished with Chris, and he's walking along the short landing to my room. My door opens. I close my eyes and try to look peaceful. Thank God, he never takes my pulse.

'Good night, Old Pige,' he says. I nod my head to make out I'm half-asleep, but I've heard him. The way he says 'Good' is the key. If he draws out the 'oo' sound, I know he's in a good mood. He's doing just that now. I don't know why I'm an 'old pigeon' to him, but he makes it sound an OK thing to be. It's better than some of the things he's called us. I once heard him say 'cow' to my mum. I lie perfectly still. He goes to bed. As his door closes, I breathe properly again. I'm so relieved he's not angry.

My mum appears at my door. Without even opening my eyes, I can tell she's there as her lighter weight makes different creaks in our floorboards. She's still dressed. She's never been one of these women who get their nighties on at 8pm. She says she needs to feel in control.

I don't have to pretend for my mum. She knows damn well I'm awake. My eyes are wide now, waiting for her report. She looks content, as though a big weight has been temporarily lifted from her shoulders. Just for tonight, at least.

'He's OK, Chris, he isn't angry tonight,' she tells me. 'He's gone to bed. Are you all right?'

I nod my head, and she kisses me on my forehead. She tucks some sheets and blankets in,

'Get some sleep now, love, you've got school tomorrow,' she whispers. I nod. She looks at me as if to say: 'You're almost five years old, for God's sake. You shouldn't still be awake at almost 1am.'

I hear her walk downstairs, calmer, slower steps altogether now. I turn onto my side. It's safe to have one ear on the pillow now. I don't need to listen out a hundred per cent now.

Minutes later, my mum comes back upstairs. She turns the landing light off and goes to bed. Sometimes, if my dad is angry, the light stays on.

My heart rate slows down, my body relaxes once more into the grooves of that lumpy mattress. At least the fear has made me warmer. I drift off to sleep, safe in the knowledge that it isn't going to happen tonight.

◆◆◆◆◆

Tonight I'm doing one of those magazine quizzes, about the various roles you have in your life. I've scored OK, though I think 'Lover' should get extra points – but I can't really go out and take a lover just to get a few extra points in a quiz. I'm not sure my husband Ian would appreciate the motive. Besides, I've nothing to wear to meet a lover in, and there's something I want to watch on telly.

Here's what I have so far:

Wife.

Mother.

Journalist.

Sister.

Daughter.

Daughter-in-law.

Friend.

Pet owner.

Finely-tuned long-distance athlete (I've just done a half-marathon).

Do-gooder (I'm raising money for charity with my runs).

'Mum, can I get out of the bath yet?' my son Jack calls. 'Have you finished your quiz? Did you win? Will you get a trophy or a certification?'

'Yes, coming,' I say, quickly checking I've added my points up right. We live in a bungalow, so I haven't really left my son upstairs in a bath while I idly sit doing a trivial quiz in some far-flung living room. I'm next door in the dining room. Six feet away from the bath really, and all the doors are open in between, just in case North Yorkshire's Social Services are reading and preparing to send a team round.

In our bungalow, we're never far away from each other, whether we're in the shower or the kitchen. All rooms lead off a main corridor, just as in sheltered accommodation, except I'm 43, not 73.

Jack literally jumps out of the bath in one of those moves that could split his head open on the bath or the wash basin if he slipped.

'Jack!' I shout, grabbing him. 'Pack that in! It's dangerous.'

'I know, Mum, but I didn't slip. Blood didn't gush out of my head. I'm never going to crack my head open, am I?'

He's disappointed.

I love him for having the confidence and courage I never had at his age. He asks questions and is eager to know things. He doesn't give a damn if we get angry with him. The very worst that could happen is I'd shout for a second, or confiscate a toy. If I threaten to tell Daddy, we all know Daddy will say: 'Jack, I hope that isn't true?' and it will all be forgotten.

How different his childhood is to mine. When I look at our school photos, he's laughing and happy, while I'm a frightened little girl with brown lifeless eyes. When I look at Jack's school photos, I get a surge of excitement and joy; yet when I look at my own, I want to scoop that little girl up in my arms and hold her head to my chest and protect her.

Jack is all clean and sweet-smelling. I wrap him in a warm fluffy towel and carry him to his bedroom. With his long legs, he seems nearly as tall as me. I cuddle him on the bed for that skin-to-skin contact I read about when he was a baby but I never wanted back then. Then I just wanted to plonk him in a cot with a dummy, while I exhaustedly tackled the washing. They could keep all their naked bonding. I didn't have time for that malarkey.

Instead I want it now. I must be a late bonder. I know my days are numbered. He's four now. He accepts his sad mother has to lie on a bed and stroke his back after he's had a bath and tell him 50 times he's gorgeous and she wants to marry him. At seven he's never going to let his mother cuddle him naked and propose an incestuous marriage. I know I have to make the most of it.

'Mummy,' he asks, with big brown eyes staring into mine. 'Why do monsters come out at night?'

'I don't know any monsters, Jack,' I answer, not completely truthfully. 'What do you mean?'

I'm struggling to get him into his pyjamas, but he wriggles and escapes and is off to the living room before I can catch him.

'Come here, you monkey!' I call, seeing him hurtling towards the door leading out into the sheltered accommodation corridor. He's killing himself laughing. He loves these games of tag when I'm completely knackered.

'The vampires in the wardrobe and the skeletons under the bed,' he tells me, nodding his head furiously as if to verify their existence.

I can't bear him to be scared. I would sit by his bed all night long to protect him, no matter how tired I was. I look at his face. I think he believes this stuff about skeletons and monsters.

'Let me just have a look,' I say, feeling courageous.

Here I am, going out of my way to make Jack feel safe and comfortable, yet my own dad didn't give a toss about his child at exactly this age. If I make Jack happy I feel like performing a song and dance routine like a cheerleader, so how come my dad didn't want to make me happy, and sometimes went out of his way to make me very unhappy and frightened?

I get on my knees and look under the double bed.

'Nope, no skeletons under there,' I say, as I turn to the wardrobes. 'Not a single vampire. Now here is Flower the super-hero Skunk, and here's Leo. They're tough and they'll look after you.'

His pyjamas are on. I'm on the home stretch. Just toilet and milk left before we can settle down and read.

'Jack, how can you be afraid when you have all these Power Rangers here too?'

I look round the bedroom. It is seriously cluttered. *Life Laundry* could do an entire series on our house and fill 300 bags for recycling, 2,000 for the crusher and 1,000 for the charity shop.

Jack doesn't look convinced that those mighty Power Rangers would spring to his defence. He's wrinkled up his nose and started to frown, implying I've lost the plot about the protection capabilities of toy Power Rangers.

'Remember Buzz and Woody and the way all the toys came alive as soon as Andy went out of the room?' I ask. I should know. I watched *Toy Story* at least a hundred times when he was three. 'They wake up and look after you!'

I'm rabbiting on in the hope he'll go to sleep early tonight. I'm pretty laid back about the washing these days. I tackle it twice a week and iron as little as possible. No, tonight, the carrot dangling before me is getting *my* pyjamas on early to watch *You Are What You Eat*. I love it when Dr Gillian McKeith piles up the food her case studies have eaten in a week. All those congealed fish and chips and bacon, sausages and fried eggs. There's fat dripping everywhere. Even better is her face when she analyses their faeces. It's as though she's astonished they're so smelly.

Even *How Clean Is Your House?* on some remote Sky Channel is a laugh. When Aggie and Kim find mouse droppings in other people's grillpans, it makes me so much more confident about my own housekeeping skills.

Jack looks at me as if I'm barmy, believing that thing about toys coming alive at night. I look at my watch. I have 20 minutes before Dr Gillian McKeith walks down the road, wearing red, to knock on the door of her latest target.

I get in bed with him, prop up our pillows and get out a *Brer Rabbit* book.

'Lovely, lovely Enid Blyton,' I say, opening the hardback book.

'Who the heck is he, Mum?' asks Jack.

'She's a lady, Jack. She wrote *Brer Rabbit*,' I answer, delighted we're having our first literary conversation. I can see us at Book Fairs and Literature Festivals when he's older.

Jack looks as me as though I can't possibly be thinking straight.

'Mu-u-um,' he says, speaking slowly because he obviously thinks I'm thick. 'Brer Rabbit wrote his own story. He's written in my book – "To Jack, enjoy my story, Brer Rabbit." He even put a kiss.'

'So he did,' I say, shaking my head to myself at such lovely innocence. Imagine a world where rabbits write their autobiographies. How fantastic would that be? And what brilliant naming and shaming for that nasty fella Brer Fox!

I lie in the double bed, stroking his slightly damp brown hair. It isn't as dark as Ian's and mine. He has the same chubby cheeks I had, the same dark brown eyes, though his are bigger like his dad's. But there's happiness and excitement in Jack's eyes, as we read about Brer Rabbit and The Teapot, not the dull fear and worry I had throughout my childhood and teens. I can't bear his sadness ever. In times of real misery, like when he has fallen over and hurt his knee, I want to pluck out my own heart and hand it to him.

'Do you know anyone as nasty as Brer Fox?' Jack asks.

'Not any more, sweetie,' I answer.

Jack knows my dad was in the Brer Fox league of nastiness. I've never given him details, just hinted at the different kind of childhood I had, but it's obvious we're both thinking of my dad now. As I look at our inquisitive little son, I wonder how anyone could ever hurt a child so small, so full of innocence. And worse still, how can they live with themselves once they've mistreated a child?

'Was your daddy worser than Brer Fox?' Jack asks, unable to grasp there could be a greater rogue than the bushy-tailed one.

But he doesn't wait for my answer. The word 'daddy' has moved that active little brain along a step or two, even though we're now settling down our pillows, getting ready to go to sleep. Or rather one of us is hopefully going to sleep. The other is getting ready to creep out and watch telly.

'Will my daddy be home soon?' he asks. Was it telepathy, I wonder. Could he possibly have read my mind, tuned in to my thoughts about my own dad coming home at night?

His voice is almost singing at the thought of his dad coming home. There's no need for Jack to lie awake and analyse his dad's footsteps.

I realize how lucky I am. My own mum must have lived in fear every single night of her married life. Imagine being terrified of your own husband coming home and hurting your children. I wonder for a minute why she stayed, then realize she probably had no choice in those days. She was totally dependent financially on my dad. She was also very, very scared of losing us kids in a custody battle, which he threatened now and then to scare her out of leaving, I suspect.

'He won't be too long,' I say. 'He's playing squash, then he'll come and say good night to you. It's the very first thing Daddy does when he gets home.'

'What exactly does he say?' asks Jack.

'He says: "Good night, little fella," and he kisses you, and then he says: "Sleep tight."'

'Bloomin' brilliant,' says Jack, with a contented sleepy smile.

I grin to myself. Jack has picked up his latest new phrase from his role model, an old man who has never travelled out of North Yorkshire.

Now, if the skies are cloudy, Jack announces: ''Appen it might rain today.' If he's not well, he feels 'out of sorts' and when we were in Jamaica on holiday, and I was running to get on the water slide, Jack shouted: 'Mum, wait for me, I'm not as young as I used to be!'

He's a strange role model, this old man, but from a doting Mummy point of view, it could be 40 years before Jack says 'fuck' and 'bollocks' if 'bloomin' brilliant' is as good as it gets.

As he drifts off, his knees go out to the side. His arms go over his head. He moves his head from side to side to get comfortable. He might be four but he still looks like the little baby he once was. The profile's still there, with his high forehead, those scrummy toddler cheeks and that delicious button nose.

He may be thinking about Brer Rabbit, his dad, Power Rangers or Buzz and Woody. He doesn't look like he's thinking about monsters in wardrobes or lying nervously, waiting for a car to bring home a man full of anger. He's like a rag doll, limp, relaxed and content. There's a bottle of white wine already open in the fridge and my programme's just starting. Result.

CHAPTER 2

Can My Friends Come Round?

The next morning, I feel a light touch on my arm. I'm lying on my back, cuddling a little floppy panda. Pandy wasn't with me when I went to sleep, so someone must have been in and put him there.

It's hard to even open my eyes. I'm so warm in bed at last, and my eyes are so tired. My whole body aches with tiredness. I've got a throbbing pain in what feels like the very middle of my head. I really hope it's the weekend. I can't get up for school. I don't think I can even walk downstairs, let alone half a mile up the road to school.

'Chris,' whispers my mum, softly, as though she can read my thoughts. 'It's 8 o'clock, you have school today. C'mon love.'

I stretch a little, but as I do, I feel every muscle in my body wants to rest. I could sleep for the whole day. I wouldn't even need looking after.

I know my dad will have already got up and gone to work. I'm not quite sure what he does. He comes home in a suit so he must have a fairly important job.

I know I love my mum and my brother, but it's hard to say with my dad. Sometimes he seems really angry with us all, yet other times he takes me for long walks, we hold hands and I ask him all sorts of questions. There are days when I feel he really loves all of us, yet others when I think he hates us. It doesn't make sense to me at the moment.

My mum gets up early every morning to light the fires so the house is warm for the rest of us. She's an early bird, she says. She loves mornings and she seems so much happier at breakfast than she does at teatime.

'Chris, c'mon, sweetheart, get up,' she urges me, now in a louder voice, yet still stroking my hair as though she doesn't really want to force me out of bed.

As I walk to the bathroom, I feel as though my legs might give way. I'm seriously tired. My mum senses this and looks worried.

'You need some breakfast for energy,' she jollies me along as she helps me wash my hands and face, but her eyes look anxious.

Once we're downstairs, we turn left through the door to go through the living room, then the kitchen, and right into the dining room.

My mum likes to keep our living room for 'best'. It's usually all tidy and clean, with our new three-piece suite with the pattern on and the fringe round the bottom and the edges of the cushions. The carpet's light grey with a diamond-shaped flowery pattern, and there's a grey square soft rug right in front of the fire.

On the fireplace there are our best ornaments, Beswick china cows and their calves, and mares with foals, which cost a lot of money. When people come in this room, they always say: 'Oooh, what a lovely living room.'

This is the room my dad sits in when he gets home from work, and we sometimes sit in here and watch television at night. I sometimes wonder what goes on in here when we're in bed. Now and then we find the odd splinter of china, a tiny piece of glass on the carpet or a stain on the carpet my mum's trying desperately to get out.

Once you're through the living room, you're into the messy part of the house. The kitchen is small, with a little fridge, an electric cooker and a few white units. It's fairly clean, but what makes it look scruffy are the rugs all over the lino. My mum says we trample in so much mud and dirt we have to have these rugs down.

Our dining room is completely different to our living room. It's full of old furniture and dog hairs. We have a red carpet that my dad chose. My mum hates it because she says it shows up all the dog hairs. She's discovered a rubber-soled shoe of hers will gather up the dog hairs if it's dragged along the carpet. Sometimes she wears the shoe on her foot to clean up the dog hairs by dragging her feet along the carpet. Other times she goes round on hands and knees with the shoe on her hand like a glove.

The wallpaper in this room is cream with a few small figures on. If you look really closely, you can see an uneven surface where my mum has scratched the pattern out. My mum has always said birds on anything in the house – wallpaper, pictures, cups, plates – are unlucky. But she hadn't spotted the flying geese on our new wallpaper until it was up and too late, so she went round with a pair of scissors one night and scratched them all off.

'We don't need any more bad luck in this house,' she said, scratching with determination.

◆◆◆◆◆

Chris is sitting at the teak table in here now. He's already wearing his school uniform and he's quickly spooning cornflakes into his mouth, but every now and then he turns to his left to the fireplace to check the clock.

He has to get two buses to his grammar school, one into town and one out again, and if he doesn't get the 5-past-8 bus from the top of our road, he'll never make it to school on time.

I don't have cereal in the mornings much. The cold milk seems to make me sick, so I have warm toast with butter on. Sometimes, if the fire's been blazing for quite a while, my mum gets out her long fork and toasts my bread on the fire. Once I've had my toast and warm milk, I start to feel more alive, and I get dressed into my bottle-green school uniform in front of the fire.

I pull my bottle-green knickers on under my nightie so my brother doesn't see anything. There's no need to bother anyway, he's in such a hurry for school.

'Tara, Mum,' he calls to my mum.

'See ya, Chris,' he waves to me, as he grabs his brown leather satchel and dashes through the back door.

'Bye love,' my mum calls back, 'be careful.'

She acts quite blasé until he's through the door, then she goes through to the living room window to watch him all the way up the road. There are two busy roads along the top of ours, separated by a traffic island. Two years ago, Chris was knocked down by a white car that drove off after it hit him. The police never caught the driver, my mum tells people when they ask. Chris was rushed off to hospital, and my mum still cries when she remembers his bruised little body.

I know, every morning when she says, 'Be careful,' she's thinking of the moment there was a knock at our door and some-one shouted: 'Your Christopher's been knocked down.'

She can't see Chris cross the road to the bus terminus as the section of road where he crosses is out of sight of our front window, but once he's on the double-decker bus, if he sits upstairs at the front, she can see him and she breathes a sigh of relief.

◆◆◆◆◆

It's just me and my mum in the house, and I'm nearly ready for school. I don't feel as tired in my arms, legs and back, just in my head, especially my eyes. I feel if I closed them, they'd go straight back to sleep even though I'm standing up. As I bend to fasten my T-bar black patent shoes, I could just keel over.

My school is a 15-minute walk away, alongside one of the busy roads that Chris has to cross to get his bus to go in the other direction towards the city centre. Once we've crossed the roads leading to two schools – the Catholic school and a comprehensive school – there's quite a wide footpath and some grass at the side of the road so we children can run and play while our mums walk and chat. It's always mums, there are never any dads. If it's just me and my mum, I hold her hand and we chat.

Sometimes my friends and their mums call at the door for me and my mum to walk with them. Some of the mums love getting into our kitchen for a chat with my mum. But this only happens if my dad's not there. If he is, my mum will say we're not quite ready and we'll catch our friends up.

But today they come in. Betty, by far the most entertaining of the mums, has just called in. She isn't even going to school. She's on her way to the shops with her new baby. Betty has short jet-black hair and she's always going to the hairdresser's to have it set to make it look like corrugated iron. She's got sharp little blue eyes that seem to narrow when she asks you a question.

Betty has a whole list of health problems that she likes to discuss with my mum, including what she calls 'time-of-month things'. I'm not quite sure what they are, but I know they put Chris off his cornflakes. When Betty starts pointing to her crotch, Chris pushes his cereal bowl away and is first at the bus stop. He'll be glad he's missed her this morning.

Now and then, Betty asks my mum questions about our home and my dad. She isn't alone. A lot of people try, but my mum never gives anything away. Whatever worries my mum, whatever she was talking to my granddad about, and to Chris on the landing, she never tells anyone.

I listen really carefully because I want to know what's going on, too. It's like there's a big secret inside our house. I wonder if that's what makes my dad so angry.

I think our neighbours Mr and Mrs Stanger might know something, too. Because their house is joined onto our house, and Mrs Stanger's bedroom is right next to my mum and dad's room, they must hear some things, especially when my dad's angry and he shouts at my mum. I sometimes think my mum will be like Mrs Stanger when she's older because they both have slim figures and a gentle way about them.

A week ago, Mrs Stanger said to my mum: 'I don't know how you and them kids cope, Margaret, I really don't.' But she said it quietly, in a tone that implied she'd never say a word to anyone else. You don't know how grateful that made my mum. She looked as though some of her worries had vanished, just like that.

Betty is probing now.

'Are you a bit tired today, Margaret?' she asks, looking carefully at my mum. Those eyes are narrowing with every word.

'Yes, I didn't sleep well,' replies my mum.

It's true, my mum looks shattered. She has dark circles beneath her eyes.

'It's this blasted cough,' says my mum, putting her palm flat on her chest. 'It's keeping me awake a lot of the night. It's one of these bugs that everyone's getting.'

Betty's face falls with disappointment. No shared intimacies, no confidences there then. Just a made-up cough.

I copy my mum, and if people ask me a question about home, I say as little as possible.

'Is your dad OK?' they ask me.

'Yes, he's OK,' I say.

When they see I'm not offering any more information, they shut up. I know my mum doesn't want anyone knowing about our lives.

'We don't want them to feel sorry for us and pity us,' she once told Chris, while I was listening. 'The less they know, the better. Besides, your dad would go mad if he thought we'd been talking.'

So I've learned to give nothing away. People probably think I'm a bit thick. I suppose I am. I don't have a clue what's happening in my own home, just my dad gets angry and my mum, brother and Granddad are worried.

◆◆◆◆◆

I love school. I love learning and reading and writing. The only thing I don't love is when we all sit on the floor near Mrs Sykes or Mrs Alderson and listen to a story. The stories are really good. It's just I get scared I might fall asleep during them. There's usually one at the end of the morning, just before my mum comes for me to go home for lunch, and by then I'm so tired.

But fresh air on the walk home wakens me. I'm glad I don't stay for school dinners. I don't know why I don't have them. Maybe my mum just likes seeing me. I know I like seeing her. On our way home, we talk about school and what my mum's been doing. Sometimes she's been to the shops, other times she's done the washing. If it's Thursday, she dusts the skirting boards.

I have a quick sandwich or some tomato or beef soup, and we set off back. Then my mum's at the school gate by 3.30pm when I finish.

◆◆◆◆◆

When we get home from school, we race straight to our garden. Because it's winter, my friends are allowed in the old shed right next to our rabbit hutches under the dining room window, as long as their mums know where they are. We make the hut into a schoolroom, or a hospital, or a vet's surgery. Sometimes the rabbits are our 'patients' at our vet's surgery.

My mum doesn't mind my friends coming round for an hour after school, but as the time gets nearer 5, she comes out to tell the children it's time to go home as she's cooking tea.

'Come along, come inside,' she says to me. 'Your dad will be home soon.'

I know better than to start arguing. When my dad's due home, my mum is anxious to please and keep the peace.

◆◆◆◆◆

My mum is rushing round our kitchen when my dad arrives home. The car makes the same noise as it does when it comes back later, but somehow it's not as scary at teatime. There are other cars around for a start. We don't dread my dad coming home from work and we don't listen for his footsteps up the drive. We're apprehensive, but we know the rules and we stay as quiet as we can. My dad's fairly quiet when he comes through the door.

'Hello, Daddy,' I say quietly.

'Hello,' he says, looking at me from head to toe and giving me a half smile.

He has a small mouth, with a top lip so thin it's hardly there. His lips barely move when he smiles, but his eyes seem to brighten up when he sees me. It's at times like this that I think he loves me.

He always looks smart in his work clothes. He usually wears a grey suit with black polished shoes. I know they're polished regularly because he does them every night before he goes out again. His short, brown hair, which sometimes looks red in the sunlight, is always tidy too.

He slips his jacket off and settles down in his armchair by the fire in the living room with our local newspaper, *The Telegraph and Argus*. We know if things go well for him at teatime, he won't be as angry later on.

'You just stay in here, Christine,' says my mum, pointing to the dining room. 'Let your dad sit in the living room in peace. He's been working all day.'

My mum's an expert at keeping the peace.

He sits down, and carefully crosses one leg over the other, with his ankle on the opposite knee. Then he rests the paper on his top leg. He grunts occasionally.

'How's your catarrh, Harry?' my mum asks, popping her head round the living room door from the kitchen. 'Are those new tablets helping?'

'Aye, I think so,' he says, not looking away from the paper.

As he reads, he rubs the tips of his fingers from the hand not holding the paper over his scalp as though he's trying to loosen dandruff. He does this night after night and sometimes, when he's gone to bed, Chris pretends to be my dad. He does exactly this with the paper and makes my mum laugh.

I sometimes gauge my dad's mood and try to talk to him about my rabbits.

'Daddy, Tiny jumped over a hurdle tonight,' I say, excitedly. 'He'd be a show jumper if he were a horse.'

'Really?' he says, semi-smiling again, before he goes back to his paper.

I'm never quite sure if he's interested or not in my rabbits, but it doesn't matter. Chris is just home from school, so I rush out to the kitchen to hear his news.

Our tea's ready now. There's a thick cloth on the dining table to stop it getting scratched and a white ironed table cover on top.

We all sit and eat. I notice my mum barely eats anything. She has cooked four lamb chops, but she has given my dad two, one each for us, and she just has mashed potatoes, carrots and gravy. I'm not sure why she's so mean to herself.

We chat and my dad asks Chris if he wants to go and see Huddersfield Town playing on Saturday.

My brother nods with enthusiasm as he finishes his apple pie and custard.

Then my dad gets up, even though the rest of us haven't finished our dinner. My mum always told me that was rude but she lets him get away with it.

'I'm just going to have a lie-down,' he announces.

He goes through the living room door and up the stairs to bed.

It's only 6pm, but it's dark outside. Chris gets up from the table and gets his football. 'Have you done your homework, young man?' my mum asks, pretending to discipline him.

'Did it on the bus, Mum,' he replies, his eyes glinting with untruths.

'So where do you think you're going now, with that ball?' she asks. 'You can't play out in the dark.'

He doesn't answer, and my mum nods as if to say: 'Go out, son, and have some fun. You deserve it. Our night is just beginning.'

I know better than to ask if I can play out. We couldn't risk having any children near the house while my dad's resting. He wouldn't be that bothered now, but he'd be really angry later.

Besides, I'm really tired. My back has an ache that makes me want to lie down and rest. My eyelids are pretty heavy, too.

There's a strange anxiety about my mum. It's as though she's tip-toeing on eggshells. I know we mustn't make a noise. I don't, at this stage, know what would happen if we did. I just know upsetting my dad is one of my mum's greatest fears and I don't want to upset her or get her into any sort of trouble.

She does the washing up, before she puts my hot water bottles in bed. Then she gets me ready for bed. She's just kissing me good night when we hear my dad stirring in the next room. It's 7.30pm.

◆◆◆◆◆

The bathroom's right next to my bedroom so I hear my dad get washed. There are long silences in between water splashing. I assume he's having a shave. If this is his usual routine, he'll go downstairs and polish his shoes. I've seen him do this at weekends, when I stay up later.

But before he goes downstairs, he bumps into my mum, coming out of my room.

'Don't have too much tonight, Harry,' I hear my mum say. 'It was almost 1 o'clock last night when you got back. You didn't used to stay out this late.'

I can see my mum through the crack in my open bedroom door, but I can't see my dad, just hear him. He sounds nicer now. His voice isn't as tired. He sounds almost excited and happy. Maybe nothing is wrong in our house and I'm imagining it, I wonder.

'I'm just going to have a couple of gills,' he says. I've heard him say this to my mum so many times, but I can tell from her face, between the two door hinges, she doesn't believe him.

'I'll be here for 20 to 11,' he reassures her.

I think of the contrast between them. He will be all smart in his suit, a different one to his work suit, and polished shoes and combed hair. He will even smell of aftershave.

My mum has cut her own hair for years and she hardly has any clothes at all, just old clothes she's had for years, or hand-me-downs from other people. Out there on the landing, he will look like the Lord of the Manor, and my mum looks like the cleaner in a pinafore dress she's had for at least 15 years.

My dad sounds like an ordinary man just going out for a drink. He's cheerful now. He even comes in and says good night to me. He ruffles my hair.

'Night-night, Daddy,' I say. The words come out fast because of my nervousness about him going out.

'Night-night, Chris,' he replies, in a relaxed tone.

In that instant I think all our problems are over. How can a dad who ruffles his kid's hair do anything but tuck her in and say 'Night-night' again a few hours later?

It's 1965 and the pubs call last orders at 10.30pm. He can drive the mile home in minutes. It's a straight road, past my junior school, with just one right-hand turn into our road. It's quite quiet at that time of night, not like when Chris crosses the roads in a morning. The police have never once stopped my dad. He's never hit anything or anyone while driving, not even our gatepost.

My mum looks worried. We've survived the day again, but our night-time worries seem to be starting now.

'Chris, are you going to sleep?' she asks nervously, putting her head round the door.

'Yes, Mum,' I answer.

I'm shattered. If I get to bed by 7.30pm, I get a good three hours' sleep before the knots in my stomach wake me or before Chris tucks me in.

My feet settle on the bleach bottles filled with hot water. I zig-zag my legs and lie on my front until I'm warm enough to sleep.

◆◆◆◆◆

It's drizzling outside. Jack pushes his nose against the French windows in our living room and stares out at the little chalet house Santa and the elves knocked up on Christmas Eve when Jack was two-and-a-half.

We live at number 11, and we call the little house 11a because it has a kitchen, a staircase and an upstairs, as well as mod cons such as a toy microwave, sink and cleaning trolley. It would cost several million in central London, but up here in a village near Northallerton, it was £600, a mere snip for a one-bed detached home set in its own grounds.

'I wish this terrible rain would stop,' says Jack, sounding more like Ian's dad than his son. 'What can I do today?'

'Well, you can start by clearing your toys away,' I suggest.

Jack ignores me.

'Can my friends come round?' he asks.

'Yes, of course,' I reply, 'but tidy up first, please.'

'Why?' asks Jack.

'Because Aidan will be here soon,' I say.

Aidan is Jack's best friend and the pair have been close since Aidan's mum Jayne, an old work friend of mine, and I started the great sleepover. The boys stay at each other's houses while we couples each have a night out, have fun and lie in the next day.

'Yes..s..s..s!' cheers Jack, punching the air.

28

'That's nice, Jack,' I say, smiling. 'Will you be pleased to see him? Are you lonely?'

I've always felt incredibly guilty that Jack's an only child. I look at him and wonder if he will blame me for his solitude as a child, for miscarrying and losing the baby that would have been his younger brother or sister. I know how much I love my brother. Have I deprived Jack of that joy? I wonder with massive guilt.

'No,' says Jack, abruptly. 'I'm not lonely. Mummy, how can I be? I've got you and Daddy and Kitty and Granny and Granddad and … six million thousand friends. I want to see Aidan because I want to tell him I'm going to be five before him.'

I start to breathe normally again.

'Jack,' I say, gently. 'You won't be five before Aidan. He was born six weeks before you. He'll have his fifth birthday before you.'

'Well, I'm going to be six before him, then!' answers Jack defiantly.

'Jack, I know how hard it is to accept, because I know you want to be older than Aidan.'

'I want to be older just once and I will be,' says Jack, with typical Aries determination.

'But Aidan is always going to be older than you, sweetie,' I say.

I really don't want to upset his feelings.

'He will be five before you, six before you, seven before you, OK?'

He looks calm. He has accepted this explanation. Wow, he's obviously growing up. No wonder he's due to start school soon. He's maturing fast.

Any minute now he'll say: 'Thank you, Mummy, for making

it all so clear for me. I shan't let it trouble me any more.'

'Waaaa! I hate you, Mummy! It's all your fault!' he wails. 'It's not fair! I want to be eight before him! You should have made me first!'

'Jack, I couldn't have done that!' I answer. 'Daddy and I made you as soon as we could, and I didn't know when Aidan's Mummy was going to make him. Sometimes it's hard to know exactly when you're going to make a baby.'

❖❖❖❖❖

There's a knock at the front door. It's still quite early. It's one of those childish knocks that goes on and on until you answer it.

I'm to blame because I have always encouraged children to call round for Jack. I want Jack to have everything I didn't have as a child – and an open house is a start. Day after day I serve our little visitors with drinks, fruit and crisps. I listen to their school stories, comment on the girls' clothes, the boys' haircuts. They ransack Jack's bedroom and play in the playhouse and garden. It's a regular occurrence.

'Is Jack playing out?' asks Hannah from up the road, oblivious to the rain drizzling on her bike helmet.

'I'll just get dressed, Hannah,' calls Jack. 'I won't play out. It's raining, but you can come and play inside, can't she, Mum?'

'Of course,' I smile, because it gives me such a joyous feeling inside to be able to say that. 'Come back in five minutes and Jack will be dressed, Hannah.'

❖❖❖❖❖

Aidan seems to love coming to our home. His own home is a lovely old five-bedroomed house with high ceilings and large rooms. It's so big he even has his own computer room. But he likes the hustle and bustle of our three-bedroomed modern bungalow with low ceilings and minuscule rooms.

The minute he arrives for his sleepover he runs from room to room, like an excited puppy. He's angelic-looking, with slightly wavy blond hair and blue eyes, and he's exactly the same size as Jack. But while Jack prattles on with his stream of consciousness, Aidan considers his speech and which words he will use.

In Jack's bedroom Aidan finds three little girls playing with a toy hamster that sings 'Kung Fu Fighting' in a Chinese accent, while doing karate moves.

'Oh hi,' says Hayley, who's Hannah's older sister, looking up. 'Hannah! Aidan's here!'

Hannah and two boys emerge from the living room, where they've been playing with Jack's castle, to welcome Aidan. It's as though children are crawling out of the woodwork. Aidan's eyes widen in excitement and he looks at me as though I really am the old woman who lived in a shoe. Our house IS so full of children I don't know what to do. His mum Jayne looks horrified at such mayhem.

'C'mon then, kids,' I call. 'Everyone outside in the garden! It's just stopped raining. The sun will be out any second. You all should get some fresh air. See if you can find me a rainbow.'

I speak firmly, pretending to Jayne that I have some authority, I am mistress of my own house and these children are not running wild. They have tremendous respect for me.

The kids ignore me completely, and go to ransack Jack's bedroom for swords and cutlasses. Jayne turns to leave, horrified at this chaotic house while hers is serene, calm, ordered and polite.

'Have fun tonight, don't drink too much!' I say cheerfully, as though all houses are like ours. 'Aidan can stay till after bathtime tomorrow if you want a day to yourselves.'

Jayne looks as though I've just handed her a winning lottery ticket. She doesn't quite punch the air but I suspect she will when she's out of sight.

'Bye-bye, darling,' she bends and whispers to Aidan, as though she's leaving him in a Thai jail for a long hard spell. 'Be a very good boy and do as Christine tells you.'

Then she turns to face both Jack and Aidan. 'No fighting with Jack.'

Both Aidan and Jack ignore Jayne. They're already Ninja Turtles.

Jayne repeats the no-fighting rule, and Aidan nods his head in a very considered way as she walks off to the front door. There's an extra brightness in his blue eyes as he looks round our house.

'I love coming here!' he says, excitedly running to the back door to go out into the garden.

'But, Aidan,' says Jack, in great awe. 'Your house is so big and there are lots of rooms and you have an upstairs. My mummy really wants an upstairs, sometimes more than she wants fish and chips!'

'Yes, Jack, but your house seems to always have so many children in it! They're everywhere! Look!' concludes Aidan, eyes gleaming as he points to children in every single direction.

CHAPTER 3

Why Can't I Mess About at Dinner?

It's spring and the daffodils are out. I'm going to buy my mum a bunch for Mother's Day later in the month. But right now I'm getting my anorak on to go for a walk with my dad and our dog Dinky.

Dinky's really my mum's dog. She's a Corgi and she doesn't think much of my dad. She growls whenever he goes to the cupboard under the kitchen sink for his shoe-cleaning box.

My mum says Dinky doesn't like men, but she seems perfectly OK with my brother and my granddad. Oh, and she quite likes Teddy the milkman, Mr Mullen the butcher who delivers our meat once a week, and all my brother's friends.

'OK, are you ready, Christine?' my dad asks in a steady voice.

I nod. I love going for walks when my dad's in a good mood. He wasn't late in last night. He was back to watch football on television with Chris and we all had such a good night's sleep, we were all up fairly early. It's still only about 9am. Even my mum sounds cheerful today.

'It might be March but there's still a chill in the morning air,' she says, forcing my hands inside mittens. She's trying to sound strict but I can tell from her voice she's happy. 'Jack Frost might still be out there. Ne'er cast a clout until May is out!'

She says this every year until June whenever she wraps me

up in coats, hats, scarves and gloves, but I don't know what she's on about, even though I'm five now.

I set off walking with my dad. He holds my right hand and has Dinky's lead in his other hand. Whenever we set off, I know we'll be gone for ages. He loves walking. Now and again we chat about animals or flowers or trees, or we just walk quietly, looking around us.

I'm never scared of my dad when we're out walking. It's as though he's a different person to the angry man who comes back late at night. I know on these walks he'd never hurt me, or let anything horrible happen to me. Mind you, he's been OK recently. He hasn't shouted at us for ages in the night.

'Will we see a fox today, Daddy?' I ask.

It would be dead exciting to see a fox, but part of me is a bit scared of them. They're always doing nasty things to people and animals and they lie in wait for you and pounce when you're not looking. I keep turning round just to check there isn't a fox right behind us.

'Maybe,' he says, smiling. 'Though it's a bit early in the day for foxes. We might see some rabbits further down. We'll have to come out at night to see a fox.'

'Can we?' I ask with excitement.

He raises his eyebrows and nods his head with short sharp movements which make a trip in the night seem highly probable.

We've turned right out of our driveway and walked down the avenue where we live. We've passed Betty's house four doors down. She was putting some rubbish in her dustbin and waved.

'Morning!' calls my dad.

'Morning, Harry! Going for a walk?' calls Betty. 'Nice day for it. Mind, it's forecast high winds this afternoon! Don't go too far!'

34

As the old stone houses end, about 20 doors down from our house, there's a public footpath leading down to the side of the school playing fields where Chris and his friends play football. But the footpath doesn't go near the playing fields. It veers to the left, through high grass, and around a grassy mound, to a stile leading to a farm field.

Dinky is off her lead. She crawls under the stile and waits for us.

'Dinky, you need to go on a diet,' laughs my dad. 'Her tummy touched the ground then. Did you see, Chris? She couldn't get much further down than she is when she's standing up.'

I nod and laugh. Our eyes meet and we hold that gaze for a second before we both look away at Dinky.

Over the next stile, my dad stops suddenly. He's seen something. Please let it be a fox, I pray, holding onto his hand for dear life. He gets Dinky back on her lead. I feel a mixture of excitement and terror.

'Sssssh!' he whispers to me.

I look at his face, then follow his eyes and see a grey horse.

My dad loves horses. When I was two, he bought a Welsh Mountain pony called Rosie and he keeps her at his friend's farm. He's talking about breeding from her.

'What is it, Dad?' I ask.

He doesn't usually make us be quiet for a horse.

'Look at the other side,' he whispers. I see something moving under the horse's tummy, then as we follow the footpath nearer, I see a foal feeding. It's struggling to stand up on its long skinny legs and it's wobbling all over as it tries to get milk.

'It's quite a young 'un,' says my dad, looking in wonderment and standing completely still. 'Look, he can hardly stand up.'

'He's got a very curly tail,' I say. 'Dad, what's that thing hanging down there?'

I point to just under the foal's stomach.

'Oh that,' says my dad. 'That's his jimmy. That shows he's a boy, he's a colt.'

I nod as though I understand and before long we're on our way through the farmyard, and on the steep climb to the path that takes us back round to our house.

◆◆◆◆◆

My dad's gone out for a drink and my mum's cooking Sunday lunch. When we got back from our walk, he said he wouldn't be gone long and he'd be back for a nice dinner. My mum looked relieved. Because things have been OK for a while, she's started to believe him when he says things like that.

But now he's late back and everyone's good mood is wearing off. I try to cheer my mum and Chris up.

'Me and daddy saw a foal today,' I say, cheerfully.

'Did you?' my mum perks up. 'Where?'

'In the fields near Judy's farm,' I answer. 'I saw his jimmy.'

My mum and Chris exchange smirks, and for a second I'm so glad I've cheered them up.

'And now I'm starving,' I add. 'Can we have our dinner, Mum?'

'Sorry, love, we can't,' she replies. 'You know your Dad doesn't like us to eat without him. He probably won't be long now.'

'Can't I just have a snack?' I ask.

'No, it will spoil your dinner,' replies my mum. 'Your dad likes us all to sit down for dinner together.'

'Well, he should be here then, shouldn't he?' chips in my brother.

My mum just raises her eyebrows as if she agrees.

I'm still on a high after the walk. Maybe all our problems really are over. Whatever they were, maybe they've gone away and we'll all be happy and go away on holiday and my mum will start eating properly again. Things have been going well for a few weeks now.

My mum laughs.

'You really enjoyed that walk, didn't you?' she asks. 'You look so happy.'

She stands still and looks at me for quite a time as though she has never seen me so upbeat.

'Your eyes are so bright, Chris,' she says, bending down to hug me. 'It's lovely to see you like this.'

But her joy soon fades and she looks at the clock on the fire-place in the dining room for the umpteenth time. For a while lovely smells of roast beef filled the house. Now all we can smell is overcooked vegetables and I'm beginning to feel sick. Glances pass between my brother Chris and my mum, as they look at the clock, worried. My mum stirs the gravy in the roasting tin.

'Will he be long?' I ask. 'My tummy's rumbling, Chris.'

My brother looks at the clock.

'No, any time now,' he says, with a half smile.

The table is laid in the dining room. My mum has been round on her hands and knees with her rubber-soled shoes. There's not a dog hair in sight.

Chris and I wander round the house aimlessly. We don't relax enough to sit. We walk from the living room bay window through the kitchen to the dining room window and back again. Sometimes we pop our head in the pantry just off the kitchen.

At the front window we look up the road for our car, then down the road to see who's playing out. A few children are playing football in the road at the front, looking up now and then to check there are still no cars.

'David! Martin!' we hear one of the mums calling out. My mum has opened some of our windows to let the overcooked-vegetables smell out. There's obviously a car coming. Both my head and Chris's turn left at the same time. It's ours!

'He's here, Mum, he's here!' I call. 'We can eat! Hurrah!'

My dad drives his car down the avenue and turns right into our driveway. He loves his cars, and every 1st August he goes out and collects his new car. Then he proudly drives home and our neighbours call: 'Lovely car.'

My mum is draining the boiled potatoes with a panlid in our steamed-up kitchen, while looking through the kitchen window to watch him put the car away and walk up the drive.

Considering we had such a lovely morning walk, he's pretty quiet now. He hardly says anything. I'm dying to get him to chat about the walk, and the mare and foal, but he doesn't seem that friendly now.

We all know better than to say: 'What time do you call this?' Even pleasantries could spark his temper.

Chris and I sit down at the table while my dad staggers off to the toilet. My mum rushes round serving our dinner. Outside the wind is getting up. The sky's looking darker now. It looks like 8pm outside, not 3pm.

She's an ace cook, my mum, but it must be so hard to keep everything warm while she waits for him to come home. She can't make the dinner for later because she can never assume he'll be late. He'd go spare if his dinner weren't ready when he got in. My mum prides herself on getting his dinner on the table within two minutes of him walking through the door.

Our dinners – melt-in-your-mouth roast beef and Yorkshire

puddings, with delicious beefy gravy – are put before us. My mum has also got a block of ice cream from the ice-cream van. It's the only thing we can get in our little ice compartment in our fridge, but we're so excited about it. It's new and you get strawberry, vanilla and chocolate flavours all in one block.

My dad's back from the toilet now. He's taken off his suit jacket and is just wearing his trousers, shirt and tie. He takes his place at the end of the table to my right, just near the fire. Chris is opposite me and my mum's going to sit to my left. My mum comes in with the first plates. The food looks delicious, not at all stinky or overcooked. Then she brings hers in and we start.

It's unlike me, because I know my dad's not in a good mood any more, but I make a comment. My stomach is growling with hunger and I am so happy to see some food. I pipe up: 'Thank God, it's here.' I don't think there's any harm in it. I'm sure I wouldn't have said it otherwise.

I'm about to get some beetroot from the jar to mix in with my mashed potato and beef when my dad leaps out of his seat. I look up in surprise. I have no idea what's going on. But it's like slow motion and he leans over towards me, and grabs my arm. With one pull, he lifts me from the table. For a split second, I am standing in front of him.

The next thing I know he has hold of my legs and he tips me upside down. I don't know how he has done it, whether he has just grabbed my legs and tipped me very quickly, but it all happens very fast and I'm scared. I catch sight of his face. He looks strange from the wrong way up, but I can tell he's very red and angry and his false teeth are almost falling out with rage.

'And I am absolutely sick of you!' he yells for the second that I'm in the air, but he's slurring and trying to hold his teeth in while I'm in the air. His voice sounds horrible, not at all like

39

the Dad who took me for a walk this morning and laughed at Dinky's fat tummy. He sounds nasty, as though he doesn't like me at all.

For a moment I'm embarrassed my brother will see my knickers, as my skirt falls over my head. I can't see Chris at the moment, nor my mum. I can just see the fireplace and my dad's face if I look up. Chris will be behind me and my mum to my right.

I hear my mum's voice.

'Harry, stop it! Don't! Be careful, oh my God!'

There's a movement behind me. It sounds like my mum has pushed her chair back and jumped up from her seat. Whatever she does, I hope she doesn't make him any more annoyed. It would be best if she just let him do what he's going to do.

I can feel the blood rushing to my face from being held upside down. My head is starting to feel very heavy. I feel as though I've been there for ages, but I know I haven't. I hear a sharp intake of breath. I think it was from my mum.

Then I feel a hand on the small of my back. I don't know if he has thumped me or slapped me, but it hurts. My face feels bright red, smarting from the pain.

It's over in a second. He lets go of me near the floor. Once I'm upright again, I can feel tears start to fill my eyes. I sit back on my chair. I feel slightly dizzy from being held upside down, and my back is throbbing. Sitting down really hurts as there is a gap in our dining chair just where I could do with support on my lower back.

My dad sits back down. I've never seen him look so scary and angry. His pale blue eyes are blazing with anger. They've gone a clear colour, almost see-through, and he's fiddling with his false teeth with his tongue.

I try to eat a bit more to pretend that we can go back to normal. I'm still absolutely starving. I will those tears to go back into my eyes, rather than roll down my cheeks as they want to. I've seen my mum fighting back tears when she wants to cry and she's been brave. I'm trying to be brave, too.

My mum and Chris don't say a word and neither of them makes eye contact with me, my dad or each other. My dad has carried on eating, and I am trying, but neither Chris nor my mum has picked up their cutlery again, despite being ravenously hungry two minutes earlier.

I am racked with guilt. With just one stupid comment, I have ruined my family's dinner. No one is speaking to me and no one is looking at me. In fact, no one is speaking at all. Only my dad is eating and he looks so angry with me.

I give up on my dinner. I must have been bad to have annoyed my mum and brother as well. They're pretty easy-going types. I've obviously pushed them to the limit this time. I put my knife and fork together and sit looking at my plate gloomily. My mum and Chris are doing the same.

My stomach is still rumbling, but I am starting to feel really sick. It's like the butterflies you get in your stomach when you're really excited about something, but there's no excitement for me, just a feeling of complete hopelessness.

I know things aren't right and I was wrong this morning. Our problems haven't gone away. My dad has never smacked me before, yet what he just did felt like more than a tap.

My dad eats the last morsel of food on his plate, then he gets up. Nobody is bothered about the block of ice cream any more. He's unsteady on his feet and has to hold the table for a moment for support. Then he goes out of the dining room, through the living room to the stairs. He's off to bed. None of us moves until we hear the creak that tells us he's in bed.

Then my mum says with a trembling voice: 'Chris, come here, let's undo your skirt, lift your top up.'

But as soon as I get to her, she hugs me, and cuddles me, and starts to cry. She cries for what seems like ages, her forehead in the palm of her right hand on the table, now full of dirty plates, and her left arm round me.

It seems ages before she looks at my back. It still hurts.

'Is she OK, Mum?' Chris asks in an unusually quiet voice.

'It's red,' she replies.

I can tell she's angry by the way she is shaking her head slowly, as though she's plotting some kind of terrible revenge. But what can my mum do, I wonder? She doesn't have any money, she has no job, she has nowhere to go. My dad's in charge.

We have a few hours before my dad gets up, but we hardly speak. It's as though we're all in a state of shock. Normally, my mum springs back to her old self when my dad's in bed on a Sunday afternoon. She makes an effort to try and be normal. But today she's very down. It's as though her worst fears have just happened, and there's no going back.

❖❖❖❖❖

As a journalist, I can persuade the most private of people to pour out their hearts to the world when their grief is raw and new. I have chatted up hospital porters to let me onto no-go wards, doctors to give me an off-the-record prognosis on someone's life expectancy, and teachers to divulge the name of a child they have expelled. But I cannot persuade our son to sit at a table and eat his meals within a reasonable time.

We're sitting in our dining room now, me and Jack, and I'm

coaxing roast chicken, Yorkshire puddings, mashed potatoes, carrots and gravy down him.

It's a slow process and could last all afternoon, but I have read in one of those toddler-taming books it's best to give children their main meal at lunchtime because they could be too tired by teatime.

I look at my watch – 2.10pm. Bloody hell, it will be teatime soon at this rate anyway. I'm so keen to do this parenting lark right. If the book says 'Eat at lunchtime,' we'll eat at lunchtime, even if it means I have to start roasting chickens the minute I get back from walking Jack to pre-school.

With every mouthful, I think what a lucky kid he is and I remember the Sunday lunchtime I was hit. Sitting at this dining table for several hours a day, I've plenty of time to muse over how my dad could treat me like that. But I wonder about my mum too, and how she felt. Surely she hated seeing her child hit like that, even though most children got smacked in those days?

I've tried all methods of getting Jack to eat. Bribery, coaxing, starvation, a year of eating the food for him (definitely not recommended for the figure-conscious).

I once left the room and sobbed with my head in my hands in our bedroom, fantasizing about being one of these parents who disappear from their world without telling anyone. But I can't leave home JUST because my child chucks his spaghetti Bolognese all over the dining room. I'd miss him by bathtime and would have to reveal my whereabouts when I rang to see if he'd had his bedtime milk.

The truth is, Jack is not interested in food. He doesn't want to sit and eat when he could chat, play, read, tell jokes or save the world with Action Man. I've read the books. I've seen *Supernanny* in action. I've watched repeats of *Little Angels* on

BBC3. I've sounded out child psychologists I have interviewed. I've tried a star chart for mealtimes, rewards for good table manners, and issued threats of never, ever, ever watching *Scooby Doo* ever again in this lifetime if he doesn't eat properly.

I'm not averse to a chat over a lovely meal, but a 2-hour chat at three meals a day leads to a hell of a lot of talking and not much else.

Jack goes to pre-school four mornings a week, and nursery for a full day on Wednesdays, so I'm spared the lunchtime session then. But breakfasts have to be spooned down him, and evening meals would turn into midnight feasts if I didn't give up after an hour and a half.

'Mummy, why can't I mess about at mealtimes?' asks my Little Angel in all innocence.

He's taken to calling me Mummy again instead of Mum and I quite like it. You know, he has a point. Why can't he? It's his life, his body that's getting starved of food. Why are we overzealous parents so hung up on nutrition these days?

'Because Mummy wants you to eat nice healthy food and grow up to be a big healthy boy. If you mess about, you don't eat and you'll stay a little boy. You'll also be very hungry,' I answer.

'Did you eat all your food when you were a little girl?' Jack enquires.

'Why do you want to know that?' I ask.

I've just read one of these self-help pieces that advise you to smile and ask that very question if you're ever faced with a question you don't want to answer. Well, I'm happy to answer this one, but I thought I'd try it out anyway.

'Well, you're not a very big girl and you're not that healthy, either,' Jack informs me. 'You've been poorly every month for the last three months. You've been picking up Germans, haven't you?'

44

'Jack, I have never picked up Germans,' I answer indignantly, casting my mind back to those long rail trips across Europe in my twenties. No, I never picked up Germans.

'But, Mum, I heard you telling Daddy every time you went to a kids' party you caught all their bloody Germans.'

'Germs, Jack!' I say. 'Please tell me you haven't told Tracy and Alison at pre-school I've been picking up Germans?'

'No,' he says with confidence. 'I just drew a picture of you in bed and said you had a lot of Germans in there. I said you'd been in there for ages with them and you haven't got any energy left any more.'

'Bloody great,' I think to myself. That makes it all OK, Jack. Not only do the leaders at pre-school now think I'm a crap mum because I can't bake cakes for fund-raising stalls, they also think I've been shagging half the continent and am too knackered to look after my kid.

But just a minute: Jack has done it again. He has reeled me into another conversation. His knife and fork are down. I will not succumb to these diversion tactics. I am going to win this one.

'Jack, please eat your food,' I say. I try and sound serious. 'It's going to be very cold soon.'

'It's cold already, Mummy.'

For a moment I berate myself for forcing my child to eat cold food, then remind myself it was perfectly warm when we started out an hour ago. I know part of me is tempted to get so angry with him, to shout and scream at him. I'm bored out of my head sitting at this table, staring at cold, congealed food.

'Tell me about when you were a girl and what you ate,' he asks. 'Did you eat with your mummy and daddy?'

'Later,' I say, pointing at his dinner. 'I'll tell you all you want to know later.'

I look at him sitting at the table and wonder how you can physically grab a child and hit them. Jack's much taller and more solid than I was, but even so, how could my dad thump me for such an innocent comment? Was he just pissed and looking for a scapegoat?

And I wonder what my mum was doing. I know for sure that if anyone so much as smacked Jack, there would be trouble. Why didn't my mum pick up the poker from the hearth and whack my dad across the head? Maybe she thought that would make her as bad as him. Or maybe it all happened so fast she didn't have time to think. It certainly took me by surprise.

Or maybe she was just scared of him. I know he told her if she ever left him, he would fight her for custody of us children. With his Mr Nice Guy image, he'd probably win. Now that would be a terrifying thought for any mother. That thought alone obviously kept her where she was, stuck in a horrible marriage.

Jack interrupts my reverie.

'Mummy, don't get mad,' says Jack, laughing. 'Why not now?'

'Why not what?' I ask, I'd forgotten what we were talking about.

Jack is still swinging on his chair, waving the fork in his hand all over the place. He follows my eyes to our carpet, not that long ago a pale grey with pink undertones, now sadly a very dirty grey.

'It's just some gravy that's gone on the carpet, Mummy,' says Jack. 'Oh and yes, I think there's some mashed potato down there too.'

He looks carefully at the carpet as though accuracy is vital in his evidence.

'Yes, I'm right, look, that big white lump is mashed potato, Mummy.'

I sit and look at his mischievous face, the bright happy look in his eyes, and those cute little baby teeth we get to see when he laughs. It's as though the world is one big playground for Jack, a place of fun and laughter.

Aware I'm prepared to sit this one out, he starts to eat. He chases cold Yorkshire pudding round his Winnie the Pooh plate with his Bob the Builder cutlery. He tries to humour me by saying, 'Yum yum!' with every mouthful. But I know it isn't yummy any more. I hurry things along and pop the final carrot into his mouth, almost 80 minutes since we sat down to eat.

'There! That wasn't too bad, was it?' asks Jack, looking at his empty plate with pride. 'Now tell me about when you were a girl.'

I think back for a moment to my mealtimes as a child, trying to think of a happy episode for Jack. I don't want to burden him with tales of doom and gloom and mealtime violence.

'I used to have sandwiches and soup with my mum at lunchtime when I got home from school,' I start. 'Uncle Chris and I often had home-made beefburgers and chips. Your grandma made the best beefburgers ever.'

'What, did she work for McDonald's?' asks Jack, wide-eyed and clearly impressed with his heritage.

'No, she made her own,' I answer.

'And they were better than McDonald's'?' checks Jack, doubtfully. 'Mummy, did you ever mess about at the table like me?' he adds.

I look on the bright side. At least he knows he's guilty.

'No, Jack, I never messed about because I would have got into very serious trouble.'

'With your nasty daddy?' he asks, pretending to shiver with fear. I'm never sure if he enjoys the little I tell him about my dad,

47

but he always wants to know more, often the same questions I have, like why he did those things and what made him that way.

'Yes,' I reply. 'He didn't like us to mess about.'

'I'm very glad he's not my daddy,' says Jack. 'I'm dead lucky, aren't I, Mummy? My daddy's not like that, is he?'

'He's nothing like that at all, Jack,' I reply, deep in thought. 'Very, very lucky, that's what you are, mister,' I conclude, getting up to wash the plates. 'Why do you think you're so lucky, Jack?' I add, testing him.

'Because I can mess about as much as I like and you never shout at me,' he says.

He's on a roll now. There are more reasons, I can tell.

'Because we sometimes have fish and chips with lots of batter on, because we can have tomato ketchup whenever we want it, and because you, my fair lady, are the softest mummy in the whole world.'

He's gone all theatrical now, going down on one knee pretending to propose. It would be quite a sweet sight, if he didn't have gravy down his top and round his mouth, Yorkshire pudding on his trousers and a lump of carrot in his hair. Oh, and I think my knight in shining armour is kneeling in that dollop of mashed potato he dropped earlier. Who said romance is dead?

CHAPTER 4

Mummy Doesn't Drink Beer

We don't talk about that Sunday lunchtime last spring when my dad hit me. My back got better after a few days and he hasn't hit me – or anyone else – in the last year. You'd think that's a blessing and things aren't as bad, but they are worse than ever. A few times I've heard him saying some of the nasty things he wants to do to us. Sometimes I think it would be better if he got on and did them.

I can tell from my mum's face things are getting a whole lot worse. Things are simmering at the moment, just waiting to bubble over into another outburst. It's the waiting that's the terrifying part. You never know just when it's all going to bubble over again. It might as well be happening all the time because it's on our minds constantly.

My dad has started going to a different pub, The Queen's Head, because he got so pissed off with people at the Duke, or the Old Duke William Inn, as it says on the sign. The Queen's Head is a bit further down the same road as the Duke.

It's Saturday lunchtime and Chris is doing some football thing with two of his friends.

My mum has put a casserole in the oven so it will be ready when my dad gets back at 10 past 2, as he's promised. As soon as his car has turned left at the top of our road, my mum says: 'C'mon, Chris, get your coat and gloves. We're going for a walk.'

My whole face must light up. My mum and I never walk, unless it's to school. My dad hasn't walked as much with me since Dinky died just before Christmas.

'Where are we going, Mum?' I ask, puzzled.

'Just to see what the Queen's is like.'

'My dad will be so angry, though,' I say. 'He won't be pleased to see us. Besides, I can't go in, can I?'

'He won't see us, love,' she replies.

'Well, how will we see what it's like if we don't go in?' I question her.

'We'll look at the type of people who go there,' she nods as though to persuade me it's the right thing to do.

We set off walking, up the same road that takes us to my school, but this time I feel as though I'm on a mission. I don't let go of my mum's hand and run through the trees. We pass my school on the hill, and continue down the road, past some farms, then past the Duke on our right. Soon, we're crossing a T-junction just before the Queen's Head.

We stop just before the car park entrance, near a hedge which is just getting its spring leaves on. The nearest window to the pub is about 12 feet away and it looks like it's in a corridor. My mum doesn't seem interested in what's going on inside anyway. She has spotted my dad's car in the car park but she doesn't seem that bothered about seeing him, who he's with and what he's doing. She's just interested in the type of people who come here.

It does look fancy. It's a new building, whereas the Duke is stone and old. It has lots of bright lights, even though it's a bright March afternoon. There's also a big sign saying: 'Food served here'.

'Blimey, there's some money here,' whispers my mum, as we see great big cars pull through the entrance and into the car park.

Couples get out of the cars. Women are wearing fur coats and men wear longish dark overcoats in a lovely smooth material.

I see the way the men put a protective hand on their wives' lower back to guide them towards the door and they hold doors open for their ladies, whether it's the car doors or the entrance to the pub. They look so fancy and rich. The women all have nice hair and lipstick on, and some even have necklaces and scarves on and they're wearing high heels.

I suddenly feel uncomfortable with my mum. She's nothing like these people. She's wearing a pair of moccasin shoes and the sole is coming away from the upper part of the shoe. She's not fancy like them at all and I'm torn between wishing she were a little bit fancy and dressed up, and feeling guilty because she's my mum and how could I wish that when I love her so much just as she is?

'Mum, let's go,' I say. 'I don't like this.'

'Me neither,' she says, in the saddest of voices. 'Let's get going.'

We walk home together, hand in hand, looking for lambs on the way, and though she makes an effort to be cheerful and chat to me, I know my mum saw something she didn't like.

◆◆◆◆◆

We seem to have been home just a few minutes when my dad's pale blue car arrives back, but it's longer than that because he never goes to the pub for just an hour these days. More like three or four now.

My mum quickly takes the casserole out of the oven before she looks out to watch my dad walking up the drive.

'Christine!' she calls, sharply. 'Do me a favour and just go and play in your bedroom, love.'

'But, Mum, it's so cold up there,' I try to negotiate.

'Well, put the heater on, then,' she replies hurriedly.

She must be keen to get rid of me. We're only ever allowed to use the electric fires when we're ill and there's no coal for the fires downstairs. Normally she would have said: 'Put an extra pullover on, then.'

I'm already upstairs when my dad gets through the back door, but I have left the stairs door ajar so I can hear everything.

'I'm fucking starving!' I can hear him speaking slowly and monotonously, as if there's a threat in every word.

'Where's my dinner?'

I cringe. I know 'fuck' is such a bad word and I have never said it. I'm not even sure exactly how you write it, and think it may actually be 'fock'. I've asked Chris but he's just laughed at me and said I shouldn't be using it anyway, so what does it matter if it's a U or an O? I don't have a clue what it means, just that it's forbidden.

I can picture the scene. My mum will be scurrying around using tea towels as oven gloves. He will be taking his jacket off and trying to put it on the back of the settee, but he'll miss the settee and his jacket will land on the floor. Then he'll start to get angry.

He stomps upstairs to the bathroom, but doesn't come into my bedroom. He obviously thinks I'm out somewhere. I stand as still as possible, looking out of my bedroom window, willing myself not to sneeze.

He's back downstairs now. It's so easy to guess what he's doing when he's drunk because he's much clumsier and the sounds are more exaggerated. That's him, pulling out a chair at the table, I tell myself. Then I hear the rattle of him using his knife and fork. He's talking, but though his voice is low, I can tell by the monotone he isn't happy.

Then there's an almighty crash, followed by a series of smaller ones. I know my mum said I'd to stay upstairs, but what if she's injured? I know I'm only six, but I know how to phone 999. I run downstairs.

Standing in the doorway of our dining room, I see my mum is safe. But the next thing I see is food dripping slowly down the walls. Great big lumps of food slathered in gravy snake their way down the wallpaper. Gravy drips down onto the fireplace and lumps of mashed potato plop on the carpet at the side of the fireplace. Bits of smashed white plate are everywhere. Some are tiny splinters of china.

My dad is trying to balance by leaning a hand on the table, where there is no plate. He isn't a big man, but he can't stop swaying. He's redder than I've ever seen him, and the tip of his nose is almost purple. As always, when he's angry, his eyes are clear with rage, as though his eyes have been poked out and replaced with fresh air.

'What's happened?' I ask. I bite my lip and cringe. I know I shouldn't have spoken, but I've never seen food thrown around like this, and it seems an obvious question. I may spark his anger, but I'm confused. My mum looks as though she wishes she were anywhere in the world but having this conversation with me. It's a look of total despair.

'What's happened? What's happened?' he says, mimicking my high-pitched childish voice. 'She's ruined my fucking life,' he tells me. 'That's what's happened.'

'Your mother,' he adds, pointing at my mum as though I don't know who he's talking about. 'She's a whore. I could have been this and that, but she has held me back. I'm finished, I'm ruined and all because of this fucking useless cow. She has always held me back.'

53

'You have got such a filthy turn of phrase when you've been mixing with that rabble,' says my mum with an air of superiority.

She's getting tougher all the time now. There was a time, not long ago, when she would never answer him back. Now it's as if she doesn't care as much. But she's obviously still miffed at the posh coats and jewellery we saw from the car park because she emphasises the word 'rabble' with venom.

'How much have you had today anyway to get into this state?' she ventures bravely.

'I've had about 10 fucking pints, and every one of them was to try and forget about you, you whore, making us the laughing stock of the neighbourhood, with your carryings-on,' he replies.

I hardly know what they're talking about, but my dad's tone is scary. I know 'cow' isn't a good word, nor is 'useless'. I know 'fuck' or 'fock' is pretty bad too, but I don't have a clue what a whore is. Whatever it is, my mum is one and it doesn't sound too good.

Ten pints of beer sounds a lot, too. Maybe that's what the strange smell is whenever my dad comes back from the pub – beer. I shudder. How can he drink so much when it smells so disgusting? It must be vile stuff.

I look at the wallpaper. The food is now clinging to the patches left when my mum scratched out the flying geese. It looks disgusting. I realize I haven't had my lunch yet and my mum hasn't had a decent meal for weeks, yet here's all this food going to waste on our wallpaper.

He walks past me and I flinch. I've lived in fear he'll hit me again since that Sunday lunchtime. Today he's angry enough to hit me, but he doesn't. He trips over a spare dining chair in the living room, before he makes it to the bottom of the stairs.

'I'm off to fucking sleep,' he shouts. 'I hate every one of

you, you're nothing to me. Nothing! I don't give a damn about any of you.

'As for you, you tramp,' he snarls at my mum. 'I'm going to cut you up. I have just the knife for it, you wait and see!'

A shiver runs through me and my stomach leaps around. The thought of my mum getting hurt makes me want to cry, but I just stand there, rooted to the spot, my mouth open in shock, a strange shaking slowly taking over my body.

I'm also shocked that my dad hates us, even though he has said it before. The horrible part is, I can tell from his eyes that he really does hate us. If he really means that, does he also mean to hurt my mum?

'Ignore him, Chrissie,' my mum, says reading my thoughts. 'It's not your dad talking, that. It's the drink. When you drink so much beer, it turns you nasty and you say some horrible things and use terrible words.

'Your daddy doesn't hate you. He loves you a lot when he's not full of beer.'

'It sounds awful stuff, Mum. Why does he drink it?' I ask, perplexed.

'Because the first one or two drinks make him feel happy, so he carries on and on, but by then he doesn't realize his mood has changed and he's not happy any more,' she explains.

'But, Mum, I always know when I'm happy or ...' I stop in mid-sentence because it's so obvious I'm not happy very much these days.

Then I have a brainwave.

'I know! If more than two drinks of beer makes my dad unhappy, why doesn't he just stop after two and he'll stay happy?' I ask.

'That,' says my mum, slightly smiling but hardly moving her

mouth or her eyes, 'is the million-dollar question.'

'But, Mum, those things he says he's going to do to you …' My voice is going wobbly and weak. 'Will he do them?'

'Of course not, sweetheart, he's just letting the beer talk,' she replies.

'But what if he does them when he's full of beer?' I question her.

'He won't do them,' she says in a tone that tells me the conversation is over.

We've just heard a loud creaking of bedsprings upstairs as Chris arrives back with his football. His happy face, exhilarated from a half day's football training, soon changes into one of worry when he sees my mum on her hands and knees cleaning up a perfectly cooked beef casserole.

'What's up?' he asks. 'What's happened, Mum?'

My mum is picking up bits of food with a distasteful look on her face as though she's handling dog dirt.

'My dad's gone barmy,' I tell Chris, quietly. 'I think he threw his dinner at the wall.'

'Why?' asks Chris.

'He was mad at my mum,' I try to explain, realizing I'm not altogether sure why he lobbed the plate at the wall.

'What's my mum done now?' asks Chris, as though this is a regular occurrence.

'Er, I'm not sure,' I say.

'Probably nothing as usual,' he adds. 'Are you OK, Mum? Did it hit you?'

I see the two of them look at each other and realize they have something so different from what me and my mum have. He's old enough now at 15 to be almost a friend to my mum. He crouches down to talk to her while she cleans the carpet and the tiles on the fireplace.

She gets up and goes back to the kitchen to change her bowl of water, so we're alone for a minute.

'Chris, what's a whore?' I ask.

He's stalling. I can tell. But I can tell that word has given him a clue as to what this was all about.

'I'm not sure,' he says slowly, as his brain works fast to piece all the evidence together.

'My dad says he hates us,' I say in a weak voice.

I feel like crying. It's awful to be hated when you try hard to be well-behaved.

'Does that make you sad?' I ask.

'Yeah, it does,' he replies, but I can tell he's far more interested in what's been going on in the dining room than discussing feelings surrounding hatred.

'What's a whore?' I repeat.

He looks at my mum as she comes through the door with beseeching eyes, saying: 'Please get me out of this one.'

'Christine, it's w-h-o-r-e,' says my mum. 'It's a woman who sleeps with other men and gets paid for it.'

'Well, why did he call you that?' I ask.

I'm puzzled that some women get paid for just sleeping. It sounds OK to me and maybe the answer to my mum's money problems if she thought it through.

'I don't have a bloody clue, love,' my mum answers me, picking up little brass ornaments from the fireplace alcove, now covered in onions and little strands of succulent beef. 'Same reason he calls us all those other names; he's got a screw loose, that one has.'

'You don't sleep with other men, do you, Mum?' I ask, very puzzled.

My mum's here with us every night. How can she possibly sleep with other men? I feel stupid asking, but it's as if I have to know.

'Of course I don't, sweetheart,' she says, now almost laughing at the thought. 'I've never slept with anyone other than your dad. I am not a whore. He has got that bit wrong, but then he's got a lot wrong recently.'

For a second I wonder if I should try and tell him my mum isn't a whore when we're out on a walk, but then I wonder if that might just stir up his anger again. Hopefully, he may have forgotten all about whores when he wakes up.

◆◆◆◆◆

I am in such a jolly mood. I'm having two nights away in a five-star hotel in Manchester. Even better, I have two of my most wicked friends with me, the type who, when you say you've had far too much to drink already, just go and order another round.

Trouble is, these two friends can take all this alcohol. Claire is 30 and Sarah is 29. They go out a lot at home and their bodies, and livers in particular, are used to regular alcohol abuse. They've both just got new boyfriends and no kids so they can get as pissed as they like and spend the next day in bed. Not for them the familiar tribal chanting of: 'Mum, mum, mum, up, up, up!' and the purgatory of knowing you have more chance of being prime minister than getting a lie-in.

I don't think they understand what my life is like now I'm a mum. I know because Claire, in particular, tells me off regularly because my nails are looking a bit ragged, my swimming cossie is apparently 'dated' and I haven't bought many new clothes since having Jack. Truth is, I HAVE bought lots of new clothes, but they're all for boys aged four to five and covered in dragons and dinosaurs.

So tonight I'm going to show them I still know how to party. I'm here to do a hotel review and a travel feature on Manchester. But this isn't your run-of-the-mill travel feature. The only people who will be interested in this are people who watch the television series *Cutting It*.

We're doing everything the *Cutting It* way. We've been to get our hair, make-up and nails done, purely for research purposes, of course. Tonight we're off to a VIP opening of a restaurant and tomorrow we're going shopping. We're taking it all very seriously, right down to using *Cutting It*-speak for getting a cab.

'Let's catch a Joe,' I say, as the others dissolve into fits of laughter. Though we're pretending to be glamorous and sophisticated like our heroines Sarah Parish and Amanda Holden in *Cutting It*, we're behaving like a bunch of pathetic schoolgirls. As the oldest, I should know better.

◆◆◆◆◆

We're almost ready. I'm wearing an olive-green shift dress, which I've read in Trinny and Susannah's book I shouldn't wear because I have a waist. But it's my only posh dress, without sequins, and it was expensive, so I always feel good in it.

Claire is wearing a white strapless number and she looks as though those enormous 34DD boobs of hers are going to make an appearance any minute. Sarah's wearing a black wrapover dress and her accessories are stunning. She has gorgeous dangly flowery earrings on, a subtle necklace and the trendiest of shoes.

'How do I look?' asks Claire, ensuring her breasts emerge from the en-suite bathroom about five minutes before the rest of her.

'Lovely,' Sarah and I trill.

Of the three of us, Claire is the most confident about her

looks. She struts around like a model, one foot firmly in front of the other, eyes looking forward. Sarah and I amble along, chatting and laughing, bumping into people, and forgetting all those deportment lessons Claire keeps giving us.

It's nearly time to leave and Claire is prancing up and down in front of the mirror, like a racehorse in the parade ring. She's flicking her long straight brown hair around and looking at her profile from each side. Sarah and I exchange glances.

'Chris, you look great,' whispers Sarah.

'So do you,' I add, with an air of conspiracy.

'It starts with a meal,' I gabble on. 'Then there's a band on and lots of drinks, and that's the bit when I think we'll see the celebrity.'

I'm getting quite excited and I feel really happy.

'I wonder who the celebrity will be?' I jabber on excitedly, as Sarah sits on the bed swinging her legs and Claire tries to straighten her hair even more.

'Wouldn't it be absolutely ace for my feature if it were a *Cutting It* star? Imagine Jason Merrells being at the same party as us. If he is, please don't let me stagger up to him and say something juvenile. Don't let me do this.'

I do an exaggerated drunken stagger, and point with my index finger, and through pretend-bleary eyes, I say: 'I think you're gorgeous, Gavin. I think I'm in love with you.'

Sarah laughs. 'We won't let you do that,' she reassures me. 'But isn't that what you said to Paul Merton at that book launch he was at?'

'Yeah.' I cringe at how juvenile I become after a single unit of alcohol. 'I told him he was one of the five celebrities I'd like to sleep with.'

'What did he say again?' asks Sarah, grinning. 'Did he laugh?'

'He asked who the other four were!' I reply. 'Mmm, he laughed. He seemed a bit surprised to be accosted at a respectable book launch. Not what he expected at all. Very funny. I blame the one glass of champagne I had.'

I'm about to list the other four celebrities when Sarah stops me.

'No, no, no, let me guess!' she laughs. 'Gorgeous Gavin from *Cutting It*, of course,' she says, touching the thumb of her left hand with her right index finger.

'Hugh Grant, you've always loved him since *Four Weddings*. Oh my God, yes, who's that bloke in *24*? He must be number one in the list.'

'Jack Bauer,' I say dreamily. 'Yes, he's top of the list. Kiefer Sutherland, lovely, lovely Jack Bauer.'

We're both so sidetracked by thoughts of sex with celebrities and we've forgotten all about number four, when Claire chips in: 'Who will it be, then?'

We'd obviously both forgotten she was there, because we look up, startled. 'Who will what be?' asks Sarah.

'The celeb at the opening,' replies Claire. 'Will he think I'm pretty?'

'He'll think you're gorgeous,' we both laugh.

Then I add: 'But he might be a she. Hey, wouldn't it be fantastic if the celeb is Sarah Parish? She's brilliant.'

Sarah nods enthusiastically.

'I just hope it's Finn,' enthuses Claire, referring to her *Cutting It* hero. 'You either love boring old Gavin for the same old, same old you'd get with him, or you'd go for excitement with Finn.'

'Yeah, it would be dead exciting, never knowing who he's going to shag next, your mum, your sister, your daughter, your best friend – life on the edge, Claire,' I grin, as we hail a Joe.

◆◆◆◆◆

We've had a gorgeous three-course meal with aperitifs and a bottle of wine. Sarah and I are keeping a lookout for the celeb, but Claire, who loves all homey stuff, is looking at the décor with distaste.

'It's retro, Claire,' I say. 'We really had wallpaper like this in the sixties and seventies, you know.'

'What, all these murky browns and greens and mustards?' she checks, wondering how we could have survived those decades with such vile décor and not be in therapy for the rest of our lives.

'Yes!' I enthuse, 'and most people had a picture of an elephant hanging over their fireplace. It's the one in Del Boy's living room in *Only Fools and Horses*.'

The bar and dance floor are already packed with people who've been invited just for drinks. They're the Manchester in-crowd, very arty in their head-to-toe black grunge.

Claire perches herself on the end of a sofa, but as Sarah and I stand and look around, we realize we're slightly tipsy. We start inquiring about the celebrity. A man wearing a trilby beckons for me to move closer so he can whisper who the VIP is.

'It's not!' I laugh.

'It is!' he laughs back. 'And here he comes now!' Our heads turn to the stairs, and there, emerging from the crowd, is Dev from *Coronation Street*.

'Oh, fantastic!' I say to Sarah, giddy with excitement, as the crowd parts for Dev and his blonde, scantily-dressed female companion.

'Here, hold my drink, Sarah,' I say, handing her a large glass of white wine. 'I just have to tell Dev what an opportunist shagger he is.'

'Chris, no!' says Sarah, as I set off, staggering by now. 'Think about it first.'

'I have thought about it,' I say, drunkenly returning to her. 'I've thought about it long and hard, and Dev never turns down the chance to get his leg over in the Street. He needs telling.'

◆◆◆◆◆

The rest of the party is a bit of a blur. I'm almost sure I didn't approach Dev. I remember vaguely dragging Claire and Sarah to look at a shopfront used in *Cutting It* after we left the restaurant.

'Chris, it's almost 2am, there's no one about,' says Sarah, trepidation in her voice. 'We should be getting back.'

But once we're back at the hotel, I'm up for cocktails. We order Brandy Alexanders and we sit on stools round the bar drinking them. We're discussing declaring undying love to our men. Claire and Sarah are in such new relationships they're not sure if it's a good idea.

I have had such a happy night I decide to ring Ian to tell him all about it. I might also joke on and declare undying love just to show off to Claire and Sarah.

'Hello,' says a bleary voice at the end of the telephone.

'It's me, Crossy,' I say, using the nickname all the reporters used for him when we worked together on a local paper.

'I thought it might be,' he says, humouring me.

'I'm ringing so late, just to say …' Every word is slow and slurred and I'm almost in a heap on the hotel bar. I can see my reflection in the mirror opposite. It isn't a pretty sight. I look as pale as a ghost, my white face a contrast to my dark hair.

Until now I've been messing about, pretending to make a

jokey declaration of love, but suddenly my mood changes and I realize I mean every word of what I'm saying.

'You'll never know, I mean, never ever, know – did I say that bit? – just how much I love you.'

And with that I collapse into great big sobs, tears dripping on the bar as I say sorry to a very concerned barman.

'Ah, that's lovely,' says Claire, who longs for a lifetime of romantic love. We've always said she'd be Charlotte in *Sex and the City*.

'Chris,' says Ian, concerned. There's no conversation between us, just my enormous sobs in between large gasps for breath. 'Put Sarah on.'

Sarah chats to Ian and she laughs.

'Did he say he loves me too?' I ask, raising my head about three inches from the bar and turning to face her.

A few hours earlier I walked through here, afraid to put a foot wrong. Now I'm almost lying on the bar, plastered.

'I'm sure he does,' says Sarah, 'but he did say I have to take you to bed and give you a very big drink of water.'

◆◆◆◆◆

I sleep for a couple of hours crashed on my bed. Just before I collapsed on the bed, we filled in our breakfast order. Sarah was reading out the options.

'I have a good idea. I'll dance and you can guess how much I want something on the menu,' I said excitedly. I know it's juvenile but it felt like the funniest thing I had ever done.

But when I wake I feel dreadful. My head is throbbing, the backs of my eyes are hurting and my body aches. I hate myself. I can't believe what I did. I torture myself with thoughts that I behaved appallingly. I was a token drunken woman in the hotel bar, all that ridiculous sobbing. Oh god, I hate myself. Will they have me on CCTV? Will we be banned for the rest of our lives from this hotel? Will I ever be let loose to do hotel reviews again?

I lie there for about four hours, unable to get back to sleep. How many health features have I written in which I state: 'The more alcohol you drink, the less you will sleep'? It's so true. I can hear Sarah's gentle snoring and I tiptoe to the bathroom. Once back in bed, I start to feel sick. I look back over the evening and berate myself. I've made a total fool of myself, and now I'll probably be too ill to go shopping. I don't deserve to have a husband or a child. I'm not fit.

I beat myself up until the bellboy knocks and he wheels in a trolley containing breakfast. I dive under the sheets so he can't see me. I'm so ashamed of myself.

As soon as the door closes, Sarah says: 'Hey, you, get out of there, he thinks me and Claire brought a bloke back!'

I pull the sheets back slowly. Any swift move will make me throw up, I'm sure. Sarah is just standing looking at the breakfast tray. It has every kind of juice imaginable – orange, apple, pineapple, blackcurrant, cranberry, mango.

'You danced a lot when I was reading out the juices,' laughs Sarah, as Claire goes into the shower.

A little bit of it starts to come back to me.

'Sarah,' I say feebly. 'Was I really badly behaved? Did I offend anyone? Do I need to send flowers?'

'No, you were fantastic!' laughs Sarah. 'You had a fantastic time, crying all over the bar. You'd still be there now if we hadn't brought you back.'

'Oh my God, I rang Crossy, didn't I?' I say, horrified. 'But was I bad at the party?'

'Well, you were gagging to go over to Dev,' she grins.

'I didn't, did I?' I gasp.

'No, we stopped you,' she reassures me. 'You were great at the party. Mind, I was a bit scared when you insisted on walking round Manchester looking for scenes from *Cutting It*. Don't mind you doing your research, but not at 2 in the morning.'

I start to hate myself again. I probably put everyone's safety in danger by dragging them round the back streets of Manchester.

'Oh God, I'm turning into an alcoholic,' I voice my worst nightmare. 'I have the alcoholic gene in me. It's come down a generation. I'm like Sue Ellen, a drunk and an unfit mother. I'm not even a nice alcoholic. I have that evil nasty streak that makes me endanger my friends.'

'Listen, you're not an alcoholic,' reassures Sarah. 'We were out for a night and we had fun. We did nothing wrong, and you were very, very funny.'

'You don't think I've pickled my liver or anything nasty?' I ask nervously.

'Well, you might if you drank like that every night,' replies Sarah, 'But not just once in … how many years?'

'Four?' I suggest.

'What's going on?' asks Claire, strutting out of the bathroom. I don't believe her. She even struts in a robe and flat slippers. 'Can you even get out of bed, you drunk?'

'Not without throwing up,' I tell Claire.

'Claire,' says Sarah, with that mischievous tone in her voice that I usually love. 'Is Chris an alky?'

'Her, an alky? Never!' she says, as though I'm not in the room. 'Mind you, I'm looking at her in a new light after last night. She's a bit of a party minx, after all.'

In between the bouts of self-hatred, I'm quite pleased I've made it. I may be a mummy but I can still party. Question is, can I get out of bed and go shopping?

◆◆◆◆◆

After a full day trailing after Claire and Sarah round department stores, I've survived the train journey with just a few trips to the loo to throw up, and I'm back home. Whilst it's fab to see Jack, it's a bit scary that I'm now back in charge of a four-year-old boy in this delicate state. I'm stuffed if he wants me to play. I give him the Buzz Lightyear suitcase I bought him.

'Wow, it flashes when I touch that button, Mum,' says Jack, excited.

Then he pulls the handle out to pull the case along.

'You do this with your case, don't you, Mum?' he checks.

'Yes, if I can't persuade Daddy to carry it for me,' I reply very slowly.

I'm absolutely shattered and lying on the settee. I still feel horribly sick.

'Mum, will you play Robin Hood?' asks Jack.

'Jack, let Mummy lie there,' says Ian, sympathetically.

My husband is very kind to me when I'm hungover. I'm not sure if he understands the mental angst I'm going through, but he treats me with kid gloves. Thanks to this, I'm starting to feel a little better about my imagined chronic alcohol addiction.

'Why, is Mummy poorly, Daddy?' he asks. 'She's just been away on holiday, hasn't she?'

'No, she's not poorly, she's a little tired, Jack,' replies Ian.

'Why is she tired?' continues Jack.

Ian tells it straight.

'Because she was out on the beer last night,' answers Ian,

looking Jack straight in the eye as though to say: 'That's what kind of mother you have, son.'

'She can't have been,' says Jack, horrified.

Oh my God, here we go. Another reason to feel guilty for getting so pissed. Is he going to say I can't drink because I'm his mum and I'm pure and faultless and mummies don't go on the razz?

'Why, Jack?' I ask nervously. 'Why can't I have been drinking?'

'Yes, why?' asks Ian.

'Because Mummy doesn't drink beer,' says Jack, with confidence. 'She says it's smelly and it makes you horrid. Her daddy used to drink it and it made him into a horrid man. My mummy would never, ever drink beer.'

'Daddy, Jack's right,' I say, laughing, though my ribs ache from vomiting. 'I don't drink beer, just kir royales, wine, brandy, banana daiquiris and Brandy Alexanders.'

Part of me is horrified at the amount of alcohol I packed away, but part of me is secretly pleased I had such fun now I'm back in a life where I have to get up any time from 6am. After a good night's sleep, I'll be OK to function and, in three weeks' time, my complexion will be back to normal.

'Mummy, those drinks are perfectly OK,' nods Jack approvingly, 'especially the banana one. That's healthy. It's OK, Mum. Don't worry. Don't you see, you didn't drink beer!'

And in that second I am redeemed in my little son's eyes. I have got away with it. Even the hotel has e-mailed to say they're glad we had such a good time. I just hope my insides are as forgiving.

CHAPTER 5

Were You a Good Girl at School?

I love school. I love it, I love it, I love it. I love my teachers. I love learning and working and getting my work marked because I always get top marks. And best of all I love going home and telling my mum how well I have done. I learn quickly. I seem to have a photographic memory. I just need to look at a picture of a statue or a cathedral and I can say instantly where it is. We've been doing lots of geography recently and learning about capital cities. Now my teacher is holding up a picture of a cathedral in Austria. My hand shoots up like lightning.

'Christine,' says Miss Williams, pointing at me. 'Vienna, Miss Williams,' I say, quietly.

'Excellent!' she says. 'You're very fast at these cards.'

Inside I'm really chuffed. The teachers say I'm doing really well at school. When they say this, it makes my mum so happy she almost cries.

Today my mum has come to school to have a quick word with Miss Williams after our morning lessons. Usually she comes to Parents' Evening and talks to my teachers without me, but Miss Williams asked my mum to stop by and have a chat today.

I'm really proud to have my mum in our classroom and I show her all the drawings and work on the wall I've described to her at home. She's remembered everything. I bet if I blindfolded her, she'd walk straight to the display we did on shapes and sizes.

I really like Miss Williams. She's about 24, I think, and this is her first job. She keeps telling us she'll be getting married in a few months and then she'll be Mrs Ramsgill. We all laugh that we'll never remember that and for months when she calls the register in the mornings we'll say: 'Yes, Miss Will … er … sorry, Mrs Ramsgill.'

'I know I've only had Christine in my class since September,' begins Miss Williams. 'That's just a couple of months so we're obviously just getting used to each other.

'Her work is absolutely excellent,' she goes on, and I feel a glow of pleasure run through me. 'Look at this writing. It's so neat it could have been done by a 16-year-old, not a girl of six.' Although she's heaping praise on me, I sense there's a 'but' coming very soon.

'But I just wish you were a bit chattier, Christine,' she continues, turning to me.

Then as she turns back to my mum, she adds: 'She seems very timid and shy in class and she has no reason to be. She's very popular.'

'Yes, I know,' says my mum. Then she adds: 'She's quiet,' as though that isn't an altogether bad thing.

'But she gets embarrassed when I ask her a question. I can see her face getting redder when the other children turn to look at her. She also seems a little bit tired in class,' continues Miss Williams. 'Do you mind me asking what time she goes to bed?'

'Around 7.30pm,' replies my mum, with confidence.

'Well, that's not the problem, is it?' says my teacher, thinking aloud.

She must notice the look of consternation on my mum's face because she adds: 'Oh well, she's doing well, and maybe she'll just grow out of the shyness.'

'Let's hope so,' smiles my mum, but I can see she's a little bit worried. I think she expected this chat with my teacher to go well because I'm so good at my work.

But Miss Williams is right. I am tired and I am shy. I don't like to be the centre of attention and I prefer to sit at the front of the class so that when I answer, no one can turn round and look at me.

◆◆◆◆◆

I'm on a total high. We've just had a spelling test and I got 49 out of 50. The closest mark to me was Susie who got 25 out of 50.

'If you were in the big school now, Christine, that would be 98 per cent. That's a fantastic mark,' says Miss Williams, who's almost as excited as me. 'The rest of you should try harder.'

I'm a little torn. I'm happy my mark will please my mum and it has earned me praise from my teacher, but I don't want to upset the rest of my class. Life would be awful if my friends stopped liking me. But they don't seem to mind. At playtime we all play outside in the cool November air, with our hats and mittens on, and our scarves round our mouths.

Once we're back in class, it doesn't seem long before the school bell rings in the hall, and it's time for home. I am dying, absolutely dying, to tell my mum my spelling mark, and then my heart leaps a little bit, too. My dad will also be proud of me. I almost fly out of the school door and down the little railed-decked ramp to my mum at the iron gate.

But I'm discreet. I don't want to brag in front of other people, so I hurry my mum to the lollipop man ahead of everyone, so I can tell her quietly. It works, we cross the road together first, and then we're ahead of everyone walking back down the hill towards home.

'That's great!' she smiles, and she stops to bend down to kiss me. I know she must be proud. It's a windy walk up and down the hill and we hardly ever stop because we know we'll get even colder. But today we stop. 'You are such a clever girl,' she says.

◆◆◆◆◆

I'm still on a high when my dad gets home from work. I rush to the back door, and his two feet aren't in the kitchen before I tell him.

'Dad, I got 49 out of 50 today. We had a spelling test and I came top. My teacher said if I were at the big school …'

I'm talking really fast and my heart is beating with excitement, but his face isn't as ecstatic as my mum's was. He stands and looks at me and, after what feels like minutes, he says: 'Only 49, hey? What was the one you got wrong?'

For a minute, I think he's joking and any second he'll scoop me up and tell me what a clever girl I am. Then I realize his face hasn't changed. He's not joking. I feel my excitement sapping down through my body, into my feet and away. All that joy and all that pride have just been drained out of me.

I can't even answer him. I can't tell him I lost a mark because I spelled out 'mister' instead of shortening it to Mr. In fact, the more I think about it, the more I'm convinced I should have had 50 out of 50, and that would have been 100 per cent. But for now I'll make do with 98 per cent, whatever that means.

He goes into the living room, and takes his jacket off, and reads the paper. I don't say another word all evening, but inside me there's a determination not to get any more spellings wrong. It has to be 50 correct answers next time. I don't want to feel like this again.

◆◆◆◆◆

I'm in bed now, and I have vowed I'll do better at school. I didn't say anything to my mum. I'm not even sure if she heard what my dad said to me. She was probably making a cup of tea to hand him when he sat down with the newspaper.

I'm still slumbering when I hear a banging. It's the door at the bottom of the stairs. My dad must be home from the pub. I must have slept through the car coming home.

'You useless cunt!'

My stomach feels as though it has dropped two feet inside my body. I can tell from the tone, it's going to be one of those nights, though I've no idea what a cunt is. I know 'useless' isn't good, so one of us is going to get it.

Some of my friends at school say they like getting their brothers and sisters into trouble, but I don't. They say they're relieved when their parents are mad at the others, not them. But when my dad's about to explode, I always hope it's going to be me in trouble if anyone. It's easier than hearing him ranting at my brother or my mum.

Yet I'm not sure who it is yet. I think quickly. No one has done anything that could have angered him so much. Chris got home from school and stayed in. He was supposed to be doing his homework in his bedroom, but when I went to see him, he was putting football teams on a wall chart. But my dad doesn't know that.

I know by now we don't need to have done anything wrong, but all the same I still try and think of a reason. Often the problem's in my dad's imagination. If my mum's bought a loaf of bread, my dad shouts at her for talking to the baker. It's as though he sometimes looks for problems that just aren't there.

I hear my mum's voice, pleading.

'Harry, calm down, come on, get to bed, leave it, please. It's already late and her teacher told me today she's tired all the time.'

'No, I'm going to sort her out,' he snipes.

Oh God, they've both said the word 'her'. I'm the one in trouble, and my mum sounds worried and scared. My dad is soon upstairs and he pushes or kicks my bedroom door open. I'm not sure which. I just know there's a gust of air as the door flies open.

'What's wrong, Dad?' I try so hard to sound strong, but inside I'm so scared. I'm about to ask why he's angry, but he'll latch on to every word and tear it apart. I hate it when he mimics me. He makes me sound so frightened and little, which I am, I suppose. I also think him mimicking me has made me hate speaking aloud in class now. Best keep quiet, I tell myself.

'What's wrong?' he repeats. 'What's wrong? I'll tell you what's wrong, you stupid fucking child. You're what's wrong. Everything about you is wrong.'

I've absolutely no idea what I could have done. I got up, went to school, came home, had lunch, went back to school, came home again, had my tea, did my homework and came to bed. I didn't even watch Benny Hill on television, which my mum sometimes lets me watch as a treat because she likes to see me laugh.

'You stupid fucking thick cow!' He pauses after every word as if to emphasize how stupid and thick I am. I hate those long gaps because I know it's giving him a chance to think of something even nastier to say.

There's a very slight slur in his voice. If I didn't know him, I'd think he was just incredibly angry, and his voice was slow through sheer emotion. But I can recognize the signs by now.

He's been drinking, his eyes are that scary clear colour and he's getting unsteady on his feet.

My mum has often said the last few pints kick in after he gets home, as he seems to get drunker and drunker after he comes through the door. It hasn't been unusual for him to come in all nice and friendly, then half an hour later he gets up and starts shouting at us. We really don't know what mood he'll be in from one half hour to the next.

I can see movement through the hinge in the door, though I can't hear anything. My mum's out there. I didn't hear my mum come upstairs. We're all such dab hands at creeping around, we should form a gang of cat burglars. My dad's standing above my bed. He's still wearing his suit. He must have stormed through the back door and straight upstairs.

'You think you're so good,' he starts, his index finger jabbing me on the top of my arm. I hate his hands being so close as I think he'll hit me. I also hate myself for flinching every time his finger comes near me.

I almost laugh inside. He's wrong. I don't think I'm so good at all. I'm just trying my best.

'You're just like the rest of them.'

I don't know who he means. My mum and Chris and the rest of our family, or the children at school? Whoever he means, it can't be that bad being like them. Better to be like them, than him.

'98 per cent,' he rants. 'That's no fucking good.'

I don't say a word. I can feel tears creeping up to the back of my eyes. I was so proud of myself this afternoon, now I just feel like a bag of rubbish.

'You've got to get 100 per cent. There's no fucking point getting things wrong, you stupid little bastard. I want to be proud of you. I want to go and tell people my daughter got 100 per cent at school, not some fucking 98 per cent.'

'Oh Harry, please will you stop this filthy language,' my mum pleads. 'This little kid did well today and you've ruined it for her. Please just leave her alone and go to bed. She doesn't deserve this.'

'Deserve this?' he questions. 'I don't fucking deserve you lot, but do you hear me complaining? I don't deserve a whore for a wife. It's not about what we deserve.'

My mum is biting her lip. She wants to retaliate but she looks at me and shuts up.

My dad goes off in a rant, sidetracking to insult my mum and her family. Then he turns back to me.

'I'm ashamed of you, that's what I am, fucking ashamed. I wish you weren't mine, you're so useless. You're never going to be anything or anyone. You may as well go and get a job in a mill.'

My mum reacts as though that's the greatest insult he could ever dish out, and inside I cringe that she's going to make the whole thing worse by speaking up.

'A mill?' she queries. 'A mill, did you say? Listen here, mister, she's a damn sight brighter than you ever were. You're just jealous because she's bright and you were so bloody thick yourself.'

With that, he leaves my room and staggers off to his bed. From that day, my mum swears he's jealous of me because he didn't do very well at school.

I lie there, tears flowing now he's gone. I can sometimes hold back the crying but there's too much in there. I have to let some sadness out. He said I'm useless and I'm thick. My mark wasn't good enough for him and I try so hard. My face and pillow are hot and wet with tears and my nose is running.

My mum sits on the side of my bed, handing me a cotton handkerchief with embroidered Spanish dancers on for my tears and my nose.

'Christine, love, don't get upset, he's nothing and he's very, very wrong,' my mum tells me. 'Please don't believe a word he says. He was hopeless at school and he's narked that you're so clever. You're a bright kid, you are.'

'Why does he say those things, Mum?' I ask. 'I'm sure I would never speak to anyone the way he speaks to us.'

'It's beer talking again, love,' she replies.

I nod as though I understand, but a voice inside is saying: 'Hang on, he wasn't very pleasant about my spelling mark earlier when he got in from work. He hadn't been drinking then.'

But I stay quiet. Is he starting to be horrid all the time now?

'She's right, Chris,' says my brother. He's standing just behind my mum and he's looking pretty pale. 'You did well. Take no notice of him.'

But I do. I feel useless and what makes me feel sad is that my schoolwork is the only good thing I can do. The other girls are funny with their one-line jokes and pretty with their long blonde curly hair and bright blue eyes. I was always the clever one – or so I thought until tonight. Now I'm not so sure what's good about me, if anything.

◆◆◆◆◆

Big day in our house! It's September and Jack's starting school. For three hours every single weekday morning I shall be as free as a bird, just like that old Nimble advert on telly. I shall float off in a hot air balloon with supertrim thighs.

It will also be less of an emotional wrench than it might have been, because for the last year Jack has been going to pre-school for two-and-a-half hours four days a week, and nursery on Wednesdays. I've squeezed all my freelance work into those hours.

After Christmas he goes full days and then the flags really will be flying. It isn't that I don't love my son, it's just that I need a bit of time for myself. Having used all pre-school and nursery time for work, I haven't shopped for clothes for myself for years. When I get my hair cut, I take my work with me, and sit reading shorthand notes when I should be reading about the Beckhams in *OK* magazine.

I know I went to Manchester with Claire and Sarah last April, but that was a one-off. If I have a work interview further away than an hour's drive, there's a major military operation to get Jack looked after.

So when Jack is at school mornings only, I'll be gaining just half an hour extra most days. I am just so excited, visualizing hours and hours of time ahead of me. I imagine I'll have time for manicures, coffee with friends, and I may even relax in the garden with a book one of these days. Yes, my life will be sussed. When I fill in those life-circle questions, every part of my life will be a straight 10.

I can see it now. I shall be so well groomed because I will have time to get the spaghetti hoops out of my hair before I rush out of the house.

My wardrobe will be all organized, plentiful and co-ordinated, and in a morning I shall say: 'I don't know which of my 12 pairs of trousers I shall wear today,' instead of 'Oh my God, I've got tomato ketchup on my one pair of jeans and I've no more clean trousers.'

◆◆◆◆◆

'Jack!' I shriek. 'Stop messing about! Come and get dressed. We have to take a photo yet and you have to be at school on time. You can't be late on your first day.'

I've been asked so many times if I'm sad my baby is starting school. Of course I'm not sad. I sympathize with mums who cry at the school gates, and sob about losing their babies, but I just don't feel like that. I'm excited for Jack. School's a treat. I loved it. And I really do need a little extra time.

'Be a very good boy today, won't you, Jack?' I say. 'Do as your teacher asks and don't get into any trouble.' I don't know why I'm saying this. He was always an angel at pre-school.

'Were you a good girl at school, Mummy?' he asks.

He's always been interested in my childhood, probably because he senses I'm not telling him the full story half the time.

'Oh yes, I was, Jack,' I say proudly as Ian chips in mockingly from the dining room: 'Mummy used to get 100 per cent and ask for extra work, Jack. Ask Uncle Chris about it sometime.'

'And Daddy's a very cheeky monkey,' I say, as I lead Jack to his bedroom for the big uniform ceremony. 'He's very jealous because Mummy worked much harder than Daddy sometimes.'

For a second I have a flashback to my own schooldays when nothing was ever good enough for my dad and I vow, there and then, that I will praise Jack for every item of schoolwork he ever produces. He will never have to suffer the pain of knowing you just can't please a parent, however hard you try.

I look at him: He's so young and so little, yet he's not much younger than I was when my dad was ranting at me all night and throwing obscenities at me. I cringe if I say 'bloody' or 'bugger' by mistake in front of Jack, yet my dad was regularly saying 'fuck' to me and calling me a 'cunt'.

I also wonder how my dad could ever have eroded my confidence the way he did at such an impressionable age. He must surely have been aware of the damage he was doing. Didn't he realize that the beliefs he drummed into my young brain would stay with me all my life? Maybe he knew that and that's what he wanted, or maybe he just didn't know or didn't care.

Jack's blue sweatshirt, white polo shirt and dark grey trousers are laid out on his bed. For the last few weeks I've felt as though I'm the one starting school. There's been so much to learn, but if I'm on a learning curve, I'm still at the bit before it bends.

There's the uniform for a start. Does Jack have to have the school logo on every single jumper? Does he have a polo shirt under a sweatshirt or are they optional? Long trousers or short? It's only just September and it's still sunny out there most days. Are socks with footballs on allowed?

Then there's the hassle of where to put your name tags. When we got the blurb from school, the name tags were emphasized so much, I felt sure they would execute any parent who forgets to label clothing.

And do you go for iron-in or sew-in name tags? Jack gets eczema on his neck, so I've sewn them in the hem. Will anyone ever see them? I didn't read the instructions and wiggled the iron when I put Jack's name tags in. Now his name is so blurry I feel pissed every time I read it. Blimey, I'm such a crap mum. I can't even get the name tags right.

'Jack! It really is time to get dressed!'

'Jack! Why aren't you answering me?'

'You haven't asked me three times yet, Mum,' he answers, blasé.

He still wriggles like a two-year-old as I bend and twist and turn and try and get him into his clothes.

'Jack, keep still!' I think to myself, 'No wonder I'm always at the osteopath with my dodgy neck.' Out loud I say, 'It's like being on *Challenge Anneka* getting you dressed.'

'What's Challenge Annie?' he asks, excited at the mention of a challenge.

'Never you mind,' I say. His vest, pants and socks are on. I pull his polo shirt over his head and admire how good he looks in white. Then his long grey trousers. Wow, he looks so grown-up. Now his sweatshirt with the tree logo. Finally his new school shoes.

I was quite chatty when we started, but gradually, as I've put more clothes on him, I've gone quieter. There. He's ready. I straighten up to go and look at him head to foot. He looks so grown-up in his long grey trousers. I look again. My annoyance at his trying to escape has evaporated. I can hardly speak a word. Why do I suddenly feel like sitting down and crying?

'Jack, you look so good,' I say, as tears start to gather in my eyes. Soon, to my absolute horror, there's a stream of them down my face. 'Just go and show Daddy your uniform.'

Daddy isn't as affected by our son's first day at school as me.

'Wow, what a smart boy,' he says. 'What's that noise? Is Kitty trapped somewhere? Listen.'

'It's Mum,' I hear Jack say, with a chuckle in his voice. 'She's crying in my bedroom.'

By now, my face is awash with salty tears and they're showing no signs of stopping either. Every time I catch a glimpse of those long dark grey trousers, my chest heaves some more and more face gets wetter.

'Sweetie, what's wrong?' asks Ian, coming into Jack's bedroom all concerned. He obviously thinks I've had terrible news in the post. Or maybe the phone has rung when he wasn't listening to say a whole family I know has been wiped out in a car crash.

'It's not h ... h ... him g ... going to s ... school that bothers me, I can cope with that, I'm l ... l ... l ... ooking forward to that. It's those b ... b ... bloody grey trousers. He looks so cute.'

And with that off my chest, I sob some more. Ian walks off confused. He'll be thinking: 'One minute she wants him to start school, the next minute she doesn't. Women.'

Aware I'm against the clock, and there is no time for emotion when you're up against a very punctual school bell, we head outside. Jack messes about and pulls ridiculous faces for photographs. As usual, I take one of Ian and Jack, then Ian takes one of me and Jack. Because we never go and ask someone to take a picture of the three of us, we always look like a separated couple, with limited access to our only son.

By the time we're ready for our walk to school, my face is swollen, my eyes puffy and my nose is all red. Neighbours are keeping a lookout for Jack going to school.

I keep my head down. Shame because I feel so proud of him, with his little blue book bag with nothing in. He's like these businessmen you see in first class on trains. When they open their briefcases, there's just an orange inside and I realize with disappointment I have more important documents stuffed in my handbag.

Lots of people chat to Jack on the way to school.

'Are you excited, Jack?' asks Mandy, whose son is in the year above Jack.

'Yeah,' he answers, part sullenness, part shyness, just like a teenager. I can see other mums looking at my red face, but I can't start to explain it was just the grey trousers that did it. They'll say: 'Yeah, yeah, you're just a clingy overprotective mother.'

At school I take Jack through to his classroom, a portakabin with little toilets and a cloakroom and a big classroom area. His teacher is to be Mrs Link, and she seems to be urging parents to leave their children in the classroom as soon as possible. It's like the second cutting of the umbilical cord.

There will be just five in Jack's Reception class, which will be mixed in with Class One. I wonder why my classes were much bigger when I was five and six, and put it down to a lack of contraception.

Jack knows three of the girls, Jessica, Roxanne and Triona, from pre-school, but one of them, Chloe, doesn't know anyone.

I'm going to start his training now. He's going to be a new man. People will congratulate me on bringing up such a sensitive soul, so in tune with the feelings of others.

'Jack,' I say, taking him aside after seeing poor Chloe clinging to her mum for dear life. How scary this must be when you don't know anyone.

But I know Jack's a sensitive soul and if I explain how Chloe feels, he will go over to her, maybe even put a friendly arm round her. How cute would that be? Her mum will go off to work reassured that Chloe has found such a caring friend and I will walk back up that road with pride. I may have been an emotional heap this morning, but my son is showing the true effect of having a mother who verbalizes her emotions so well.

'Chloe is new to the area,' I tell him, as he looks excitedly at the books, toys, jigsaws and trays with arty things in. He's barely listening to me. He's wide-eyed at blackboards and little desks and chairs. 'She doesn't know anyone here today. Will you make friends with her and play with her? Look how sad she looks.'

'Why doesn't she know anyone?' he asks, with the confidence of one who knows half the school already and has spent the summer playing in the park with them.

'She hasn't lived here very long,' I say, pulling a sad face to try and conjure up some empathy in him.

'Why?' Oh my God, why is he so matter-of-fact? Can't he grasp the idea that a little girl may be scared and he could help? I suppose he is only four-and-a-half himself.

'I don't know, I think her family lived in town before; she's new to this village,' I'm going on now but he's not listening. He's spotted a Year One boy he plays with in the park. 'Listen up, Jack, just be nice to her, OK?'

'No, sorry, Mum, can't,' he replies, looking me straight in the eye. 'I won't have any time. You see, I've got my friends from pre-school here. I need to see them and play with them.'

'Jack! Don't be so mean,' I say. 'Imagine how you would feel if you were new to the area and you didn't have any friends.'

'I'd make some, Mum.' He's so matter-of-fact about this. But he has more to say.

'Anyway, Mum, if you're so bothered about Chloe, you stay and play with her.'

I look at him in horror. He knows he's got me there. But I've done my time, thank you very much. You don't see prisoners begging to stay inside on their release day, do you? I kiss him goodbye, I walk towards the door and I look back once before I escape. He's playing with the girls he knew at pre-school, not remotely bothered he's the only boy in the Reception class.

I'm up that road in a flash. I don't even wait for the green man before I cross the road. You see, four-and-a-half years inside but I still have that rebel streak when it comes to obeying the rules. There really is hope for me yet.

CHAPTER 6

Why Don't You Like Christmas, Mummy?

I'm almost bursting with excitement. My mum and I have got the bus into town and we're just coming to Lingards, a department store in the centre of Bradford. You have to walk through rows and rows of women's tights and knickers near the entrance, but we don't even stop to look – we are going upstairs to Father Christmas's grotto.

Lingards is very cramped. The aisles between displays are so narrow I have to walk slightly behind my mum, still holding her hand. It's important I stay with my mum because the displays are piled high and she would never find me if I went out of sight. I don't usually get lost anyway – the only time my mum lets go of my hand is when she's in the shoe department.

She loves shoes, my mum. She's always telling us that before she was married she had a pair of shoes on every step on my grandma and granddad's staircase. Now she doesn't have that many, but it doesn't stop her looking at them. Sometimes she strokes their soft leather, tries them on and admires them in a mirror, but she never buys them.

She always looks nice in them. When he's being nice to us, my dad says my mum has the best legs around because her calves are shapely and her ankles are slim. She puts the shoes back on the shelves, giving them a long lingering look, as though she'll be back for them one day.

She's always very keen that we have good-quality shoes. She once told me: 'If you only have enough money for decent shoes or food, go for the shoes. Your feet are very important and they carry you around all your life. It won't do any of us any harm to miss a meal.'

We're getting into the lift now. It has two cage doors, one on the inside and one outside. My mum always makes a big thing of shutting the two doors. Every time we come here she says: 'It won't work if they're not both shut properly.' And she even tuts at people who don't close both of them if they get in after us.

We're finally in the queue to see Father Christmas. There are a few decorations up and we passed a tree so it must be Christmas in a week's time. There are three more children ahead of me.

Soon it's my turn and my mum sort of pushes me through the little grotto entrance when I stop and look back.

'You'll be fine, I'm just here,' she says, laughing.

I sit on Father Christmas's knee. He's a bigger build than my dad and there's more space on his knees. I don't feel as though I'm going to wobble off any minute.

'So what would you like for Christmas?' he asks me in quite a deep voice.

'I'd like anything you could find for me,' I say. 'I'd like a doll or a game ...'

I stop, afraid Father Christmas thinks I want all these things. I should have made it clear I'm giving him a choice. I know we only ask for one thing at Christmas. I hate asking but Father Christmas is richer than my mum so maybe he can afford what I really want. I'm going to ask him, I may not get a chance like this again.

'But I would really, really like a record player,' I say timidly, expecting him to roar and ask me if I know how much they cost.

But he nods and asks: 'Does your mummy know this is what you want?'

I shake my head.

'Very well,' he replies. 'I shall see if we have any spare ones. Have a lovely Christmas, and would you ask your mummy to pop in and see me for a minute?'

My mum crouches down to go into the little grotto and comes out smiling at me, but I can see a worried look in her eyes, as though her mind is doing some overtime.

'Why didn't you tell me that's what you wanted, Chris?' she asks.

'I would have, but I was afraid you might worry you couldn't buy it for me. I told Father Christmas because he's got more money than you, hasn't he?'

'You are daft,' she says with appreciation. 'C'mon, let's go and have a strawberry milkshake at your favourite place.'

We head across the next two roads to the market, where we find the café with the high stools. My mum lifts me up to my seat and we order. I love sitting so high, right up to the counter, looking at all the different flavoured milkshakes.

'We'll just have a drink,' she says, her mind elsewhere. 'Christmas is an expensive time, you know.'

It's Christmas morning and the whole house is quiet. There's no light coming through the curtains. I can tell it's still dark outside. My mum and dad's bedroom door is closed, and so is Chris's. How can they all sleep on when Father Christmas may well have been down our chimney last night? He might even still be downstairs.

I tiptoe downstairs to the living room to see if he's been. There's always a draught as we pass the front door. As I open the living room door, I gasp. There, to my left, on the little cards table, is a record player. There are some selection boxes too and some presents for Chris. Father Christmas has used our full names – Christine and Christopher – so we don't get muddled.

On my record player there's a note, which I can just about read. 'Dear Christine, I hope you like your record player. Please don't play with it until your mummy or daddy are with you. You must be careful with it, as the needle is very fragile. Have a lovely Christmas, Father Christmas.'

My mum usually has a lie-in on Sundays and I stay in my room until I hear her getting up so I'm not usually downstairs on my own in a morning. But I'm very excited and want to shout out and tell everyone I have a record player of my very own. Now I won't have to ask my dad to take his Dusty Springfield records off the old gramophone so I can play my *Songs from Peter Pan* record.

I tiptoe upstairs and push open my mum and dad's bedroom door. As soon as the door creaks my mum leaps out of bed, as though she wasn't asleep anyway. She doesn't even speak, she just ushers me out, moving me towards the door with her arm, pulling on a quilted dressing gown with lace trimmings round the collar and pockets.

'He's been, Mum,' I say on the landing, so happy I'm almost in tears. 'He brought me that record player. You don't have to buy it for me after all.'

I look for signs of joy and relief on her face. She smiles but she doesn't look as though all her money worries are over.

I gabble on: 'It's really, really lovely, and he left me a note.'

'Happy Christmas, sweetheart,' says my mum, gently touching

the back of my head. 'I'm glad you like it. We'll have a go with it when everyone gets up.'

'And to think I nearly didn't ask him for it. It just shows, you should ask for what you want, shouldn't you, Mum?'

'Yes, always,' she replies, obviously hoping I don't make it a habit.

◆◆◆◆◆

We've had a lovely day. I've played *The Little Drummer Boy* so many times, even my grandma knows it by heart now. We had roast turkey for dinner and my grandma found a sixpence in her Christmas pudding. Now Grandma is sleeping in my bed for the night, and I'm on the sunlounger at the bottom of my mum and dad's bed. Even my dad has been quite nice today. He has watched some television with us and shared his Christmas chocolate bars.

She's an old lady, my grandma, but she's still a tough nut. She's at least 65 and she's my dad's mum, the last of my grand-parents. She's so deaf we have to shout at her or write her notes. She has snow-white hair with dark eyebrows and she smells of talcum powder.

She has arthritis so bad her knees have started to point out-wards, making her two legs a diamond shape. She needs a stick all the time and it takes her a good half an hour to get up and down our stairs. We know she's tough because she has threatened to clout us with her stick, and once tried to whack Chris when he'd been using the stick as a pretend golf club, hitting balls around the house.

She's been living in a council flat since my granddad died, but she hates it there because there's a girl called Susan who's about my age, seven, and she stares in the window and pulls faces at my grandma. So far my grandma has just sat there, but

I wouldn't be surprised if she doesn't try to get to the door and give that girl a clip round her ear with her stick.

My mum and I sometimes walk down to her flat. I have never seen Grandma happier than when my mum suggested she came to stay with us for Christmas.

'Our Christine will be OK on the sunlounger in our room for a few nights, won't you, love?' my mum asked me, to reassure my grandma she would have a bed, and wouldn't be putting anyone out. 'We'd love to have you, Grandma.'

'Oooh, thank you, Margaret,' she said. 'I love coming to your house, that would be grand.'

I always think it's strange the way my mum gets on so well with my grandma. After all, she's my dad's mum.

I like having my grandma here. She sits in her chair and plays with me a bit, and I sometimes read to her. I didn't mind giving up my bed for her, but I don't really like being in my mum and dad's bedroom.

◆◆◆◆◆

Now I'm wide awake because there's some shouting downstairs. I'm not used to sleeping in my mum and dad's bedroom, above the living room at the front of the house, so I need to get my bearings. I can't hear the kitchen and dining room as well from here.

But then the hallway door opens and the shouting is clear.

'Harry, don't be stupid, you can't do that!' I hear my mum saying. 'You can't wake her up now.'

I stiffen. Oh no, what have I done wrong now? I go through the day, like a film reel running backwards, but there was nothing I did wrong. Maybe he was just fed up with *The Little Drummer Boy* song.

The footsteps are heading upstairs. My heart starts beating

fast and I turn to my right-hand side so I can see the door open, even though their wardrobe is in part of my line of vision. I always like to face him when he's angry, as though I need to be prepared for what he's about to do. But the door hasn't opened and the shouting continues.

'C'mon, Mother, we're not having you here,' I hear my dad shouting. I realize he's in my grandma's bedroom. He's shouting extra loud because of my grandma's deafness. Our neighbours will hear every word. My mum will be so ashamed tomorrow morning.

I hear a frail, weak, half-asleep voice say: 'Harry, what's the matter? What's up, lad?'

By now my mum's upstairs, and she's saying loudly: 'Ignore him, Grandma, he's been drinking, you get back to sleep. C'mon, Harry, come back downstairs, leave your mother. It's the middle of the night.'

'Mother? She's not my fucking mother,' he rants. 'She was no fucking mother to me. She never had any fucking time for me.'

'What is wrong with you?' my mum asks.

She sounds appalled that he can speak to his own mother like this, an old lady who's done none of us any harm. My mum's voice seems braver tonight, maybe because my grandma is there.

'She never did owt for me, no time for me,' he continues, with some whimpering in his voice.

There's some quiet and it's a moment or two before I realize he's crying. He's whining like a dog.

My grandma speaks again: 'Harry, pull yourself together. You shouldn't touch that stuff if it makes you like this. Look at yourself.'

'Look at myself, look at myself!' he mimics her doddery voice.

91

No wonder she's doddery. It's the early hours again, and she's tired out, like the rest of us.

'I'm the useless bastard you made me. This is what you made me, you fucking cow. And don't pretend to be deaf. I'm not stupid. You might think I am but I'm not.'

I'm still in bed, rigid, and I wonder if Chris is listening to this too. We've accepted that my dad shouts at us like this, but it sounds terrible when it's directed at my grandma.

'You fucking old cripple!' he rants.

I feel as though he has put a knife through me. My grandma hates being crippled. How must she feel to be called a cripple by her own son?

'C'mon, c'mon, get out of bed, I'm taking you home. We don't want you in our house, you're not fucking welcome here!'

I expect to hear my grandma getting out of bed. I expect to hear my mum fussing around to help her get dressed but there's no sound from my bedroom, where all this is going on.

Then I hear my grandma's voice. She seems to gain strength with every word and she's no longer a feeble old lady.

'You can shout as much as you like, Harry, and call me whatever you like, but as long as it's all right with Margaret for me to be here, I'm not going anywhere, lad. So best thing you can do is get yourself to bed and sleep off that skinful you've had.'

I am amazed at my grandma. What a tough woman she is. I would have been up and getting dressed the minute he told me to. Not my grandma, she's not afraid of him. Ha.

'Go on, bugger off, and sleep it off!' she says.

I tense up even more. This is it. He'll hit her now, I'm sure. No one answers him back like this. I hope she has her stick handy. If anyone is going to belt him, my grandma will. Oh God, I hope it doesn't turn into a fight, between my drunken dad and a crippled old lady. But he doesn't hit her. He's gone quiet for a second.

Then I hear him stomp out of the room, downstairs and out of the back door. I think he may have gone into the back garden or to the garage but, because I'm at the front of the house, I can't hear any more. Damn, if I'd been in my own room, I would have been able to look through the window to spy on him if I dared.

I start to wonder what he's gone for, but he's back within seconds, and I hear terror in my mum's voice as she cries out: 'Harry, what are you doing with that?'

He's obviously got something from the garage or the car, something scary. But he doesn't come upstairs. I'm bracing myself to run downstairs and check my mum's OK when I hear sudden crashing and hitting for a few moments, but there are no screams from my mum. Then he slams the living room door, comes upstairs into the bedroom. He doesn't realize I'm there too.

Seconds later, my mum comes to bed. Already my dad's breathing is louder. He's gone straight to sleep. I can tell from my mum's red eyes she's been crying. She bends right down to kiss me good night. The camp bed is so much lower than my own bed. I gesture for her to give me her ear so I can whisper.

'What's been happening, Mum?'

She presses her mouth close to my ear: 'He went berserk with an axe and smashed up that little chest of drawers your granddad made for me. His own dad made them for us and he's gone and done that.'

Her voice is going wobbly now. She's going to cry again.

'I loved those drawers,' she whispers. 'Granddad made them especially for me. Your grandma will go mad. She knew how much I loved them.

'But listen, Chris, don't be scared. I'm coming to bed now. I'll be right here and I probably won't sleep, so you close your eyes. It's Boxing Day tomorrow. Christmas isn't over yet.'

I'm terrified and I realize I hate Christmas. My dad gets drunk on and off all year, but at Christmas it's a dead cert, and whatever happiness I feel on Christmas morning is replaced with horrible memories by Christmas night.

◆◆◆◆◆

It's the week before Christmas and I'm in a foul mood. My to-do list is as long as my arm. I know because I have taped two pages of A4 lengthways together and it's so long I have to hold the whole list quite a way from me to read it.

I keep ticking things off, things like 'Buy Jack's teachers interesting presents.' I love buying presents normally, but this Christmas lark is so time-consuming. I feel as though I haven't done a proper day's work since mid-November, so I'll be skint by January. I've turned into a shopaholic, scouring chocolate shops, delicatessens, toy shops and Woolworths.

I know I should have been organized and set aside a week-end in November to do the whole lot, then celebrated with after-noon tea at Betty's, but I wasn't and I didn't, and here I am the week before Christmas, deadline girl once again.

It doesn't help that Jack won't tell me what's on his Christmas list.

'Away then, Jackie, give us some clues what you have asked Santa for,' I ask jovially, as we get ready to go to town for the zillionth time this week, and it's only Tuesday late afternoon. I'm trying to be cheerful with Jack so he'll confide.

'Why?' questions Jack, perplexed. 'Why do you need to know?'

'Oh, just interested,' I reply. I feel hopeful and pick up a pen and paper to make notes. 'Just in case I see Santa and he wants to check.'

'No worries on that score, Mum,' says Jack. 'I'm on holiday now. Where you go, I go. I'll be with you if we see him.'

'And don't I know it,' I mutter under my breath, putting down my pen and paper. Aloud I say: 'He may well ring when you're in bed. Santa's moved into the 21st century now. They have telephones in Lapland these days.'

Jack heaves a sigh of despair.

'Look, Mum,' he says in a slow careful voice as though he's speaking to a foreigner who has mastered just a handful of English words. 'That list is between me and Santa. There are some things you keep to yourself. OK?'

OK, OK, OK. But my stress levels have just gone off the Richter scale.

◆◆◆◆◆

We're in Northallerton now and I'm not the only stressed-out mother. There are a lot of mums dragging school-age children round the shops. They all look as knackered as me, if not more so.

Jack is bombing up and down the High Street, like a creature demented.

'Jack!' I yell like a fishwife. 'Slow down, there are a lot of people with walking sticks in town today. Don't knock any of them over or Santa won't come.'

'He will, Mum,' answers my son, returning to heel. 'He came to school last week and said he would definitely drop by at my house. Santa doesn't break his promises, so you see, Mum, I can do whatever I like now and Santa will come.'

With that parting shot, Jack is off again. I can see people in the distance looking up and down the street for someone in charge of a five-year-old boy running wild, apparently unsupervised.

'I'm so sorry, he's mine,' I say to an elderly woman who's just nearly been knocked flying.

'It's all right, dear,' she says, to my enormous relief. 'He'll be excited. It's such a special time of year for little ones …'

I try to escape but she wants to talk. I can see Jack waiting for me at a pedestrian crossing. I feel I have to hear her out. If she weren't so friendly, she'd be issuing a writ against us now and I'd be in Northallerton magistrates' court tomorrow for being in charge of an uncontrollable child in a public place.

'Yes, Jack's very excited,' I say, faking a doting mummy tone.

'I bet he is,' replies the woman. 'You mark my words, Christmas with little ones is such a magical time, but I expect you've discovered that these last few weeks.'

Oh yeah, I feel like saying, dead magical. I'm totally knackered. He's so excited he won't go to sleep till well after 10 and he won't eat any meals. I can't control him. He won't concentrate on anything.

On top of that I don't know what my only son wants for Christmas. Everyone's saying the shops are selling out. I have had more magical moments in my life, mostly on a beach while the ocean tickles my toes.

Unable to pretend any more, I nod, apologize once again and rush off after Jack.

'Jack, you nearly knocked that poor lady over,' I say, grabbing his arm and bending down slightly to speak to him.

'Which lady?' he asks looking round, but totally unconcerned.

Oh dear me, this kid is going to get it any minute.

Sensing he is standing at Danger's Door, Jack takes my hand and walks into Woolworths with me. He has a revelation for me.

'Mum, you know the Santa that came to the party the other week?' he asks.

'Yes,' I lie. Truth is, he's been to so many parties and seen so many Santas I've lost count. I'm just relieved he's calmed down.

His face is all serious. 'It wasn't the real Santa!'

'No!' I feign horror. 'How do you know that, Jack? Was it an impostor, pretending to be Santa?' I ask.

'He had a string round his beard!' whispers Jack, as though he's just revealed the secret of life itself.

I make some wide eyes in horror, then ask casually: 'What did you tell him you wanted again?'

'Oh, good try, Mum,' says Jack. 'You tried to trick me, didn't you?'

'Tell me Jack, go on,' I say in a teasing voice.

'No, definitely not telling now,' he says.

Bollocks. I'm definitely losing my questioning skills. If I weren't self-employed, I bet no one would hire me as a journalist. I've lost it.

◆◆◆◆◆

Mooching around the vast aisles of tubs of sweets in Woolworths, I ask: 'Jack, how much do you want to spend on Daddy this Christmas?'

'Five hundred pounds,' he replies, excitedly.

'That's very generous of you,' I reply, impressed he's such a giver.

'Shall we get him a new television?' asks Jack. 'I'll choose one with a really big screen for him to watch football and cricket on and you can give me the money. Daddy would like that and I really want to make my daddy happy.'

I start to explain.

'Daddy's present comes out of your pocket money,' I say.

I sense passers-by giving me the evil eye, as though I'm the skinflint parent from hell. I imagine them going home and telling their other half: 'This miserable woman in Woollies today was making her kid buy his dad's present out of his own money. Poor little thing, he only gets a pound a week and she makes him spend it on other folk. He's going to have a crap Christmas, isn't he? Are there charities that will help kids like him?'

But I'm adamant. I want my child to learn the value of money, yet be thoughtful and generous.

'So, Jack, what do you want to get Daddy? Look, there are some nice heart-shaped chocolates here for £2.99. That's three gold coins. Do you want to get those?'

Jack's gone all sulky now. 'Will I like them?' he asks. 'Are they just chocolate? There's nothing in them, is there?'

'They're not for you, Jack,' I say. 'They're for Dad, and yes, I think he will like them. They're praline, he likes praline.'

'I'm not buying them if they're not for me!' he stomps around.

'Jack, it's nice to buy presents for other people, especially people you love the way you love Daddy.'

'Well, if it's so nice to buy presents, you buy him them, then!' he retorts.

Bugger. Now my persuasion skills are up the creek too.

◆◆◆◆◆

Shoppers are getting more and more stressed by the minute. In the yummy chocolate shop down the arcade, one woman is about to hyperventilate because two boxes of chocolates she ordered three weeks ago haven't been made up.

'We haven't had time,' explains a young assistant. 'It's the busiest week of our year.'

'That's why I ordered them,' snaps the customer.

As we emerge and go back towards the High Street, we see the Christmas decorations have been switched on. The clock no longer chimes on the hour. Instead it gives us a rendition of *Hark, the Herald Angels Sing*. I'm hungry, desperate for a cup of tea and I just wish the Herald Angels would piss off. Every chime is a reminder of what I still have to do before the big day.

I try to fake it. 'What pretty decorations, Jack,' I chirrup. 'Have you seen them before?'

'Yeah, yesterday when we were in town,' he replies in a bored teenager voice.

'How many more jobs to do now, Mum?' whines Jack.

'Last one now, the shops are closing anyway and it's freezing, isn't it? Just to the cashpoint, then we'll go home,' I say.

But even home doesn't hold much fun for me. I remember the pile of washing-up from lunch I left behind.

There's an enormous queue at the cashpoint. I stand in line while Jack tries to put his head in a bin, pick up a cigarette stub, sit on the pavement and take his coat off, all within the space of a minute. No wonder I'm all nagged out.

'Jack, get your head out of there, please,' I snap.

I look wistfully at young scantily-clad couples emerging from Bargain Booze with carrier bags of alcohol. One or two people stagger across the road, obviously pissed after Christmas parties. I can remember those carefree days when all I had to do was be sober enough to drive home to my mum for Christmas dinner. Blimey, I didn't even wash up afterwards.

It's nearly my turn at the cashpoint, then I can hurry to my car and go home. At least our house is warm.

'Mum, look!' says Jack excitedly. 'What's happening here?'

I look through the parked cars to see a group of six women walking towards us. They're all wearing antlers. I'd forgotten antlers, and I'd certainly forgotten how ridiculous adults look wearing them. I realize they're all heading towards the Town Hall for a slimming meeting.

'What are they, Mum?' asks Jack, excited we may be being invaded by aliens.

'They're ladies, getting excited about Christmas,' I reply.

'They're all really, really fat,' says Jack, just before they get to us.

Normally I'd explain 'fat' isn't a very nice word, and saying that within earshot will hurt their feelings, but I'm too knackered. I let it go. There's a limit to the bollockings even I can deliver in a day.

'They're off to a meeting where they'll get weighed and be told what food to eat to help them lose weight,' I explain to Jack once they're out of earshot.

'Hey, Mum, cheer up!' laughs little Jack. 'We don't have to get weighed. Don't we have some chocolates for the car? Why don't you like Christmas?'

I look at his big excited eyes. It's no fun being a kid and being dragged round the shops. I ruffle his hair and laugh.

'I'm sorry I'm a bit grumpy, Jack. I'm just a bit fed up with Christmas at the moment,' I say. 'It's wearing me out and I want to use my energy for other things.'

'But Mum,' he says, wide-eyed. 'What if you get everything you want?'

I look at him, with his hair long overdue for a cut and slight dark circles round his eyes from lack of sleep, and I realize I don't even have a Christmas list. I haven't asked Santa for anything, not even the entire collection of *24* on DVD or, better still, Kiefer Sutherland himself delivered to my bedroom.

At the end of the day I already have absolutely everything I want: I have a happy, healthy, high-spirited boy who can run the length of the High Street. I have money to spend on presents and nobody's asking me to wear a pair of antlers in public. Hallelujah.

◆◆◆◆◆

Still slightly concerned about my son's capitalist streak, I listen carefully to his nightly conversation with God. Now he's five, every night, after his story, he puts his hands together and closes his eyes. It's purely voluntary. I'm not a religious maniac who makes her son praise the Lord at every opportunity. But I'll be down on him like a ton of bricks if he mentions money to our Lord Jesus Christ even once. I remember how my poor mum scrimped and saved every penny and how grateful I was for the tiniest thing.

'Would you mind not listening, Mum?' he asks me. 'This is between me and God.'

'Of course,' I reply. 'Don't mind me, I'm just thinking about things I have to do tomorrow for work.'

I can't believe this. I'm excluded from conversations with Santa and now God. I'll soon say to people: 'I used to be a mother, but my son let me go. He didn't need to keep me on.'

I'm dreading this prayer, I really am. If Jack asks God to make Santa bring us an entire toy shop on Christmas Eve, I'm going to donate all his presents to charity.

'Dear God,' he starts, peeping from one eye to check I'm not looking. 'We thank you for houses and beds, and knives and forks. Amen.'

And that's it. Hark, my Herald Angel has sung. I'm going to go out tomorrow and buy him even more for Christmas. How quickly and easily I can forgive one so humble.

◆◆◆◆◆

It's Christmas Eve. Ian bought the castle Jack wants for Christmas yesterday and it's wrapped and hidden away. I've spent the whole day cleaning the house. Ian's mum and dad and his sister Catherine are coming to stay tomorrow and we're all going to meet my brother Chris and his wife Eva for Christmas lunch in a village pub.

'Mum, I've just realized, everyone I love in the whole world will be in the same room tomorrow, won't they?' asks Jack.

I can see his heart leaping with joy. He's the only child in both families and naturally loves the attention and affection he gets. I've worked through my to-do list, which Jack wrote for me. Everything is ticked off apart from the last item, with the 'D's and 'B's the wrong way round.

'Leave out carrots, deer, mince pies, a dottle of wine for the reinbeer.'

'Daddy can be in charge of Santa's food,' I say, flopping down on the settee, exhausted.

Ian leaps at the chance to cater for our midnight visitor. He quite likes playing the host.

'Shall we leave Santa some cocktails, Mummy?' asks Ian, humouring Jack.

'Ooooh, I think a Brandy Alexander may well warm him up on this cold night,' I reply.

I'm relieved my weeks of chores are over and I can relax. I'm bang on deadline once again. I hear the ice being cracked with a hammer, then that delicious sound of the cocktail shaker working its magic.

'I'd better just try one, Jack,' I say. 'We want it to be just right for Santa, don't we?'

'Oh yes, definitely,' replies Jack seriously.

He's so excited he can't keep still for longer than a minute. I feel a surge of joy in my heart when I see him and remember the crap Christmases we had when I was a kid. I wonder, as I look at those bright shining excited eyes, how you can ruin a kid's Christmas and live with yourself. How can you not get carried away with their excitement? How on earth did my poor mother feel when she had hardly any money and no means of getting any from my dad? It must have been heartbreaking trying to get us what we asked for for Christmas.

It's almost bedtime and the feast is ready. Santa has got a tray of Brandy Alexanders, red wine, beer, a giant chocolate bar and some luxury nibbles.

'I hope that's enough,' says Jack, thinking aloud.

'I'm sure it will be,' I say gratefully, as I kiss Jack good night and send him to bed with his dad for a story.

'C'mon, little fella,' says Ian, sensing the feast may begin without him.

I hear the two go to Jack's bedroom, then I gather up all three remote controls. Before me are three of my favourite things. It seems only right to offer thanks. 'Dear God,' I say. 'Thank you so much for Brandy Alexander, giant chocolate bars and series 1 of *The West Wing* on DVD. Amen and Happy Christmas!'

CHAPTER 7

Were You as Rich as Us When You Were a Girl?

My mum's off to school tonight to see my teacher. I heard some of my friends saying their dads are going too, but I don't think mine will want to go.

Parents' Evening starts at 7pm, when my dad's usually in bed napping, and it goes on until about 8.30pm when he's usually gone to the pub, so it's not really a convenient time for him to go to school anyway. Besides, I can't even imagine my dad at school. I don't think he even knows my teacher's name.

I'm in Class Three now and my teacher's Mrs Tough, though we sometimes call her Toughie. She is quite tough, too. She's forever hitting us on our hands with books, straps and belts. When we've been naughty we have to go up in front of the whole class and stand with our palms facing upwards. Then Toughie selects her weapon and whacks us. Her mouth goes into a tight line when she hits us.

She's quite short and she has grey hair with strands of darker grey, which she wears in a tight bun.

◆◆◆◆◆

My mum has tried lots of different outfits on, but they're all quite baggy on her. She has a few nice suits from the old days, but they're too dressy, with their fur collars and short pencil

104

skirts, to wear to school. She settles for a pair of dark trousers and a pink blouse, but now she's trying on coats.

'Too scruffy!' she says, discarding her anorak with the flowery pattern round the edge.

She's almost despairing when she remembers a coat my dad bought Chris when a salesman came to the pub a few months ago. It's a grey, black and bottle-green tweed three-quarter coat, with big buttons up the front and a small neat collar. I don't think Chris has worn it yet. He doesn't like it, that's why.

'Can I try it?' my mum asks my brother in desperation.

'Yes, course you can,' says Chris, very keen to get rid of the dreaded coat.

My mum tries it on and it looks nice on her because at least it's new, doesn't smell of cooking and is a dark colour so you can't tell it's a bit big for her. I can see hope on her face as she stands on a chair to look at it in the mirror above the fireplace. My dad's in bed so she can't use the full-length mirror behind their wardrobe door.

'Great!' she says, unable to see her head or her feet, just her middle part.

'Can I borrow this, Chris?'

He nods. He looks sad at our mum in his coat as she fumbles as she tries to button the coat up. We just accept that my dad has a lot of money and my mum has none.

'Oh, bugger!' she says under her breath. 'I'd forgotten the buttons do up the other way. Damn, damn, damn. Everyone will know it's a man's coat. Damn! Oh, I'll just leave it open.'

'Mum, it's freezing out there,' says Chris. 'You've got a good 20-minute walk to school, you'll get really cold. Do it up, then unfasten it when you get to school.'

It strikes me as odd that we have a perfectly good car in the garage and my dad's upstairs in bed, sleeping. He could get up and take my mum to school to save her getting cold, but it seems he doesn't offer and she doesn't ask.

She settles down near a chair to do her make-up. Out comes the tiny, worn-down brown eyebrow pencil and she draws a thick line over her eyebrows. Sometimes when she's in a hurry she goes off on a tangent and she looks a bit like Mr Spock.

Now she's stretching out her lips, as though she's saying: 'Ah!' for the doctor, to put her lipstick on. But she doesn't do like other mums and twirl the lipstick up. My mum's lipstick is so worn down she uses a matchstick to get a bit out, then she smears it on her lips and moves them together to merge the colour on the top and bottom lip.

Finally she runs a comb through her hair, which has no style because she cuts it herself. I can't ever remember my mum going to the hairdresser's. She probably doesn't have enough money, or maybe she's so worn down by all the names my dad calls her, she doesn't feel like looking after herself.

'I won't be long and Christopher's going to stay in with you while I'm out, aren't you?' she says, tilting her face slightly, almost in a threat, but relaxing when he says: 'Yes, I'm staying in all night. I won't leave her, Mum.'

With that, she puts on her headscarf and ties it in a knot under her chin. As she opens the back door to leave, a blast of cold air rushes in and we shut it almost immediately.

◆◆◆◆◆

The minute my mum has gone we hear creaks upstairs. My dad's getting up earlier than usual. He goes to the bathroom and we hear bath water running.

We're not scared of being on our own with my dad at this

time. If we don't bother him, he doesn't bother us. There isn't even a problem about him getting his shoe polish out from the kitchen cupboard since Dinky died. We've got a new dog now, a border collie called Lassie, and she's nothing like as vicious as Dinky.

We children have baths once or twice a week and my mum sometimes jumps into our bath water when we've got out. But my dad baths when he wants and he gets out his aftershave. When he comes downstairs he smells lovely, and his clothes are all uncreased and clean.

He's wearing a new dark grey suit. He always looks very smart when he goes out, especially when he puts his new camel-coloured overcoat on. I looked at the label the other day and spelled out the words.

'It says, "Cashmere",' my mum had told me, quite proudly. 'It's a very good make.'

She didn't look upset or angry that my dad can buy such a lovely coat while she has old worn-out clothes in their wardrobe.

'I'm just popping down to the Duke early,' he says to me and Chris.

He's started going back to the Duke, so whatever they all fell out about must have been forgotten. He's preening himself in the mirror above the fireplace in the living room, straightening his burgundy-and-grey striped tie.

'Where's your mum?' he asks, suddenly realizing she isn't there.

'She's at school,' I answer.

I'm taking my doll Babykins's school uniform off, and putting on her pink pyjamas.

'School? School? At this time?' he questions. 'Funny time to be at school.'

'It's Parents' Evening, Dad,' says Chris in a very matter-of-fact voice. 'If she'd known you were getting up early, you could have given her a lift.'

But my dad doesn't hear any more. We can see his mind is whirring, his thoughts elsewhere. He's thinking about my mum, and where she is, and what she's doing.

'Did she say what time she'll be back?' he asks Chris.

'Yes, she said it finishes at 8.30 but if she can see Christine's teacher first, then the head, she might be back by 8,' says Chris.

My dad's thinking.

My mum only ever goes out to PTA events at school, and on Parents' Evening. She doesn't ever go out with friends. I don't think she has any.

Two seconds later, he snaps: 'Well, I'll be off then.'

We both say 'goodbye' at the same time, but he seems to go without hearing us.

◆◆◆◆◆

'Oh, shit,' says Chris. 'He's not happy she's gone out. He thinks she's as bad as him.'

I grin at him saying 'shit' in front of me, but quite like the fact he thinks I'm grown-up enough now, at eight, to hear naughty words. I'm not sure what he means about 'being as bad as him', though.

'But she's only gone to school,' I say.

'I know, but he doesn't like her going out,' explains Chris. I don't understand at all, so I change the subject.

'Chris,' I ask. 'Why doesn't my mum ever go to your school?'

'Ssssh!' he whispers as though we're not alone in the house. 'Don't ever ask *her* that. I don't give her the letters about Parents' Evenings.'

'Why not?' I ask. 'Don't your teachers want to tell her about you?

'Oh yeah, they'd love to see her. You see, Christine, I'm not as good as you are at school. Some days I don't even go. I go into town instead. I don't do much of my homework, and I don't get good marks like you. But I don't tell my mum because I don't want her going all that way across town at night, just to be told bad things that will worry her.'

'But aren't you scared they'll send her a letter?' I ask.

'Oh they do send her letters, lots of them, but I don't deliver them,' he grins.

I am shocked at him and would give it a lot more thought, if my dad hadn't left in such a bad mood. Something tells me Chris's poor school attendance is the very least of our worries tonight.

◆◆◆◆◆

My mum comes back, glowing. I can tell from her happy face Toughie is pleased with me. My mum bends down and cups my jaws in her hands so we're almost nose to nose. I flinch slightly when I feel her cold hands.

'You are such a good girl,' she says with pride, punctuating each word.

'Why?' I ask, excited. 'What did Toughie say?'

'Mrs Tough,' says my mum, emphasizing the name, 'said you are a model pupil, you work hard, and you're very clever. She said you're a bit shy in class and you speak too quietly when she asks you a question, but your reading and writing are excellent.'

I'm really pleased I've made my mum happy. No wonder Chris doesn't want to risk letting her see his teachers.

'Go and get ready for bed,' my mum tells me. 'It's later than a normal school day. You'll never get up tomorrow morning if you don't go to bed.'

Then, almost as if the two are linked, she turns to Chris and asks: 'What time did your dad go out? Was he OK?'

'About 7-ish,' Chris replies.

'Bit early,' says my mum, eyebrows slightly raised. 'Did he say why?'

'No, not really. He was a bit mad you were out,' says Chris.

'You did tell him I was at school, didn't you?' asks my mum sharply.

'Course we did,' says Chris, implying that wouldn't make any difference. Although we don't say it, I think we all know tonight is going to be hell.

We're right, of course. My dad comes through the back door bawling, shouting, calling my mum a whore, accusing her of seeing a man.

'Harry, don't be ridiculous,' I hear her defend herself. 'It was Parents' Evening at school. Here's the letter.'

She's obviously producing the letter from school, but my dad's having none of it.

'You fucking liar!' he screams. 'I bet you were with him from the café. Do you think I don't know what you do in the day, while I'm at work. They talk in the pub, you know, you fucking idiot.'

I'm lying in bed rigid. I'm scared there will soon be banging and smashing. I get out of bed and creep to Chris's room. He sleeps at the front of the house in the smallest bedroom, but he's far from asleep tonight. He too is wide awake, listening. We can't normally hear as well from the front bedroom, but tonight the whole of the avenue will hear.

'What is wrong with you?' asks my mum, her voice only slightly raised. 'I've been at school, hearing how hard-working and bright your daughter is, and you come back like this. You're absolutely barmy, you are, you know. Barmy.'

'Hardworking?' he questions. 'Bright? She's as fucking thick as they come.'

He raises his voice and does an impression of me, asking a question. I can feel the colour draining from my face as I listen to the things he says about me. I wish I were alone listening to this. I'm embarrassed to hear it in front of Chris.

'Bright?' he questions again. 'She's always fucking half-asleep,' he says.

'Yes, because you keep her up all night, with your shouting and swearing,' retorts my mum.

I'm swinging my legs nervously on the side of Chris's bed, with an eiderdown over my shoulders, and I'm devastated that even my mum is agreeing I'm always half-asleep.

'She is bright, Harry, and you're doing a lot of damage with the things you're saying and doing!' she tells him.

'I'm doing the damage?' he roars. 'You're the one who's carrying on, the one they talk about in the pub.'

'Don't be ridiculous!' she tells him. She never actually says 'Who would look at me? I'm skin and bone, with no decent clothes.' Maybe she doesn't want to spell out just how far my dad has worn her down.

They carry on for what feels like ages. He accuses her of seeing other men, she denies it vehemently. For a while I lie in Chris's single bed with him, while we both listen to them.

'I can't get comfy, Chris,' I say in a complaining tone, as though I'm planning to stay the whole night.

'Wriggle around, then,' he tells me, far more interested in what's going on downstairs than my comfort.

Eventually my dad starts heading for bed.

'I'm going up there tomorrow, I'm going to sort that bastard out once and for all,' he snarls. 'Don't you think I won't. I'm tough, I am. I can make him sorry he's ever messed around with my wife.'

'Harry, don't be stupid!' says my mum. 'You're talking rubbish. I just went there for a tin of soup for Christine for lunch. I couldn't afford anything else anyway.'

Both Chris and I cringe. My mum loves domestic detail. She loves telling us how many brown loaves she has bought, and how thick the butcher cut the bacon. I suppose looking after us and the house is her life. But my dad isn't into talking about tins of soup when he's after revenge for an imagined act of adultery.

'Buying soup?' he starts. 'That's about all you're fit for, you useless cunt! You're not getting any more out of me. Don't treat me as though I'm as fucking stupid as you. I'm going to tell him I know exactly what filth has been going on behind my back.'

Chris and I hear him almost fall on his bed, like a dead weight being dropped from a height.

I creep back to my own bed. I'm terrified it's going to get out what my dad's really like. If we could just contain it and keep it in the house, I could cope. But if other people find out, I'm going to die of embarrassment. I'm going to be even quieter. That way, people might not talk to me, and they won't ask questions.

◆◆◆◆◆

I wake up and check who's in my bed. I'm not promiscuous. It's just there are so many variations with Jack's erratic sleeping patterns. I could be in our own bed with Ian, but I'm more likely to wake up in Jack's bed alone because he got into ours at 3am and insisted on lying lengthways across the bed between the two of us and I stropped out. Or I could even be on the sofa bed in the third bedroom because I couldn't get to sleep after 2am in anticipation of Jack's regular 3am visit.

It's a glorious Saturday morning in July. The sun is streaming through the curtains and I am actually in our bed. What a joyous feeling that is. Admittedly, I'm in there with Ian, Jack, Flower the Skunk and a racoon who masqueraded as a skunk before we found Flower. The racoon is called Skunky and his tail is stripey like our cat Kitty's tail, so I'm often to be heard urging Skunky to come and have a bowl of tuna, much to Jack's amusement.

'He's a toy, Mummy,' Jack tells me, pityingly. 'He doesn't really eat proper food.'

'Yeah, I know,' I answer seriously because I'm usually concentrating on making a cup of tea, putting the washing in, returning phone calls, packing lunches, answering mail and washing up. 'He just looks like Kitty first thing in a morning.'

'No, he doesn't,' pipes up Jack. 'He's a racoon, she's a cat.'

I know I whinge about our overpopulated double bed, but I secretly love waking up with Jack in our bed on a weekend when we don't have to rush to get ready for school. I love looking into those deep brown eyes and seeing them transform from sleepy to happy, playing stupid games and chatting about a lovely weekend ahead.

'Daddy,' says Jack.

'What?' groans Ian, who's not a morning person.

'There's a skunk in our bed,' giggles Jack, starting the little routine he loves.

'No! Not a skunk,' says Ian, time after time. 'I'm not having a skunk in my bed. That skunk has got to go.'

Jack giggles with delight. He loves the routine of saying the same thing, week after week.

'He's not going to spray us with his tail, Daddy,' says Jack, reassuringly.

'He's not going to do anything because he has to go!' says Ian, pretending to be seriously angry. 'I am not having any skunks in our house, and that's final.'

Now it's my turn to chip in with my lines.

'We do need another pet in this house, Daddy,' I say, praying no one has ever planted a bug in our bedroom to listen in to this nonsense. 'We have the most gorgeous little cat but we really need a skunk to keep us all company. A skunk would be a friend for Kitty.'

It all gets a bit confusing because, at this point, Jack starts pretending to be the skunk. He starts edging his bum towards us, as though he's going to emit a strange smell from that skunk's tail any second.

'I promise I won't emit any funny smells,' he says, killing himself laughing at our faces, contorted with pretend disgust.

'You certainly won't!' says Ian, getting up. 'You're going out with the binbags, you are!'

Jack is almost beside himself with joy, and begs: 'Dad, get back in, let's do it just one more time!'

'No,' says Ian.

'Please, Dad!' pleads Jack.

'No,' answers his dad, looking at me and Jack as though he's trying to figure out which is the barmier of the two of us and how many doctors he'd need to get the pair of us certified.

◆◆◆◆◆

I know why I woke in such a sunny mood. I'm off to York. I'm spending the whole day shopping. I'm going to drop the skunk at my in-laws' and let Granny and Granddad play skunks and knights.

I'm in the mood for retail therapy. How decadent is that? I ask myself, noticing a tiny spring in my step as I load the car.

It's at least six months since I bought any new clothes. I never seem to have the time to try things on. I've always more urgent things to do.

◆◆◆◆◆

I've been to one department store and got some freebie cosmetics. Admittedly I had to spend £59 on cleanser and moisturizer to get the 'free' little red bag with six mini-products, but I still feel as if I've got a bargain. I've also stocked up on children's party presents, often not knowing how much I'm spending as I hand over my card to pay.

I'm in another store now and feverishly going through the rails looking for the bright bold colours that suit me, with not too low a neckline. I've watched every episode Trinny and Susannah have ever recorded and it is all stored in a microchip in my brain.

'Are you looking for anything in particular?' asks a pretty assistant, who looks a bit like Ulrika Jonsson.

'No, I just need clothes,' I reply, happily.

'What kind of occasions do you need them for?' she asks, as though she's trying to coax a big secret out of me.

'Oh, for going out, for work, for doing the school run, for going walking, for our holidays ...' I answer. 'I haven't bought any clothes for ages.'

The assistant looks at me as though I've just announced I have leprosy in its most hideous form.

'Have you been ill or something?' she asks. 'Or saving up?'

she adds quickly, obviously embarrassed about her first question.

'No,' I say vaguely, starting to answer before I know what the answer is. 'I've just been ... er ... busy for what feels like ... er ... years.'

I must have lost a bit of weight because suddenly all the clothes look quite good on me.

As I try on dress after dress, top after top, skirt after skirt, I realize I love them all. The gorgeous black fitted dress with those sweet cap sleeves and 20 buttons up the side just for decoration is my absolute favourite. It even gives me cleavage: how fantastic is that? The floaty strappy dress looks better in burgundy than black, but the tangerine and pale blue flowered dress is to die for. I hear my mum's voice from years ago, saying: 'Gerrit! You deserve it!'

At first I berated this shop for not having a mirror in the changing room. I hated going out into the communal area to check what I looked like, but the more my confidence grows about these perfectly fitting clothes, the more I twirl in front of the mirror.

Ulrika goes off in search of shoes to match every outfit – silver sandals, red slingbacks, pointy purple numbers: they all fit and look ace. I'm a bit carried away with the excitement of clothes that fit. I make a note we must go to more cocktail parties, then remind myself I probably haven't even been to more than two cocktail parties in my whole life and there's no point having a cocktail party wardrobe.

I'm in there so long I'm startled when a woman comes through to the changing rooms with a dripping wet umbrella.

'It's terrible out there,' she says, shaking raindrops off her mac.

'Really?' I ask in amazement. 'It was gorgeous when I came in.'

'Well, it hasn't stopped raining for two and a half hours,' she tells me. 'I came out of the restaurant at 1.30 and the heavens just opened.'

Two and a half hours I've been in here! Claire would be so proud of me. I must text her soon. I want to share my shopping joy with everyone.

In the end I buy two dresses, the red slingbacks, a turquoise twinset and a short cream linen skirt, all wrapped in tissue paper, and I walk on air, with a carrier bag almost as big and heavy as me. Then I ring Ian to share my total shopping joy.

'Have you had a nice day, sweetie?' I ask Jack on the way home.

He's in the front seat of the car and he hasn't stopped chatting since we left my in-laws' house.

'You've bought a lot of things, Mum,' says Jack, worried. 'Do we have any money left?'

'Of course we have some money left, Jack,' I reply. 'I wouldn't spend all our money. I just needed some new clothes because I haven't shopped for ages.'

'Yes, you have,' he says in an accusatory singsong voice. 'You went to Tesco yesterday. You told Dad you'd spent almost a hundred quid.'

It sounds funny hearing Jack say 'quid' instead of 'gold coins'.

'Yes, but that was food and we needed that,' I explain.

I can barely concentrate for thinking of occasions when I can wear my red slingbacks.

'Mum, are we rich?' asks Jack.

'Well, we have enough money for the things we need,' I answer.

I don't want him to think we have money to burn, but I also don't want him to think we're broke.

'Were you as rich as us when you were a girl?' he asks.

I think back to my poor old mum, who scrimped and saved and never spent a penny on herself. How hard her life was. She didn't have the joy of new clothes and a shopping spree.

Tears start to fill my eyes as I remember how she struggled to pay for things while my dad drank all our money away. But hey, I'm driving, I can't cry. I try and focus on my hands on the steering wheel when I register that my nails are a delicate pink from the manicure I had yesterday.

I am so lucky. Now and then I can have beauty treatments, get my hair highlighted, buy people presents, have lunch and spend hundreds of pounds on clothes, while my mum borrowed my brother's clothes, used her inheritance from my grandparents to buy us food, sold family heirlooms so we could go on school trips and got her lipstick from the tube with a matchstick. She even saved Green Shield stamps to buy family presents.

'No, me and my mum weren't as rich as we are, Jack,' I finally answer. 'But…'

I pause.

'Your daddy was.' Jack finishes the sentence for me, nodding without understanding.

He must be very confused that I had an impoverished mum who couldn't afford new clothes and worried about money all the time, and a well-off dad who bought only the best in clothes and cars. I wonder about our relatives. My mum's brothers knew she was broke and helped her from time to time, but I think she was too proud to ask for help from my dad's family. I know my dad's mum gave her the odd pound note here and there and she was very grateful.

'Why didn't your mummy work and then she could have got some money, couldn't she?' queries Jack.

'She wanted to work, Jack,' I explain, quickly. I'd hate him to think my mum was lazy. God, she'd have loved to have got out of that house when she was younger.

'But my dad didn't want her to go out to work because he liked her being at home. He liked knowing where she was, and I think she liked being at home for me when I was at school. He was what we call "possessive". He wanted to know where she was.'

'We're well lucky, aren't we, Mum?' he concludes.

I look at him briefly as I drive and laugh at his use of 'well'. He's already speaking like a teenager.

He's on a roll now.

'Aren't you lucky my daddy lets you work?' he asks. 'That way, you can earn loads of money to spend on me, and when we run out of gold coins, Dad gives us some more to buy ice cream. Yes, well lucky, that's what we are, Mum, well lucky.'

CHAPTER 8

Mum, Am I a Handsome Prince?

My mum has done her best and cut my hair over the years, but it never looks as though it has a style. It's fine and wispy and, although it's quite long, there doesn't seem to be much of it. On some of my photos it looks sleek and long, but on others it looks like it's been cut with hedge trimmers by someone with pretty poor eyesight, which is probably not far off the truth.

I've started secondary school now I'm 11. It's a comprehensive school near the Catholic school you can see from my bedroom window. To get to school I start off in the same direction as though I'm going to primary school, but instead of walking up the hill, I veer to the left where there's a path alongside the school road.

I usually walk to school with my friend Jackie. She went to a different primary school, but I got to know her in the first few weeks and we get on well.

One of the girls from our primary school went to the grammar school, and some others went to better schools in the area. The rest of us have gone to the comprehensive school. You can imagine what my dad called me when I failed the grammar school entrance exam. He even offered to pay for me and send me private, but I failed the entrance exam for that as well.

'You see, she's so thick, I can't even pay for her to get a decent education,' he roared that night. 'She's a fucking thick bastard.'

'I don't understand it.' My mum spoke as though she were thinking aloud and it was the most natural thing in the world to call your daughter what my dad just called me.

'She was the brightest kid in the whole of the primary school from being five, yet she failed. I don't know what went wrong,' pondered my mum.

Even I don't know what went wrong, except that I was scared in the big strange school hall where I didn't know anyone when I did the entrance exams, and I was tired out. My dad has been getting worse at night over the years, and in the old days I could cope if I got about four decent nights' sleep per week. Now I'm not even getting that, and on some days I can't think straight. The entrance exams were on bad days for me. That's what happened. Simple as that.

◆◆◆◆◆

I've started reading *Jackie* magazine now – my mum gets it for me every Thursday when she goes to the newsagents. I've seen a range of hairstyles suitable for different face shapes. I've scraped all my hair back and figured out my face is a heart shape. In *Jackie* it says I should have jaw-length hair.

I look in the mirror and see my long hair. It's down to my shoulders and it shines, so I'm sure it's healthy. I sometimes wear it in a ponytail – that's when strangers ask if I'm French. My mum likes that, as though it adds a touch of glamour to our lives.

Three years ago when I was eight, my mum tried to cut me a fringe, after Louise, the girl opposite, had her lovely long hair cut into a bob with a fringe. I thought Lou looked so glamorous with her big blue eyes and black eyelashes that I wanted a fringe too, so my mum cut me one. I looked good but not as gorgeous as Louise. Problem was, the next day, I couldn't find my fringe as it was all mixed in with the rest of my hair again.

But now I've spotted a hairstyle in *Jackie* and I want it.

'Mum,' I ask tentatively, 'do you think I could go to a hair-dresser's and have this done?'

I hate suggesting this because I know my mum doesn't get her hair done, probably because she can't afford to, but then I have never asked before, so surely once isn't asking too much. I also need to be careful because I don't want my mum suggesting she does it for me. I'd hate to hurt her feelings. My dad criticizes her for so much – everything she does, in fact. I'd hate to add to her worries. But I'm wrong to worry.

'Yes, you know, Chris, I've been thinking, you should go and have a perm,' she says. 'I have a bit of money to the front, so let's book you in.'

I'm dead excited. Not only am I going to get my hair cut, I'm going to be a different person with curly hair. I really can't wait. I feel really grown up. I've started listening to Radio Luxembourg. I like the New Seekers and now I'm going to a hairdresser.

◆◆◆◆◆

It's Saturday morning. I usually go riding. My dad bred from our pony Rosie, and I now ride her foal, Prince, who's three. But this morning I am going to the hairdresser's along the main street near our house. It's called Marilyn's and it's full of women between 30 and 60 sitting under hairdryer hoods. I've never been inside a hairdresser's shop before so I'm amazed at the number of washbasins and the seats in front of mirrors. I don't know what I expected, but I hadn't pictured so many of everything, all in rows.

There's a distinct smell around, a bit like the stuff my mum

122

uses to clean her paintbrushes when she's decorating. My mum comes into Marilyn's with me, then goes off to do some shopping. She says she'll be back to see me in about an hour.

I don't feel comfortable here. I feel too young and I don't know what to say to start a conversation. I've shown Barbara, the hairdresser, the photograph from *Jackie* and she's looked at it fleetingly, and grinned.

'We'll see what we can do,' she smiles at me.

I look around the walls. They're full of pictures of women's hairstyles torn from hairdressing magazines. Some of them look gorgeous. There's one just like the singer Dana that I particularly like. I wonder if I could look like that?

Barbara starts by washing my hair. There's none of the rough stuff I get when my mum washes my hair, sometimes with a plastic shower spray attached to the taps in the kitchen or bathroom, with an old vest over my eyes to protect them from shampoo and water. Barbara is gentle and she rinses every last trace of shampoo. I'm beginning to relax.

After the shampoo, there seem to be hours and hours of treatment. My hair is cut considerably shorter, all sorts of lotions and potions are put on, my hair is put in curlers and I sit under the dryer hood. Then I need lots of rinsing, another neutralizer, then more rinsing. I'd no idea it would take this long. My mum obviously did, because she isn't back yet.

After the final rinse, Barbara dries my hair with a towel and puts her hands on my shoulders.

'There!' she says, pleased. 'It's taken very well. It will stay like this for three months.'

I can't believe what I see. My stomach does one of those flips I get when my dad starts shouting at night. My hair is in tight little curls and I look about 35. That lovely sleek French look has gone. I look chubby and old. Barbara must read my mind.

'Don't look like that,' she laughs. 'It doesn't dry like this. It will be wavier. You'll see.'

But she's wrong. It dries slightly looser, but it still looks vile. The curls are there, the fat face is there, and I look so old. I feel like crying, but I know I mustn't cry in front of her.

'What do you think?' she asks, finally showing me the back in a mirror she holds behind me. I nod and start to get up. I can't speak. If I spoke I'd cry. Oh, how I wish I'd just gone out for the day on Prince. I've just seen my mum coming through the door. She's beaming at me. Oh God, she obviously likes it like this. I've wasted her hard-saved money to look like this. I feel sick.

When I get home, Chris takes one look at me and says in a singsong voice: 'Ooooh, curly!'

I just ignore him and go to my bedroom. It's early afternoon and it's a gorgeous spring day, but I'm not going anywhere. I don't want anyone to see me like this. I look hideous. Then I realize. I have that corrugated-iron look that Betty has. I don't have a mirror in my bedroom, so I go to the bathroom, and break down into floods of tears.

'Hey, what's wrong?' asks my dad, coming through the door, taking me by surprise because I thought he was at the pub.

'My hair! Look! It's all curly!' I sob.

Normally I'd be reluctant to tell him because he might have used it against me later, but today I don't care. He can't make me feel any worse than I do already.

'It looks lovely,' he tells me. 'You look grown-up.'

But grown-up to me means looking like an old woman and I

cry again. I lie on my bed for ages. I hear my dad go out in the car. My mum and Chris come up to try and coax me out, but all I want to do is lie on my bed and cry. I'd so looked forward to this day, the day when I changed the way I looked, and I've made a real hash of it.

I think of Louise and her lovely bob, then my mind drifts off to school on Monday. Oh my God, no one at school has a tight perm. They'll absolutely pee themselves laughing at me. I'm a freak, and to think I was so normal this time yesterday. I'd love to be the old me again. She wasn't so bad after all.

◆◆◆◆◆

My dad is back in a couple of hours. I was in the hairdresser's longer than he's been at the pub today. He must be OK. He was quite nice to me earlier, even though he lied about my hair. Maybe he'll come back and have a nice chat. Oh, but I can't stand anyone to look at me.

As usual, he comes straight upstairs to the toilet, then he pops his head round my door.

'Hello, old mate,' he says quietly. 'How are you?'

'I'm fed up,' I say, grateful I'm not getting shouted at today. 'I hate my hair, and there's nothing I can do about it for three months. I will never, ever have another perm again.'

'It'll grow, lass,' he says, almost philosophically, before he goes back downstairs to eat the dinner my mum has been cooking him since we got back home.

I'm starting to get a headache from crying, lack of food and sitting with those curlers so tight for an eternity. I wonder which is best: having crap hair but my dad being nice to me, or having my old hair, which now seems fantastic, and my dad being a pig to me.

I'm still pondering when he comes up for an afternoon lie-

125

down. He even calls me 'Old Pige' just as he did in the old days. I just potter around in my bedroom. I don't want Chris calling me 'Curly' and there's nothing my mum can say to make me feel better, so I stay out of their way. They're in the back garden anyway.

◆◆◆◆◆

An hour later, my dad's up and roaring – living proof that the last few pints kick in after he gets home. He's shouting before he even gets to my room. My head is thumping with pain, so every syllable goes 'Boom! Boom!' in my head.

'You are so fucking ugly!' he yells at me. 'Have you any idea how disgusting you are to look at?'

I can't even answer. I felt miserable before but I feel lower than ever now. But he's in full flow.

'I can't bear to look at your disgusting face, you're hideous. There's absolutely nothing right about your whole face. With your crooked little teeth, you look like a fucking witch.'

I'd normally look up and face him, if only to check what he's about to do, but today I remain face-down on my bed to stop him from seeing my ugly face.

'You take after your mother, she's a fucking ugly twat too, with her four eyes,' he goes on. 'You'll be too ugly and too thick to make anything of your life. Nobody will ever want you, you ugly little bastard.'

I wonder why my mum isn't here by now. Then I hear voices outside. I'd forgotten they were in the garden when I looked out earlier. They obviously haven't heard that he's up and shouting at me. In a way, I'm glad. I wouldn't want my mum to hear him calling her 'four-eyes' and 'ugly'.

He goes quiet, but he hasn't moved. The silence forces me to turn over and look at him. I'm scared he's doing something to try

126

and hurt me. Maybe he's picked something up. He's never hit me since that lunchtime when I was four, but I still expect him to do something nasty. He's angry and drunk enough and I feel as though he's been building up over the years to something terrible.

As I look into those clear eyes, I see, for the first time, just how ugly he is. He has a massive Roman nose and thin mean lips. He actually looks like a rat.

He pretends to turn away from me in disgust at my face.

'It's not your hair that makes you look so revolting,' he says, after considering my face for a few seconds. 'It's you, it's who you are, you're an ugly little twat, that's what you are.'

He's clever. He's no longer shouting at me, because the lawnmower has stopped outside. He's speaking in a monotone, threateningly, so my mum and Chris can't hear, not that that normally bothers him.

I know I should look him in the eye and inform him he's the ugly one, with an ugly personality and ugly behaviour, but I don't. I tell myself he's right. I am pretty ugly. How stupid I was to think I might look like Dana after my hairdo. I could never look like that in a million years. He's right. I'm ugly.

'One day soon, I'm going to get rid of you, so I don't ever have to look at you again,' he goes on. 'I'm planning what I'm going to do to you. Your mother, too, she's had it as well. I'm going to cut her in half. I am. You watch me!'

He staggers off to bed and as soon as I hear him crash onto the mattress, I get up off my bed and look out of my window. There's a blanket box I can kneel on. In the back garden my mum is pottering about with a fork and spade, and Chris is sitting on our back wall chatting to her. She straightens for a minute, leans one of her forearms on the top of her fork, and laughs at something he says.

They look happy together, and I'm so glad they've missed out on the afternoon that has totally changed the way I feel about the way I look, probably for the rest of my life.

◆◆◆◆◆

Today I shall start afresh. I won't eat anything naughty. Just three meals. My usual porridge for breakfast and a sandwich with an apple for lunch. Tonight I'll have some protein, maybe a piece of salmon, with some steamed veg. I'm going to give my insides a bit of a detox. Nothing nasty, just a little spring clean.

I've been feeling a bit porky around the middle lately, and chocolate all winter has been a great comfort, but now it's spring and I don't want rolls of fat showing through T-shirts, do I?

When Ian asks the nightly question: 'Red or white, sweetie?' I shall reply: 'Thank you for asking, but I shan't be having wine for a week or so.'

I'll definitely be saying no to the five chocolate bars I had yesterday. No way will I make a blackberry crumble for three and eat it all myself today. From now on, I'll be a paragon of virtue, the epitome of self-control, the personification of willpower.

I'll always remember this day, 29th March, as the day when I became The Woman Who Doesn't Like Chocolate, who can stop after just the one glass of wine and who turns her nose up at a piece of chocolate fudge cake oozing gooey chocolate sauce.

I will float through the rest of my forties and fifties a trim size 10, maybe creeping up to a 12 by my mid-sixties. I don't want heart disease or diabetes. I want to live long and see my son marry. And I will, all because one morning, during Jack's Easter school holidays, I turned over a new spring leaf.

I quite like school holidays for the lie-ins we get. With no pressure of getting to school on time, we can lie in bed till 11 if we like, playing skunks. I'm not up till all hours washing and ironing school uniforms, polishing shoes and putting his flash-cards with words like 'again' and 'away' back in their envelope.

But once we're finally up and we've had breakfast, the buck stops with me. I am the entertainment, and on some days I'm pretty crap entertainment. We were up at 9am today, which was still quite a treat after 7am starts.

I like to think I'm a fair mummy and my son has freedom of choice for most things. Not for Jack the *fait accompli*, but an open discussion on what we do with our days. I'm game for most things – football, walking, cycling, park visits, having friends round or, better still, going to soft play with friends so I can either sit and read magazines, or chat to their mummies.

'Hey Jacky, what fun shall we have today?' I ask, as I finish the washing-up.

We're the only family I know not to have a dishwasher, but we don't trust them to get the food off our pans when we burn them. Having spent much of my childhood seeing congealed food dripping down the walls, I try to discourage it in any form now.

The washing-up is stacked to dry, but I look round the kitchen/dining room. I could spend the whole morning tidying and cleaning. It looks such a mess.

There are cat biscuits on the kitchen floor, from where Kitty has sorted the meat from the biscuits, bits of toast and sausages under the table that Jack has dropped, and a mountain of junk mail on the dresser that Ian can't bring himself to throw away or sort out. I mean, those travel leaflets are lovely, but are we really thinking of spending Christmas in Sri Lanka when Newcastle United are playing on Boxing Day? Get real.

The blue-and-white tablecloth which was a wedding present is full of splashes of tomato sauce, but our only other tablecloth is in the ironing basket. I run my hand through my hair. How can I keep on top of this place? How do women with husbands and kids and full-time jobs have immaculate homes?

'Shall we go out?' I encourage Jack.

'We could just have a nice cup of tea and then go,' I add.

'And a choccie biscuit?' prompts Jack, hopefully.

'You've just had breakfast, sweetie,' I say, but I know he's right. You can't have a cup of tea without a choccie biscuit.

I hand him his tea and unwrap his biscuit for him, hoping that inner strength of denial has already kicked in.

'Oh, have one with me, Mum. I can't have one all on my own,' he says.

'Well, I'm trying to be a good girl today, Jack,' I explain.

'Well, eat it all up, every last bit, and don't get any sticky chocolate on your face or your hands, and that way, you'll be a good girl,' I'm told.

It's such a matey thing to do, having a cup of tea and a biscuit together. This is what life's all about, enjoying these special simple moments with our children – not sparkly-clean kitchens and cellulite-free thighs.

Just as I'm tucking in and savouring every crunch, Jack decides: 'I want to go into town and have an ice cream. Can we do that thing, you know, Mum?'

My heart sinks. I stop eating mid-chew. Here I am, eating chocolate, while planning an ice cream. And it isn't 10am yet. This is not a good start. In fact, this is worse than the old days. At least I made it till lunchtime back then.

◆◆◆◆◆

Before we go to do 'that thing', we call into the barber's. I've never been to a barbershop before. Jack usually gets his hair cut by Vanessa, my hairdresser with bright red hair, but she's 20 miles away and he desperately needs tidying up. We go through the door, and see men are sitting in the chairs. There's a padded bench running along the back of the shop. It all looks very simple and straightforward.

'Can I make an appointment to have Jack's hair cut, please?' I ask.

I'm hoping we'll get a time for later and we can come back.

'Sit down,' says the hairdresser, slightly gruffly, signalling towards the padded bench.

What the hell does this mean? Am I waiting for an appointment? Am I waiting for a haircut?

Within seconds a woman comes through and shouts out: 'Next!'

I look around, but no one is making eye contact with me.

'Are we next?' I ask.

The hairdresser gets a board to put across the chair, and she says to Jack: 'Sit here.'

It's fascinating to see him being spoken to so gruffly, because he obeys first time and climbs up onto the board.

'What do you want?' she asks, acknowledging my presence for the first time.

'Just a trim, please,' I reply timidly. 'Just so he can see through his fringe and we can see his ears again.'

She starts cutting, moving Jack's head here and there, but he never complains. I sit down on the bench, and as other people come through the door and take a seat, I realize it's barbershop etiquette to just go in, sit and wait your turn. Within minutes Jack is done, and he looks a proper little man.

'How does it look, Mummy?' he asks me quietly.

He's obviously as intimidated by no-nonsense barbershops as I am.

'Fab, Jack, you look dead grown-up,' I reply.

He smiles and looks very pleased with himself as I hand over my £6.95. He catches a glimpse of himself in a mirror, and swivels round from side to side to admire himself.

'Co-ool!' he says, happily. 'Hey, don't I look good, Mum?'

'Gorgeous, Jack,' I say as we get the hell out of there.

◆◆◆◆◆

I can't resist. I really can't. It's a tradition that on a fine day, when we are not in a hurry, Jack and I buy an ice cream from Thornton's, then sit on the steps of the market cross and eat it.

'Bamilla, please,' he asks the assistant. 'One scoop. Mummy wants wum and waisin, thank you. I don't want the chocolate stick. Mummy will have two, please, and thank you.'

We take our cornets, along with about 300 tissues, and head for our favourite spot on the second step up on the market cross. We're right by a pedestrian crossing, so small crowds gather every few minutes as they wait for the lights to change.

'That thing,' as Jack calls it, is people-watching. We watch them come from the department store or the arcade where there are nice chocolate (oops, that word again) shops, jewellers and florists. Some are older, dressed in their country casual clothes, with matching scarves round their necks.

I'm particularly interested in mummies and how they cope with their kids, so I can compare notes. It's a bit depressing as most mummies look about 18.

There's one heading over the road towards us now. Jack's speaking but I can't make his words out, for the beep-beep-beep of the green man.

'Mum, you know last time we talked about girls who wear trousers halfway down their legs,' repeats Jack.

'Yes, they're called low-slung jeans, Jack,' I explain.

'Why do they wear them?' he asks.

'Because everyone else is wearing them. That's called being in fashion,' I say.

'But you can see their pants, Mum,' he says, perplexed.

'Yes, I think they like us to see their G-strings,' I continue.

Oh no, I've opened the floodgates now. Amazingly, there are no questions about thongs or G-strings. Sometimes I just get too nervy too soon and need to calm down.

'Well, I think they're rude,' he says, swapping cones so I can lick the dripping vanilla ice cream off his. He doesn't lick my cone, just holds it for me.

'Oh, look,' he nudges me. 'That lady's skirt is very short. A bit longer would be better with her legs.'

Then he spots a woman in sky blue.

'That's a nice shade of blue, Mum,' he says, nodding his forehead in the woman's direction. 'It suits her, doesn't it? It's because she has white hair.'

'It's very light blonde, Jack,' I say.

'No, it's definitely pale blue, Mum,' he argues. 'We did colours at school last term.'

I let it go, just as a soldier comes by. He's obviously from Catterick, just a few miles up the road. Jack is wide-eyed at the khaki. He has obviously seen his role model.

Just as the soldier passes us, Jack pipes up: 'He's quite handsome, isn't he?'

The soldier slows down to hear the reply, so I say girlishly: 'He's lovely, Jack, very handsome.'

It's that kind of day when you feel you can be a bit cheeky. We're all full of hope that spring may well be here. All the blacks and browns of winter have gone and the light pastel colours are out in hope.

'He looks a bit like Action Man or the Handsome Prince,' I carry on, now confident that the soldier is too far beyond us to hear.

Jack goes quiet for a minute. Please, oh please, not more thongs. I look around to try and guess the next social comment. Then he asks: 'Mum, am I a handsome prince?'

'Oooh, yes, you're gorgeous,' I say, putting my arm round him and cuddling him very carefully so his ice cream doesn't fall. He grins, then he goes back to being serious.

'Why?' asks Jack.

'Because you have a gorgeous little face, enormous big brown eyes, a cute, cute, cute little button nose, that rosebud mouth and chubby toddler cheeks.'

He's already bored with my description. I know I go on, but I want to go on and on so he realizes he IS a handsome prince. I don't ever want Jack to have any hang-ups about the way he looks. I never want him to feel the pain of being called ugly by anyone.

◆◆◆◆◆

'Let's go to the park,' I say, getting up. 'Otherwise it will be time for lunch.'

'Shall we have lunch in town?' asks Jack.

'Why not?' I reply.

I shall persuade him to go somewhere where I might get a plain jacket potato to make up for all this dietary sinning. 'Where shall we go?'

'I know!' he says brightly. 'Let's go to the pub, where they do Pie of the Day. You can have pie, I'll have scampi, and we'll finish off with a big pudding and custard. Let's do that, Mum!'

I nod. As I said, it's one of those days where you just want to be nice to people. I'll re-start the diet tomorrow, after steak pie and apple crumble. Who would believe I regularly write about dieting?

CHAPTER 9

Do All Grown-ups Work as Hard as You?

I'm on my way home from school for lunch and it's blowing a gale. I'm bent so far over trying to protect my face from the winds that my torso is almost at a right angle to my legs. I've got a heavy black bag full of schoolbooks on my shoulder.

Every night before bed I go through the next day's timetable and get out the books and things I need. That way, I don't have to do much thinking in a morning, especially if we've had a rough night.

Today I'm glad I did the preparation because last night was pretty rough. My dad swapped jobs a couple of years ago after his doctor suggested working outside might help his emphysema. I found out that previously he had been an architectural iron-monger, whatever that means, but his doctor thought fresh air would do his breathing a lot of good.

'There's nowt wrong with his chest,' grumbled my mum at the time. 'He kids his doctor. He goes out and has a load to drink the night before his appointment. We'd all wheeze if we drank the amount he drinks. Then he goes to the surgery, pretending to be gasping for breath. He can't half put it on.'

'But why, Mum?' I asked, confused. 'Why pretend to be ill?'

'Because he's bloody bonkers, that's why. Uses his illness as an excuse for all this boozing.'

It didn't take him long to find a new job and he's now a

groundsman for Bradford University at their playing fields near Leeds. He got the job because he knew the man in charge of recruiting. I was quite impressed that he walked into a job so quickly, but my mum pointed out that when you go to pubs as often as my dad you get to know a lot of people.

At first, he quite liked the job and was very proud of his cricket pitch. He stopped wearing a suit for work, but still wore quite smart casual clothes, trousers and a checked jacket. Sometimes, when he worked on Saturdays he took me with him and I went looking for cricket balls. I loved exploring the changing rooms and the groundsman's office, running from one little room to another. Even the lemonade there was yummy. It tasted extra sweet. I've been trying hard to forget some of the things he says to me when he's drunk, like how ugly and stupid I am, but it isn't easy. I'm always on my guard, whether he's sober or drunk.

But things have started to go wrong with this job now and he's falling out with his boss. He doesn't take me there any more. Last night, we were all in bed when he started ranting at my mum.

'That fucking bald-headed bastard, he's going to get it tomorrow. Fucking twat,' he yelled.

'I thought he was your friend,' said my mum, sleepily.

'Friend? Did you say friend, you dozy cow? He's no fucking friend of mine. He's snooping round corners trying to catch me out, but I'm the fucking worker there. He's the lazy bastard.'

'Well, he got you the job,' I heard my mum retort.

Blimey, she sounded tired. Maybe she didn't jump out of bed on the defensive last night because the shouting wasn't directed at one of us.

'He got me the job? He got me the job? I got the fucking job.

It was me. Me. Me! Do you understand, I got the job?'

'Stop prodding me, Harry,' she said angrily. 'You'll have forgotten all about this by morning, and you'll be mates again. Anyway, remember you need that job, so don't go messing things up there like you did last time.'

'Don't you fucking lecture me,' he snapped, and he carried on slating his boss.

'Oh, I've had enough of this,' my mum said, and I heard her getting out of their bed.

'Yes, that's right, you piss off and go and sleep with that ugly little twat. You belong together, you and her. You with your four eyes and her with that ugly face. She's going to be an ugly little cunt when she grows up.'

He was still jabbering on as my mum opened my door.

'Chris, move over. Can I get in with you?'

I moved over, but my heart sank. I never sleep well when my mum's in my bed. Even though we're both little it's a squeeze in a single bed.

My mum slept and I lay awake most of the night, wondering what she had meant when she told my dad not to mess up this job like the last one.

◆◆◆◆◆

You can see our driveway from the school path. I always look over there to check my dad's car isn't there. Thank God, he has a job and is out of the house at least eight hours a day, and sometimes on a weekend. Despite what my mum says about him bunking off work, he seems to be at work more than he's at home, for which I regularly count our blessings.

My mum will have seen me coming home from the kitchen or dining room window and she gets my lunch on. Today it's

Tuesday and it's just beans on toast.

'Oh, no little sausages?' I ask, disappointed.

It's a new thing, adding little pork sausages and sometimes bacon burgers to baked beans, and all us kids love them. It feels like hunting for treasure as you tuck into beans when there's something meaty hidden in there.

'No sausages but plenty of butter on your toast,' laughs my mum.

For a fleeting moment I remember back to that Saturday afternoon when my dad started calling me ugly. The kids at school didn't laugh too much and my perm grew out eventually. My hair is straight again now, but I've never forgotten what he called me. Ever since then, whenever he gets drunk, like last night, he says I'm ugly. Sometimes I'm fat and stupid as well.

I know from reading my mum's magazines I shouldn't have too much butter or I'll get even fatter, but I'm starving hungry and my mum's always telling me there's no way I'm fat.

'Is too much butter fattening, Mum?' I ask.

'Oh no, not that again,' she replies, almost in desperation. 'If anything, you're too thin!

'How can anyone say you're fat when you weigh just over 6 stones?' she asks, shaking her head. 'How many times do I have to tell you: don't, don't, don't listen to him. You're lovely just as you are. You walk miles every day to and from school, you need food for energy. Please don't ever think you're fat. You're not. You're 13. You're just developing a few curves.'

My mum looks close to tears and I don't want to upset her, so I sit down and eat. I have a strawberry yoghurt for afters, and then a chocolate digestive biscuit with a cup of tea.

Even though I know she slept for a good part of the night, my mum looks tired today. She's 51 and still as thin as a rake, but just recently she's been complaining that her nerves are bad. She says she feels worried all the time and she's started buying phospherine drops from the chemist because they're good for bad nerves.

I cheer her up with gossip about teachers having affairs at school.

'Blimey, who'd look at Mr Shepherd?' she laughs. 'He's short and bald, isn't he?'

My mind jumps ahead as we talk about Mr Shepherd. He takes us for English, and though he gives me brilliant marks for my essays and stories, he sometimes puts me down in front of the class.

He fancies himself as a bit of a photographer and he's always asking good-looking girls to stop by his classroom at lunchtime so he can photograph them. Then he puts his lovely black-and-white prints up in his classroom for us all to see, and the boys to drool over. He's really into beauty and good looks, and sometimes I think that's all that matters to him.

He has never asked me to be photographed. I'm not sure I would want to be anyway. I'd be dead embarrassed if I had Shepherd peering down a lens at me and all my imperfections. I've never mentioned this to anyone, but it's obvious why he's never asked me. It's because I'm so ugly. And I'm sad, too. I don't have that happy fun look about me that he likes.

I'm lost in my own little world when I hear the back door go. My mum's just sat down with a cup of tea. She always believes gossip is best with a cup of tea.

We both look at each other, alarmed. No one but Chris and my dad walk straight in. Chris is away at college and my dad's at work. My mum goes into the kitchen.

'Harry! What are you doing here? Is everything all right?'

Her voice is softer and more respectful towards him in the day. At night, she sometimes has real venom in her tone.

'No, it's not all right,' he answers in a clipped voice. 'I've packed it in. I'm not going back there. I've told him where to shove his job.'

'You can't pack it in,' says my mum.

I get up to go into the kitchen, but I sit straight back down, and put my head in my hands, my elbows resting on my knee. I've started to do this a lot when my dad's around. I think if he can't see my face, he'll be less reminded of how ugly he finds me. My mum has told me time and time again not to sit like that, as though I'm ashamed of myself and the way I look, but that's exactly how I feel.

'What do you mean, I can't pack it in? I have. I'm not going back there,' he says. '"Do this, do that!" He thinks I'm a bloody slave. I'm not going to be his lackey, working my guts out while he's swanning off down The Farmer's Arms.'

He gives me a nod on his way to the bathroom. My mum comes back into the dining room and heads straight for her phospherine drops on the fireplace.

'If he's given up his job, he won't be able to claim any money at all,' she says, thinking aloud. 'Thank God, he has a bit put by in the building society. Oh, bloody hell, Chris, when will life get any better for us, lass?'

I'm thinking about money when my stomach drops about three flights in one swoop. I've just realized what's so awful about this. From now on, my dad will be at home every lunchtime.

◆◆◆◆◆

How wrong I am. He emerges back downstairs with his suit on and he goes to the mirror above the fireplace in the living room to check his tie is straight.

'Harry?' questions my mum, hopefully. 'Are you going to the employment office?'

Her voice is bright.

'Of course I'm not going to the employment office; I'm going to the bloody pub!'

He gives one of those ridiculous cocky, screechy laughs of his as he leaves, and my mum and I exchange a look that acknowledges our lives have just got a whole lot worse.

◆◆◆◆◆

I go back to school but I can't concentrate on anything. I have double maths and I usually love algebra and my teacher Mrs Winter, but I'm not interested in anything today.

As double maths becomes geography with Miss Tomlin, I mope through the corridors and sit and listen to her talk about oxbow lakes. But why should I need to know about lakes when all I want to do is drown myself in one?

Finally it's 20 to 4 and the buzzer goes to mark the end of school. The other kids jump up and run out. I almost heave myself up from my desk and walk slowly. I don't want to go home today. I know life will be hell this afternoon, and every afternoon from now on. There's no way he'll get and hold down a job. He's going to be at home or in the pub every single day.

◆◆◆◆◆

As I walk down the avenue to our house, Jackie is chatting away and I'm nodding but I'm hardly listening. I'm trying to get a look at my mum and dad's bedroom window. If the curtains are closed upstairs at the front, that means he's back and he's in bed. They're open. That must mean he's up.

'See you tomorrow, Jackie,' I say, turning into our driveway. The garage doors are closed. He's obviously put the car away. I open the back door quietly. My mum's cooking in the kitchen. It seems early for her to be doing tea.

'What mood is he in, Mum?' I ask. 'Is he OK?'

'I don't know, love,' she says, feigning brightness. 'He's not back yet.'

'Oh my God,' I say slowly, 'that means he's been drinking for at least three hours. Oh my God, Mum, oh God.'

I start to panic and cry and turn to look round the room as though an answer lies in the furniture, on the walls, even on the carpet. My eyes are darting everywhere, searching for a solution. I realize my mum isn't cooking tea. She's keeping his lunch warm. Then my mum speaks.

'Listen, love, we've got to be strong through this. We stick together and look after each other. We won't let him get to us,' she says.

I listen to her, but just look at us. I'm almost dizzy with fear and she's a nervous wreck. He's already got to us.

◆◆◆◆◆

He's back just before 5 and he can barely get up the two steps to the back door. His legs seem to be buckling beneath him. He reeks of beer.

'That was better,' he slurs. 'Better than working for that fucking cunt. That bald-headed bastard, all those pitches I cut, and he takes all the fucking credit for it when the bosses come. I'm fucking glad I'm out of there. I wish I'd never set eyes on that twat.'

143

He goes to the staircase, but he doesn't walk upstairs. He must be crawling. After using the toilet, he collapses on his bed.

'There! That wasn't so bad, was it?' says my mum. 'Sometimes we worry about things too much, you know. He'll sleep it off and he'll be OK. He might not even go out tonight!'

The two of us look at each other, ecstatic at the thought of a night's sleep. But 20 minutes later, just as I'm starting my maths homework, we hear him getting up. He's in the bathroom.

'Nellie! Nellie! I need help,' he shouts. 'I'm dying.'

'I bloody wish you were,' I say aloud, and for a tiny moment, my mum raises a smile as she heads upstairs. I go quietly behind her.

The smell hits me first, followed by a sound of wretching, then loud farting. He's laid out on the bathroom floor. He has been sick all over the pale green bathroom suite, and the green-and-white patterned carpet. He's also had diarrhoea. He just has his vest on – no underpants, so I turn away just as my mum tries to lift him up.

'Why have you got into this state, you daft bugger?' asks my mum, heaving him up, but from what I can see, he's behaving like a dead weight.

'Harry, I can't lift you, can you get up and get onto the toilet at least?' she asks, quite reasonably.

'No, I fucking can't,' he slurs. 'Do you think I'd be lying here if I could get up? You'll just have to clean it up.'

I can't stand the smell any more, and I can't stand to hear my mum being ordered to clean up so much shit and vomit, so I go back downstairs.

My mum comes back down about 10 minutes later and starts filling a pale yellow bucket with hot soapy water, gathering up old rags and getting her rubber gloves from the cupboard beneath the sink before going back upstairs to clean up after that filthy disgusting animal. My poor, poor mum, I sit and sob. What on earth has she ever done to deserve this kind of life?

◆◆◆◆◆

When I finally stop crying, I can hear my mum cleaning the carpet upstairs. It sounds like a cat plodging on material, with constant regular movements. I pick up a magazine and start reading a feature about How To Improve Your Life.

By the time my mum comes down, with what looks like brown sludge in the bucket, I feel quite hopeful.

'Here, Mum, give me that,' I say, taking the bucket from her.

It really is stinky. I mustn't wretch.

'I'll do it, love,' she says. 'It needs to be swilled down the drain.'

'I can do that, you get washed and changed and put the kettle on for us.'

I remember the feature. It said treat those you love well. I take her rubber gloves and put them on, then I make about eight trips to the drain by the back door, rinsing and emptying the bucket until it's clean. Then I shove a load of bleach in and leave it outside the back door.

When I go back in, I say quietly: 'Mum, I really love you, you know. You know I do, don't you?'

It takes her by surprise, and, unable to speak with emotion, she starts waving her hand at me to shut me up.

'Don't, Chrissie, don't set me off. If I start crying now, I'll never bloody stop!' she says, and we both start to laugh at our crap lives as she hugs me.

◆◆◆◆◆

I really am trying to simplify my life. I make Jack wear his school uniform several days running to cut down on washing and ironing, which I now do on Mondays and Fridays, giving me the weekend off.

I plan supermarket shopping like a military operation. I even have a Master Shopping List on my computer, and once a week we tick the things we need and off I go.

The reason for this manic organization is I now have six hours a day while Jack is at school to get all my work done, but even that is never enough.

At the start of this month, March, I had 15 features to do, ranging from a little half-hour review of a hotel to great big reports, requiring case studies, experts to comment and photographs to organize.

I've also listed all the other jobs that need doing, like planning Jack's party, putting four years of photographs into albums, recycling Jack's old clothes to a friend, replying to wedding invitations, booking hotels and buying presents, and renewing car insurance, AA membership and car tax. Bloody hell, it's endless, and there's a job a day till I'm 93.

I know I mustn't take on any new work. I must clear the decks, start a work spring-clean and empty my notebook so that, one day in the near future, I will wake up feeling free and square-shouldered, rather than hunched and stressed about the amount I have to plough through. No new commitments, I chant to myself, and feel pretty good … until I check my Inbox.

◆◆◆◆◆

I've been asked to be a judge at this year's North-East Press Awards. How exciting! Ian and I used to go to the Press Awards before we had Jack. We had great fun, eating and drinking and cheering on our former colleagues. Ian won an award before I moved to the north-east. I've only entered twice and never won a thing. I never knew they asked unimportant people like me to judge. I thought the judges would be editors and managing directors and top PR personnel, not writers like me with 15 deadlines looming and no time to do anything.

I walk to the kitchen with a bit of a spring in my step. I've been asked to be a judge.

I give myself a day to think it over just in case it's a wind-up. The next day, I tell Ian as though it's no big deal to me. He doesn't mock. As usual, he's supportive. He's always supported everything I have done – an amazing contrast to the way my dad treated my mum.

'You should do it, sweetie, it would be a great experience.'

'Do you think I'll have time to read all the stuff?' I ask nervously.

'Of course you will,' he says. 'There won't be that much anyway. People submit just six cuttings per category. It'll be easy and great on your CV. Do it, sweetie.'

◆◆◆◆◆

Two weeks later the entries arrive. I'm quite looking forward to taking them from the postman and sitting down for a nice read over a pot of tea.

But it isn't the postman at the door. It's a burly special delivery man who heaves a large brown box inside our doorway.

'Blimey, that's a lot,' I comment, waiting to sign for them.

'That's not all, love,' he says. 'There's plenty more where that came from.'

He heaves two more boxes crammed with cuttings through our door, then I sign. The boxes are almost too heavy for me to carry so they must be absolutely stuffed full. My heart sinks at the number of cuttings I will have to plough through. Instead of downsizing my diary, I need planning permission for an extension. 'Judge press awards' makes it on to the To Do List and merits four whole days, which takes me up to my 94th birthday.

◆◆◆◆◆

I've ploughed through women's, features, exclusive and consumer and I have just three days left until the official judging day. To be honest, once I got started it was very interesting.

Now I just have to look through the photographs ready for Judging Day on Sunday.

◆◆◆◆◆

'Jack! Please go back to bed,' I say wearily. 'I've read you a story, cuddled you, you must go back and go to sleep. It's 8 o'clock and it's your Easter play tomorrow. You need to rest.'

I'm going on at him, the way I always do when I'm in a panic about how much I have to do. You'd think I'd shut up, save my energy and do what I have to do, but no, I rant on … and on … and on like a demented woman on a very short fuse.

'What are you doing, Mummy?' asks Jack, ignoring my orders and my impending state of madness.

'I'm judging the newspapers,' I say proudly. 'Tonight I'm looking at photographs.'

Ian's right. He says I try to discipline Jack, but then Jack asks a very sweet question, wins me over, we start chatting, and discipline is forgotten.

Just as I speak, a very sweet squirrel appears on my computer screen, with a slice of white bread. Jack's little face lights up. He loves squirrels almost as much as skunks. It must be their bushy tails because he likes foxes, too.

'Please, Mum, can I help? I won that competition at school, remember?'

It's true. He won a pets photography contest at school with a picture of our cat Kitty in some daffodils. He's probably better qualified than me to look through these photos.

Once again, I give in. But it would be a fun thing to do together, and he could help me, by getting the discs out. I settle him down next to me on a stool and we're off. I look at the clock: 8.15. If we can crack this in an hour, I might catch half an hour's telly before I crash out.

We look at Michael Owen with his daughter, silhouettes of chimneys on Teesside and Tony Blair from all angles, including right up his nose. Jack loves the newspaper that does all the cutesy animal photos. If he had his way, a little puppy dog would win. He starts to speak with great authority.

'Nah, that doesn't do anything for me, Mum,' he says. 'Nah, I don't like that shirt the boy's wearing. Too many girls on that one.'

I wonder for a minute if this kind of judging was used when I have entered. Has some five-year-old looked at my cuttings and said: 'No, this one makes me cry, Mummy. I don't like stories where people die. Don't vote for her'? No wonder I've never won! It's not that I'm crap, it's because I don't write for five- and six-year-olds!

I'm still wondering when a photo of nudes flashes up on my screen. Jack is mesmerized by so many bottoms.

'Wow, Mum, why have all these people taken their clothes off?'

'They didn't have to, Jack. They chose to take their clothes off. They wanted to be in the photograph,' I explain.

'Why?'

'Dunno.'

Ah, here we have the close-ups. The photographer has submitted several from the nude photoshoot. I must admit, it's refreshing to see bums with dimples of cellulite in, tummies sagging over pubic hair, white pale skin and couples hanging around together, as though they're in the queue at the supermarket.

'Wow, look at that man's willy,' exclaims Jack. 'It's quite big, isn't it, Mum?'

'Er, yes, I suppose so,' I reply quickly, scared he will tell his teachers Mummy was letting him look at naked men with big willies on her computer late into the night. I move on quickly.

'We're working really hard, aren't we, Mum?' he asks. 'Do all grown-ups work as hard as you?'

'Some work as hard as me, Jack, some don't. But it gives me a nice feeling when I have worked hard.'

'Me too, Mum,' he says earnestly, handing me the next disc.

Now this is sad: It's a close-up of an old lady who has been beaten up. Her eyes are purple from the beating, and her lined face sad.

'Why has that lady coloured her face, Mum? Has she used crayons?' asks Jack.

'No, Jack, some nasty people have attacked this old lady and hit her in the face. That purple is a bruise.'

I could sob when I think of how she is someone's gran, but Jack has beaten me to it. He's crying. For a minute I wonder if he shouldn't have seen this. I cuddle him close to me. He's tired and should be in bed now, but I can tell he's genuinely sad.

'Who did it, Mummy?' he asks.

'I don't know, sweetie, but that's why we need policemen and -women. They will hunt down the people who did this.'

'Mummy, do people sometimes do things like this to boys and girls?' he asks, almost terrified of my answer.

'Yes, they do.'

I may as well be truthful. He needs to know what's out there. I'm sure every parent remembers little Jamie Bulger when a child asks a question like this.

'That's why you mustn't go anywhere without your mummy and daddy knowing where you are. That's why we look after little boys and girls, to protect them from the type of people who did this.'

'That poor lady,' says Jack.

'You'd never do that to anyone, would you, Jack?'

I need reassurance our boy won't be a thug. He doesn't strike me as a thug. His father is as soft as anything, but I sometimes worry about those rogue genes from my side of the family.

'Never, ever, Mummy,' says my angel, and we cuddle up for the last batch of entries.

Needless to say, Jack has given me his list of winning photos to mention on Judging Day, when the final decision will be made. I just hope I can hold my own in the debate on Sunday when the other judges will root for arty silhouettes, the closure of mines and the other 2,000 pictures that symbolize life in the north-east of England.

I will look straight ahead, with my chin resolute, and vote with conviction for a picture of a duck walking behind a man, a tabby kitten and the squirrel with a slice of bread to be shortlisted for the region's Photograph of the Year.

CHAPTER 10

Can I Have a Gun, Mummy?

My dad loves his gun. It's a 12-bore double-barrelled shotgun. He used to shoot rabbits with it at my mum's uncle's farm in Wales. I've no idea when he got the gun or why. It seems to have always been here.

He gets it out now and then. He's usually sobering up when he goes upstairs to his wardrobe, gets the gun and proudly walks downstairs, like a gamekeeper. It's often a Sunday teatime when he settles in his chair in the living room, with his legs wide, leaning forward to lay out the gun on the carpet and rug in front of him.

While the coal fire crackles in the grate, he arranges his cloths, then he rubs and polishes to his heart's content. Every now and then he holds a part of it up to the light, to check it's gleaming. He nods to himself slowly, as though he's admiring his work. It's all legal. He has a gun licence for it. He has just got a new box of cartridges for it. He didn't have any at all left until he got the new ones.

He sits cleaning his gun while in the dining room my mum has *Songs of Praise* on television. They rarely spend time in the same room. Different interests, I suppose. Occasionally he'll shout if he needs something.

'Nellie, sharp knife!' he'll call, if there's a corner he can't get into with cloths. My mum will tear herself away from Salisbury Cathedral on TV and rush off in search of a knife. She humours him, but she doesn't have much interest in his life.

We can cope with the gun when he's sober and just cleaning it. I'm 14 now, a miniature of my mum in shape, but I still have that scared look in my eyes that I had 10 years ago, and a pale complexion from lack of sleep. I look at him cleaning the gun. It's eccentric, we admit, but each to their own. It's when he's pissed and the gun comes out that I get scared.

Every now and then, when someone has wound him up, he starts the threats.

◆◆◆◆◆

He's absolutely plastered today. It's Sunday afternoon. He rolled in about an hour ago, at 3 o'clock, and thankfully went straight off to bed.

Then, after an hour, the floorboards upstairs started to creak.

'Oh, bloody hell,' says my mum, listening.

Chris is home from college for the weekend, and we're all sitting chatting, very quietly, after a late Sunday lunch. I love it when he's home. Now he's older I know he'd never let my dad hurt us if he could stop him. I can relax my shoulders a little and share the worry for just a few days. Trouble is, my dad's so crafty he sneaks up on us. It's hard to keep one step ahead of someone as mad as him.

We hear my dad coming downstairs. He's always at his worst when he's slept a bit, then wakes up. We dread him coming downstairs. We know we'll get the full onslaught of 10 or more pints of beer.

We get a blast of beer fumes as the door opens.

'Do you know what that bastard Derek said today?' he slurs, staggering around. He's half-dressed, with his puny torso in a baggy vest and his trousers on but undone at the front. His body is so white it's almost grey. He's obviously tried to get undressed and given up halfway through.

He's looking at me. His eyes are almost clear.

I feel like saying: 'No, of course we don't know, you moron. We weren't in your shitty pub, and, what's more, we don't actually care what Derek said, bastard or not.'

One day I will say that, I swear I will. I will have attitude. I will swear and insult him as much as I possibly can. But for now it must all stay inside. I can't risk winding him up some more. It's OK being tough while Chris is home, but he's off back to college this afternoon, and my mum and I will be on our own again from tonight.

'No, Dad,' I say timidly.

I don't find out what Derek said. Instead my dad goes into a massive tirade of abuse.

'I'm going to fucking teach him to say things like that!' he rages, with his fists clenched in front of him, like a boxer about to start a match. 'He'll be sorry he ever messed with me.'

He looks ridiculous pretending to be Mr Tough Guy in a vest. At least it isn't a string one.

'Harry, what did Derek say?' asks my mum patiently.

'Never mind what Derek said!' he shouts, mimicking my mum's voice. 'I'm going to get my gun. I'm going back up there. I'm going to sort him out!'

He sets off upstairs, but we're after him immediately.

'Harry! Don't be stupid!' My mum speaks as though she's talking to a little boy. 'You'll get into trouble with the police. Don't be such a fool!'

He loves it when we beg and plead and cajole. He lets us all have a try, then he pretends he's just realized we're right and he abandons the idea of shooting a man he regularly drinks with.

'He thinks he's some bloody Wild West hero,' my brother scoffs quietly, as my dad goes back upstairs.

'Who would he be?' he adds.

My mum goes back to the washing up. We turn the television on. John Wayne's face fills our black-and-white screen. We give quiet whoops of delight when we see the film is *True Grit*. We may have a total nutter sleeping right above us, but for the next hour or so we can escape.

'Definitely not Billy the Kid!' I laugh.

We love westerns, me and Chris, especially *The Sons of Katie Elder* and *Cat Ballou*. I look at Chris. I wonder why he bothers coming home for weekends, but I know he loves me and my mum, and he just has to put up with my dad. I bet all his friends go to nice civilized homes for the weekend, and Chris has to come to this loony bin.

'Would he be in *True Grit*?' I ask.

'More like True Shit,' my brother quips, and we grin. Then we both laugh out loud.

My mum comes though and sits with us. She gives a wry smile when she sees what we're watching.

We're just about coping with the drunken ranting these days, but when the weapons come out, it scares the hell out of all of us. He's so plastered he doesn't know what he's doing half the time. He has quite a collection, too. As well as the gun, he has knives and some truncheon-like thing he brought home from the Second World War.

'How much harm could that gun do, Mum?' I ask. I wonder how close he has to be to shoot something.

My mum looks at the screen.

'Which one, love?' she asks.

She's looking at John Wayne.

155

'My dad's,' I say quickly. It's a hard question to ask, and I'm scared I might cry.

'A hell of a lot,' she says quietly. 'Don't ever ask him any questions, Chris. Don't remind him he has it and don't let him know you're remotely interested in it. If he thinks it bothers you, he'll do it all the more.'

Later, Chris packs our old holdall and gets the bus to the station to go back to college. I hate him going. I love him being home to cheer me up and I know if he can he will protect us. But when it's just me and my mum, it gets scary.

◆◆◆◆◆

I go to bed that night worried about the gun. My shoulders are tight again. It's as though the worry of my dad was passed back to me when Chris left.

But I also have another worry. I'm reading *Jackie* magazine to try and find out how to kiss properly. Not that anyone has offered. I just want to be sure I know when the time comes. I've got a bit of a crush on Howard, a boy at school. I know I'm a late starter compared to most of my friends, but they'd live like nuns too if they were as scared of their dads as I am.

I heard the other day that you should turn to God if you have a problem, so I have. Tonight I have spent a good 20 minutes telling God I don't know how to kiss. I'm not quite sure what to do with my tongue or whether to open my mouth or not. Will I still be able to breathe, I wonder? I'm completely honest. I can't expect God to help me unless he has all the info.

At the end I expect to be a snogging expert, but nothing happens. I just say aloud: 'So there you are, God, that's my problem, please see what you can do for me.' I feel a bit better for getting it off my chest.

I'm still awake when my dad gets back on this particular night. He is completely off his head, topped up from lunchtime. He's swaying, and talking gibberish, but I make out the word 'whore' again. Oh God, please no, not another go at my poor old mum, who never even looks at another man. I wish Chris hadn't gone back to college. We felt more protected when he was here and my dad was better behaved.

Suddenly my door bursts open and he's there.

'You filthy fucking cow!' he rages.

'What?' I say, looking around before I realize he's talking to me, not my mum.

'I know what you've been doing,' he rants. 'You're disgusting, nothing but a whore.'

'I don't know what you mean,' I plead. 'I haven't done anything.'

'Letting those lads at school mess around with you; you're filthy, fucking filthy!'

'Dad, I haven't let anyone do anything,' I say. 'Honest, I haven't.'

We had the talk on puberty three years ago at school, but I'm still not quite clear about it all. I'm still confused about what it is a man leaves inside a woman that actually makes the baby. Soon after the talk I asked my brother if a man wees inside a woman.

He just laughed, so I'm no wiser.

'Harry, leave her alone!' my mum intervenes. 'She hasn't done anything.'

'You can talk, you dirty bastard,' he yells at my mum. 'I know all about you and that fella from the shop.'

It would be laughable, but we're both so scared of what he's going to do next. My poor mum wouldn't have the confidence to pursue another man.

But he doesn't seem bothered about the 'fella' from the shop tonight. It's me he's after.

'Why are you doing it?' he roars.

'I'm not, Dad, honest! I'm not doing anything.'

'I know about these things, people are talking in the pub; you're a whore!'

The name-calling goes on and on. My denials go on and on. All the time he's swaying and staggering. He seems to be getting more pissed by the minute, though he isn't drinking. Eventually he goes off to his bedroom. I breathe a sigh of relief. I'm shattered. I fall to sleep almost immediately, vowing to deal with whatever I'm supposed to have done tomorrow.

◆◆◆◆◆

I don't know how long I've been asleep. I'm dreaming. It's as though I have my forehead pressed against cold iron bars. There's no give in them and the pressure against my forehead is huge. The bars are horizontal, not vertical like prison bars. I'm not sure where I am.

Slowly it dawns on me I'm not dreaming any more. I'm waking. But the pressure is still there. Maybe I'm getting one of what my mum calls a 'worked-up headache', one that strikes when I'm worried, which is most of the time these days.

As I open my eyes, I see the underside of machinery. All dark grey and metal with what looks like lighter brown wood at the end. A split second later I focus on my dad, eyes flashing with anger, swaying, dribbling as he curses, his arms bent to get the barrels square on my forehead. The barrels seem huge. They take up the whole of my forehead. They never looked that big when he was cleaning them by the fire.

I can't believe it. He has the gun to my forehead. I can't hear anyone else in the room, just me and him. My heart suddenly registers panic and starts to race so fast I wonder if it will wear itself out beating.

I don't know whether to speak. I can't see how he's holding it, if he has his finger on the trigger or not. It seems too far away. I wonder if it's loaded. I assume it is. Damn! If I'd stayed awake, I would have heard him loading it. I could have been out the back door. But it must be about 3am and I was so tired I slept.

Where's my mum? I wonder. She's started sleeping in Chris's room when he's away. But surely she's not sleeping through this? But then I slept through him coming into my room. He obviously crept quietly. Or maybe we're so bloody tired we'll sleep through anything. If I survive this, I'm going to put a wardrobe behind my door every single night.

'Now, tell me everything you've done with these lads,' he says. His tone is steady, but his words are slurred.

'Nothing,' I say. I'm too scared to move my head or my mouth a fraction, so my voice comes out zombie-like. My body is so rigid with fear my voice can't be anything but terrified and staccato. I'd love to shrug him off and say: 'You don't scare me, you bastard.' But he does and he knows he does.

'I don't know what to do, even if I wanted to,' I say. There. That's the absolute truth. Surely now he'll believe me, and maybe even have some sympathy.

'Fucking liar! Well, you're not going to lie to me ever again, you're not going to get the fucking chance, you slut. You're nothing but a tramp, a no-good fucking tramp!'

I think I'm going to die right there and then. He's getting angrier. My whole body is shaking with fear. Just one slight movement on that trigger and it could all be over for me.

Thoughts are racing through my mind. They're so fast they're hardly there before another one comes. But the one that comes back time after time is: What chance do I have? He's so pissed, he might well do it tonight.

I look around the room, moving just my eyes, not my head. Because I'm still lying down, I can just see the tops of things, the wardrobe, the door, the airing cupboard. There's nothing I could get to whack him over the head with. The telephone is downstairs in the dining room, directly below my bedroom. Besides, you need time to get through to the police, time I don't have.

My bed's as far away from the neighbour's wall as it could be. I can't even get over there and hammer for help. They won't suspect anything either. He's been so quiet even my mum hasn't woken. Let's face it, I'm not going anywhere. I'm not able to move an inch. Not even a quarter of an inch. He's making sure of that. He may be very drunk and his body swaying, but his arms are holding these barrels as steady as anything.

My stomach is gurgling and I'm going to get horrendous diarrhoea any minute now. I wonder if he'll let me out to the toilet. Will he come with me and watch me? What if he doesn't let me out and I do it in bed? I don't often let myself be so self-pitying, but oh God, why is my life so awful?

Maybe he'll let me go to the bathroom and I could bang the toilet seat and wake my mum and pretend it was a mistake? I wonder if I should shout out: 'Mum, get the police!' But my dad might just pull the trigger then.

I want my mum. I just want to hug her, touch her, anything, just be with her, and feel her arms round me.

But then what could my mum do? Let's face it, she can't tackle him. I'm not sure she could persuade him to stop this. He's adamant. He really believes I've been up to things with

160

boys at school. I think of my mum. Her heart would break if she saw this. I've often found her crying alone, sobbing: 'What am I putting you kids through? You shouldn't have to live like this.'

Then a new thought replaces the panic. I don't want my mum to see me being held like this. The shock could be too much for her. It would literally break her heart. Besides, it's OK like this. It's me he has the gun pointed at. It's me he might pull the trigger on. It's a whole lot better than if he had the same trigger on my mum. Imagine how that would feel. Now I feel sick as well as having diarrhoea cramps.

Imagine if Chris were home and he had the gun at his forehead. That would be so much worse. At any minute he could take away one or both of the two people dearest to me. Imagine losing my mum and Chris and being left with my dad. No, it's better that it's me. Now I don't want my mum to wake. I don't want her in here, witnessing this. How contrary am I? A minute ago I wanted her.

I look him in the eye, aware I have to squint a bit, as I still daren't move my head the slightest bit. His face is at an angle.

'Oh go on, then, shoot me,' I say in a quiet calm voice that doesn't sound like mine, a voice I've never heard before. I hate myself for giving up but I can't live like this any longer. Yet my contempt and hatred are so raw you could almost reach out and touch them. 'Get it over with.'

I cringe inside. I know I don't mean it. I do want to live. I want to be with my mum. But I've just told him to shoot me. What if he does?

He looks astonished at the sudden change in me. He raises his Dennis Healey eyebrows and I can see the surprise on his face. He loves the pleading and the 'Oh, please don't do it, Dad.' He's thrown by this sudden toughness.

161

'No, I'm going to save you for another time,' he says, finally taking the barrels off my head. As he turns to stagger back to bed, I lie completely still. I feel as though my head has been frozen on the pillow for days. I am rigid. Every muscle in my body feels locked. Although he's taken the gun away, I can still feel the barrels there for hours afterwards. I'm haunted by the words 'another time'. I know I can't ever go through that again.

I hear him open the wardrobe door in his bedroom, replace the gun, then get into bed. I move my head a fraction of an inch, then get braver and move it from side to side. My neck doesn't jar as I expect it to, but my shoulders are so tense they're up round my ears.

I don't sleep at all. I lie there. I'm happy to be alive and to know I'll be with my mum, but I know I can't cope with this life much longer. I go to the bathroom and painful wretching is followed by the diarrhoea I dreaded, as though my bowels have gone into spasm. I'm terrified of waking him again. I go back to bed, and lie there, as if in shock, getting up only when more cramps send me dashing to the loo. I feel clammy all over, from where the sweat from my fear has dried cold.

After about two hours I creep along the landing to my mum's room. She's lying there, fully clothed on top of the bed, snoring gently. She goes to bed ready for action these days. I stand over her for a while but she's obviously so knackered and will sleep through anything.

I want to wake her. I want sympathy. I want to lie in her arms and sob: 'He held his gun to my head, Mum. He was going to pull the trigger, I know he was.'

But I can't bring myself to wake her. I can't worry her. Besides, I could never convey how vile that all just was. I go back and lie in bed, focusing on the cord that turns the light on

162

above my bed for hours and hours.

◆◆◆◆◆

The next day, I go home for lunch from school as usual. I am totally knackered and feel very, very down. All morning I've wondered if the gun was loaded. The thought of what would have happened if he'd pulled that trigger has haunted me.

I have pictured police cars and bright lights and ambulances and my mum crying and my dad being led away by police officers. That last bit was quite good. But then I start to picture my own funeral … and I have to stop. It's too new and raw, and could so easily happen yet.

I haven't seen my dad yet and don't want to. I wonder if he'll be pleasant. I know he won't be apologetic. If I remind him of what happened, he'll pretend he can't remember. I'm getting sick of that charade.

'Where is he, then?' I ask, my voice drained of all enthusiasm.

'At the pub,' answers my mum. 'Went early, just after 11.30. Why, Chris?'

'I'm just sick of him, totally sick of him,' I answer.

She raises an eyebrow. I'm usually the upbeat one, who cheers her up and keeps her happy. However I'm feeling, I usually put on a bright face for my mum, but today I just can't do it.

'Just not in the mood for him today,' I say.

Thank God, he's already gone to the pub. I eat my lunch, the yolk of a boiled egg. I can't stand the whites and use a baby teaspoon to make sure I just get the yolk on my toast.

My mum is setting her ironing board up in the dining room. I check out of the corner of my eye that she's still engrossed, then I go to my dad's bedroom and find the new box of gun cartridges he bought by the gun in the wardrobe. I don't want my mum to

163

know about this. This way, she can never be forced to say where the cartridges are.

Even though it's the middle of the day my eyes are so tired I do a double take. The box has been opened. All morning at school I fantasized the gun wasn't loaded and he was just on a power trip.

I look at the dark red cartridges. They look so inoffensive. I thought they'd be black, not a pretty red colour. I knew he'd used his cartridges up so any in the gun are from the new box.

I look carefully, willing the box to be full. But there's an empty space in there for one cartridge. The space in itself looks chilling. He had loaded the gun with one of the cartridges. I wonder if he loaded it while he was drunk last night, or when he was sober? He must absolutely despise me if he loaded a gun to hold to my forehead.

I don't dare fiddle with the gun to unload it. I wish I could. But I carefully take the box of cartridges and put them at the very back of my knicker drawer in an old sideboard in my bedroom. Then I cover them with as many pairs of pants as I can find.

It's a very small consolation that there's just one cartridge in the gun now. For some reason I think there's space for two – isn't that what a double-barrelled gun is all about? I should be grateful there's just the one, but I'm so scared I'm losing a sense of what's rational.

At the very worst, he'll only get one of us. After realizing he could kill my mum or Chris, I hope it's me. What kind of a thought is that? I should be thinking about my whole life, not which one of my family is going to get bumped off and hoping it's me so the others live.

Then another thought flashes through my mind. How fantastic it would be if one night he got so down, he turned the gun on himself. It could so easily happen when he's all maudlin and sorry for himself and harping on about how depressing his pissed-up life really is. Unfortunately, the three of us are too normal to take the gun and shoot him. We wouldn't have a clue what to do. It's quite heavy for a start. But just as I can see him using the gun on us three, I can also see him shooting himself.

I pray to God again, but not about kissing Howard this time. That problem can go on hold for a while. I pray my dad uses that loaded gun to shoot himself.

As I say the words, my mind is racing ahead and I see my mum and me living in our house, perfectly happy, my friends calling round whenever they like, and Chris coming back for weekends. I can't imagine a single worry we would have. With my dad gone, all our problems would go, too. I already feel lighter and more hopeful and energetic as I run back to school to see if Howard's hanging around the playground.

◆◆◆◆◆

It's a glorious summer's evening and the sky is bluer and the clouds fluffier and whiter because I'm off to my weekly yoga class. I know yoga is hardly sex and drugs and rock 'n' roll, but since I had Jack, my yoga class has been my one big night out.

For one night a week, I can do yoga without having to wipe noses, do bath-time or read bedtime stories. I feel a bit guilty saying that. There must be thousands of women who'd love to put a child to bed. It's just so good to have a night off. I even get a snooze at the end of yoga in relaxation. As a mummy, you can't ask for more, can you? Well, the odd champagne cocktail, maybe.

It's a bit of an ancient ritual in our house. Ian is supposed to be home at 6.30pm on Wednesdays to be with Jack so I can have a leisurely 20-mile drive to yoga and arrive all calm, poised and serene for a 7.30pm start. But that never happens. He usually gets back just before 7pm and I bomb up the country roads, swerving to avoid rabbits, and arrive with that tired worn-out look that characters over 50 have in soaps. Except their dark circles under their eyes are painted on in make-up and mine aren't.

'Where the hell is he?' I curse, looking out of the window, my mouth set in a straight line. I'm all ready in my black leggings with the white stripe down and a grey T-shirt.

The great thing about summer yoga is I can go in sandals. In winter it's a different story – I have a jumper, fleece, a scarf, gloves, thick socks, boots and a hat. I'd probably take crampons if I had some. But tonight, the perfect evening for sitting outside a country pub, it's sandals.

'No sign of him, Jack. What is your father playing at?' I say, each word clipped with annoyance.

'Squash?' ventures Jack cheerfully.

He's drawing some pictures of knights for me, with his tongue sticking out in concentration.

'He'd better not be! He's supposed to be here!' I rage. 'This is my one night off, and where is he? My one night!'

I stomp from the front window to the kitchen and back again. No sign of his car coming round the corner, just a cul de sac crammed with cars and kids on bikes. Two minutes later, Ian rings.

'Sweetie, I'm running late. Can I meet you at yoga and we can swap Jack over?' he asks.

I jump at the idea. I've always wanted to show off my son to my yoga friends. They held him once as a baby, but they will love him even more now he's an interesting little person with news and views.

'I want you to be a really good boy when we get to yoga,' I

166

tell him as he settles in the front seat of my car. 'Be nice and calm. That's how yoga people are.'

'But you're not calm, Mum,' says Jack, opening the glove compartment so all our cassettes tumble out, cases breaking apart. 'You shouted at me yesterday. And what about yesterday after yesterday when you were going to snap Daddy's head off?'

'Yesterday after yesterday' is Jack's version of 'the day before yesterday'. No points for guessing when 'tomorrow after tomorrow' is. It gets a bit confusing when we're talking weeks and weeks, though.

'Sometimes even us yogis get a bit annoyed, Jack,' I answer, reversing and avoiding even more kids on bikes. 'We have to let it out.'

As we trundle up the country roads, I encourage Jack to look for cows and sheep, while he wants to look for Zurg from Toy Story. We both see the red sky together.

'Is it delight or warning, you know that shepherd's thing, Mum?' he asks as we park. I'm thrilled he remembers all the garbage I tell him.

As we walk through the smoky bar at the Arts Centre, Jack holds my hand tighter. He may be a tough warrior some of the time, but when faced with a bunch of long-haired, cigarette-smoking teenagers with sullen looks on their faces, he becomes a little boy again.

I love holding his hand. I feel as though I'm saying to the world: 'Look, he's mine, this gorgeous kid with big brown eyes and such a happy laugh is all mine.'

We go through the door to the room where yoga is held. We're the first. There's no need for the light on this bright evening. As soon as Jack sees the size of the empty room, it's as though a switch is turned on inside his head – the one that says 'go berserk'. He runs, just like a horse let out for spring, after winter in a stable. I smile at his coltish freedom.

But then he starts bombing up and down the hall, from side to side. It's as though he has to cover every single inch of this space.

I watch in horror. He's going absolutely barmy. He wasn't cooped up in the car that long, surely. Where's this energy come from? I wonder. I calm down. He's just letting off steam, I tell myself, but as soon as I see him pelting around, I know he's as high as a kite. Did he inhale walking through the bar, I wonder? I haven't given him sweets for months.

I look at my watch. Quarter past. Serious yogis will arrive any second now. They'll saunter in, mats under their arms, and quietly greet one or two people. They will spread their mats ready to enjoy their quiet time, and lie down. What they won't expect is Mr Energy Bags here tear-arsing around the room, crashing into anything and anyone in his way.

'Jack,' I try to whisper loud, just in case anyone is right outside the door and about to come in. You can't do yoga and be heard shrieking your head off.

'Come and sit down on this mat with me,' I say, patting it, trying to make it look attractive. I put so much effort into the patting you'd think I was offering a hammock in St Lucia. I can see he's considering coming to sit down, he starts heading back towards me, but he gets a glimpse of the space and he's off again.

I'm getting so angry now I want to go over there, grab him and shake him. I want to shock him so much he calms down. I can feel anger surging up from my stomach, up to my chest and down my arms. But I know I couldn't hurt him. I'd hate myself for a start. And how could I justify a good duffing when all the kid has done is run around an empty room? I start to wonder if

168

I'm the one going bonkers. I think of my dad. I bet he never had any dilemmas like this. Then I start to worry I'm turning into him. Maybe there's a lone gene that causes you, from the age of 40, to start mistreating small children and animals?

But I so want my yoga friends to see the real Jack, to see why I'm so proud of him and adore him so much.

There are two doors, one after the other, to get to our yoga class. We hear the squeak of the outer door. People are arriving.

'Jack,' I say, beckoning. I hate people who beckon. I think they're so patronizing. 'People are coming in now, be a good boy and calm down.'

Hurrah, hurrah, hurrah. Thank you, God. Jack sits on my mat, smiles and says: 'Goo gooo, ga ga.'

'Jack, don't be a baby,' I whisper, while smiling at the first to come in. I listen to my voice, constantly criticizing him. Am I asking too much for him to sit quietly and be pleasant to people?

'You must be Jack,' says Mary. She was in my yoga class when I was pregnant, when Jack was an enormous bump in my tummy. In those days when I went into bridge position I was more of a humped-back bridge.

'Yeah, I'm Jack,' he says sullenly, still sitting on my mat, embarrassed at the attention. I look to smile at Mary, and in the second my eyes are off him, Jack jumps up and bombs off again.

'You have your hands full,' says Mary sympathetically, as I scrutinize her face to see if she thinks he's adorable or a complete monster high on E numbers.

I'm aware more people are coming into the room, as there's the sound of squeaking doors and shuffling of footsteps.

'Oh, he's just excited,' I reply, wondering what has happened to send him so batty. I look round for him, hoping he's struck up a conversation with someone's granny. But no, he's trying to

169

swing, chimpanzee-style, from the curtains at those 10-feet high windows.

By now the room is filling up. Mats are being laid side by side. No one wants to go on the front row as usual. I'm glad I'm at the back. No longer do I want to show off my cute son. I want to tie him down, gag him and bundle him into his father's car. With a few clips round the ear.

Just as everyone has arrived and is sitting or lying on their mats, chatting about their week to their neighbour, Jack settles down.

I am so relieved I smile at him. The room starts to quieten as people start to lie semi-supine, preparing for some twists and stretches. I have my eyes fixed firmly on the door now. I need Ian to come and take Jack away so I can go back to being that nice normal person, not some stressed-out mother who's going to be in juvenile court in a few years. Ah, silence is golden.

'Mu-u-u-um?' says Jack.

'Ah,' say one or two older women, who haven't heard him speak until now. The sound of that cute voice gets all their attention. They look over. They're going to hang on to his every word. I'm beginning to feel proud again. Please, please, please, let him say something sweet about helping hurricane victims or small homeless animals.

'Mum, are guns allowed in yoga?' he asks.

He nods as he asks the question, obviously hoping against hope the answer will be yes, and I'll produce a sawn-off shotgun for him to play with. I must stay calm. I must be nice to this child.

'No, Jack, they're not very yogic,' I reply.

Any mention of guns always reminds me of my dad. They're always a constant reminder for me of how strange my upbring-ing was, and how blissful Jack's is.

170

Besides, I'm embarrassed at the very mention of guns in front of all these lovely calm people, most of whom have spent the afternoon at the Women's Institute or doing their gardens.

I just wish he'd stop being so aggressive.

'In yoga you're supposed to be relaxed and nice and friendly,' I try to explain.

'Not blasting each other's brains out?' questions Jack, with relish.

His face is all animated again and his eyes get wider as he adds: 'Getting blood everywhere and deading people?'

'Absolutely not!' I try and say it calmly, but at the same time I fake horror as though he's never behaved like this before. Oh, how I wanted them to love him as I do. I was so proud of him. Oh, where is Ian?

Our teacher Noreen is heading to her own mat. I take the hint. But before I take Jack out of the class, they must see he's a nice kid really.

'Jack, say goodbye to everyone here,' I say, as I get up from my mat and take his hand. 'These people have known you since you were a tiny baby in my tummy.'

But tonight he has no interest about life in my womb.

'I will say goodbye,' he says, about to bargain with me in front of about 20 people sitting cross-legged. There are 40 eyes on us. My heart is pounding, embarrassed at the attention. My parenting skills have never been more under scrutiny.

'I'll say goodbye, Mum, but only if you let me have a gun. Can I have a gun, Mummy?'

My hand isn't quite over his mouth as we leave but it's not far off.

I call 'Bye!' in a faked bright, breezy, bunny-boiler sort of voice.

Any psychologists in there will know I'm suppressing an urge to do something very sinister to our child. We walk through the first door and straight into Ian, who's just come through the squeaky door. I hand over our trigger-happy boy.

'Here, take him!' I snap, with no desire for our usual pleasantries. 'Just get him as far away from here as possible,' I snarl. 'He thinks he's some lunatic gunman. He's obsessed with bloody guns.'

Ian looks in shock. He knows my yoga-practising alter ego would never use bad language, even as mild as 'bloody', within a mile of my yoga teacher.

'Hello, Daddy,' Jack says sweetly.

I look at him, my mouth deliberately open. He gives me a sly look, then looks at Ian adoringly.

'Hello, little fella,' says Ian, laughing and ruffling Jack's hair. 'How've you been doing? Have you done some yoga?'

My mouth is still open for dramatic effect. Jack is back to being an angel. The pair of them hold hands and walk towards the staircase and smoky bar.

'Bye!' I snap, in a voice that reminds them they haven't said goodbye to me, before they breeze off happily hand-in-hand.

They turn and look at me as though I have a screw loose. I can see from the look in Ian's eyes he thinks *I'm* the lunatic with potential for violence.

I return to my class. Thankfully, most of them are lying facedown. I avoid all eye contact. I don't want to speak to anyone. I certainly don't want to explain my gun-obsessed bloodthirsty son and my very un-yoga-like snappish attitude towards my perfectly amiable husband.

CHAPTER 11

Do You Like Playing with Knives, Mum?

I've had a Saturday job on a fruit-and-vegetable stall for the last two months and I hate it. I don't hate the job, though my legs are knackered after standing for a whole day. It's just some of the other Saturday kids nick money from purses. It gets quite depressing working among a bunch of robbers, especially when I go home to a psycho, too. The highlight is the four £1 notes I get come 6pm, followed closely by the chocolate biscuit my mum puts in my packed lunch.

I'm saving the money to take my mum back to see her cousins in Wales. We're going to get the train and stay at my Auntie Alwena and Uncle Glyn's. Now Chris has left college and is back home he will look after my rabbits and, dare I say it, my dad. But first I have to save up, and not blow my money on the khaki military-style dress in the Marshall Ward catalogue.

When Chris came back, we swapped bedrooms and he now has the bigger room at the back and I have the little room at the front, which my mum often sneaks into as well. It doesn't make much difference because my dad's still ranting at us all night and we don't get any sleep wherever we are.

I have kept asking my dad, when he's been sober, if he'll try and cut down on his drinking. I've tried to tell him what he's like, what he calls us and says to us, but he always says, 'I would never say that.' It's hard to tell if he understands and is in denial,

173

or if he thinks I'm making the whole lot up. He's tried once or twice to reform, but his abstention from alcohol lasts no more than three hours. Last week we found him half in the back door after a lunchtime drink. It was quite a warm day so we didn't rush to get him in and get the door shut.

'Are you OK down there, Harry?' I asked, with contempt in my voice.

My mum grinned at my tone. Most mothers would give their 16-year-old daughter a clip round the ear if they spoke to their fathers the way I do. But I've no respect for him or the way he lives his life.

'Christine, Christine,' he wailed. 'I want to change, I have to change.'

'Too bloody right you have to change, you smell as if you've wet yourself,' I said, turning my nose up.

I've become quite good now at joking about the situation. Sometimes, when I feel my heart and head are going to explode with worry, stress and fear, the only way I can get through it all is to laugh at what's going on. Call it black humour, whatever, but it has helped me get through quite a few very unfunny days.

'I don't want to live my life like this any more; I can't go on,' he moaned on.

I was about to comment it would be very difficult to live your life when your top half is in the kitchen, your lower half is hanging over the back door steps and you're face-down on the doormat, but maybe I should give the sad old git a chance.

'How would you like to change, Harry?' I asked, faking sympathy, but he's too pissed to realize I'm taking the mickey and believes it's genuine.

'I've got to stop drinking,' he slurred. 'I can't do this. I'm killing myself.'

I widened my eyes with exaggerated delight and grinned at my mum, aware he couldn't see me. She smirked.

'Well, stop drinking, then. It's as simple as that. That's the only way you'll change your life.'

I know I'm harsh, but I've had years and years of this now. Of course he wants to change now he's crashed out on the doorstep. Most people vow when they're pissed they'll never drink again. Isn't that what this was all about?

Well, that was a week ago and we've had just two proper nights' sleep since then. He's often more pissed in the afternoons now, and just tops it all up in the evenings.

Whenever I get in from school, I say: 'Is he in?' If my mum nods, I then ask: 'What mood is he in?' A thumbs-up from my mum is good, but very rare. A thumbs-down is bad and happens often. A hand in the middle, tipping from side to side, means: 'It could go either way. He could flip any minute now and shoot us, or he could just sleep it off. Who knows?'

My dad has never made any effort at all to look for another job, and he managed to kid his doctor again that his emphysema is too bad for him to work. He gets some form of sickness benefit, but if you ask me, he's not all that sick if he can get sloshed twice a day. He also claims money for me and my mum, which my poor mum never sees. I sometimes think the Department of Health and Social Security should just make the giro out to the Old Duke William hostelry.

My mum made an appointment with my dad's GP to see what the verdict was. She told the doctor she was thinking of leaving my dad, but the doctor told her: 'He's a very sick man. He's an alcoholic.'

We were all shocked because my dad never drinks at home so we thought he couldn't be an alcoholic, but the GP confirmed he is. Then he added: 'With his chest problems as well, he won't live more than two years.'

It was the best news I'd had in years, in some ways. It felt like we were going out into daylight after a long stretch inside. But in other ways, it's not so good. I know my mum will never leave him now. If she stays she won't have to leave the home she's made for us all these years, and if he pops his clogs her wedding vows will still be intact. They're important, those vows, to my mum.

◆◆◆◆◆

We're at my Auntie Alwena's in Wales now. They live high on a hill in a three-bedroomed semi. Uncle Glyn is at work, and me and my mum and Auntie Alwena are going for a walk, then to look round some shops. The train fares took most of what I'd saved up. There was just £10 left over for spending money and to buy Auntie Alwena a present for having us to stay.

Chris has just got engaged to Eva, a girl he met at work, so we're full of chat about the wedding.

'I bought them some mats and a dishwasher for their engagement present, Auntie Alwena,' I say excitedly.

'A dishwasher!' exclaims Auntie Alwena, with even more excitement. Dishwashers are starting to come into fashion for people with lots and lots of money.

'No, not one of those posh machines,' I laugh. 'A little mini-mop with a wooden handle to use when they wash up in the sink. I thought it was cute.'

We all laugh at the misunderstanding, and how funny it was that Auntie Alwena thought I could have afforded a dishwasher. It's so nice to live a normal life, talk about normal things and get some sleep. I love it here.

Alwena and Glyn know a little about what my dad's like, but they never talk about it in front of me. I've heard Auntie Alwena saying: 'Is Harry still drinking, Nellie?' and seen my mum just nodding, but that is as far as it goes.

♦♦♦♦♦

We're in the middle of nowhere in North Wales, but my mother has found a shoe shop. I'm sure she sniffs them out. Now she has her face against the window. She has spotted a pair of two-tone suede shoes. True, they look dead comfy, but immediately my eyes look at the price tag. They're £5.

I know my mum doesn't have any money with her, apart from a few pounds I gave her for spending money – and most of that went on ice cream. I can tell she doesn't want to say much about money in front of Auntie Alwena, but I whisper: 'Go and try them on, we can use some of this money, we're not spending much here.'

She dithers a bit, looks more longingly, then announces she'll have a think about them. That night, when we're alone, I try to persuade her again.

'I can't justify a fiver on shoes, Chris, we need all the money we have. Who knows what might happen in the future?'

I'm not sure, but I think sitting in that doctor's surgery and announcing: 'I'm thinking of leaving my husband,' has put the idea into her head. I bet she hadn't even thought it before she was faced with the GP. She's always said she got married for life, whatever life sent her.

♦♦♦♦♦

Despite having a return ticket, we don't even get the train home. It's Saturday and Chris has arrived in my dad's car to pick us up.

Auntie Alwena and Uncle Glyn hug him for ages. They have fond memories of him when he was little.

It's a bright sunny day and we chat and laugh in the car.

Inevitably, my mum asks about my dad.

'How's he been, Chris?' she asks my brother. 'Has he been boozing a lot?'

'Quite a bit,' laughs Chris.

He never seems as scared as we are of my dad. I suppose he's grown-up now. He's also spending more time at Eva's house so he doesn't have to put up with as much of the crap as us. Now and then he's got in the middle when it's looked like my dad was going to clout one of us, but most of the time he accepts that's the way our dad is. While I've struggled to get my dad to change, I think Chris is realistic. He knows our dad won't change at this stage of his life. So Chris doesn't try that hard. He just gets on with his life.

As we pull up by the house, I look around the avenue to see if anything has changed in a week. This is the longest I have ever been away. It's exactly the same as it always was.

Except our house. As I go through the door, it looks as if it's been burgled. No one has washed up for a week.

'Bloody hell, Christopher, what have you been playing at?' says my mum, shocked, with a hint of anger in her voice.

'I haven't been here much, Mum,' he answers. 'I've been at Eva's all the time. I just came back to feed Christine's rabbits and to sleep.'

It's early evening and my dad gets up from bed when he hears us. My mum and I have talked about a new start. We're going to try and treat him well. We agreed we have to stick it out for two more years while I do my A levels. If his doctor's right, he'll be dead by then anyway.

Then we can escape – me to university, my mum to another house if dad hasn't died yet. I get such a lump in my throat at the thought of leaving my mum, but I know it has to be done. Better that she's not with my dad when it happens, though, or I'll never settle anywhere.

Here's my dad now, in a vest and trousers, looking like he's been on a beer drip for a whole week. God, he looks rough. His greying hair is sticking up and out. His eyes look like two little holes in his face.

'Hello, Dad,' I try to say pleasantly, remembering the 'new start' agreement. 'We've had a good time.'

'I don't fucking care if you had a good time or not,' he snipes. 'I wish you hadn't come back, none of you. Not one of you is any fucking use to me. Look at you, look at the three of you.'

In a second all that hope about a new start disappears. I came back happy and hopeful, and now that's been taken away from me, I feel more despondent than when I left. At least I felt I could just about cope then. Now I feel I can't face another night of this.

I try one last time.

'It was nice of you to lend our Chris the car to get us,' I say.

'Nice? Nice?' He does that repetition thing again. 'I wasn't being nice. I couldn't give a fuck how you got home. I wouldn't care if you never came home. I wouldn't mind never seeing you again. I lent him the car because I hoped you were all killed and mutilated in a car crash on the way home. I hoped not one of you would be recognizable in the wreckage. That's why I lent him the car, you fucking stupid idiot.'

◆◆◆◆◆

He goes back out to the pub and comes back like a lunatic. He's obviously just topped up his week's beer because he's back quite early, about 10pm, long before Chris gets back from seeing Eva.

'Blimey, you're early, Harry,' says my mum, jumping up from her crossword.

I've been reading *Persuasion* for English at school and put it down when he walks through the door, at least 2 hours earlier than we expected. I'm still wearing my jeans with sew-on patches everywhere. I'm nowhere near ready for bed.

'Yes, I'm early,' he says in mock despair. He looks at the two of us, as though we're disgusting, and shakes his head with revulsion.

'I wish you'd never fucking come back, either of you,' he says. 'You're nothing to me at all. I wish you'd died on those roads, I really do.'

He's talking in a normal everyday tone, as though it's perfectly natural to wish your wife and daughter dead in a car crash. What's even more ridiculous is we're nodding as though he's entitled to have his say, and we're taking on board what he's saying.

'I really had hoped I would never see either of you again,' he goes on.

He's standing perfectly still, his hands fidgeting. I start to tense. I know this sign. When he stands still, it means he's getting mad. If he paces around, or staggers about, he's happy to rant. When he's still, he's thinking, and that's the scary part. His eyes are going clearer. Oh God, I feel so sick.

'If I can't get you killed on the roads, I'll have to do it myself,' he slurs.

My legs start to feel weak, yet I can feel blood whizzing round my body, and my brain feels like it's whirring round at a rate of knots. I look at my mum. She, too, has recognized the signs.

'I'm going to have to finish you off myself,' he says.

He's looking round the room, still rooted to the spot. Oh God, where's Chris? He'd help us.

Both my mum and I dread him going upstairs for his gun. I never told my mum there's the one cartridge in there. I don't know which one of us he'd go for first. Just the thought makes my knees go.

'Mum, please, let's get out! Let's just go!'

I'm in a total panic. Normally I don't let him see me scared, now I can't help it. My mum just looks at me and shakes her head very slightly. I don't know what she's thinking. My dad finally moves, and, thank God, he doesn't go to the stairs to go and get his gun. Instead he goes to the kitchen.

Thinking it's over, my mum follows him, and asks if he would like supper. I stand by the back of the settee so I can have a good view of the kitchen. I don't think it's over. It's just beginning. They're both facing the sink with their backs to me, when my dad reaches into a drawer to his left and gets out a carving knife.

It has a big cream-coloured handle with an uneven blade that's fatter in the middle then tapers to the end. In a second he turns round, with his left arm round my mum's chest, holding the top of her arms down, and the carving knife in his right hand, right up against her throat. My mum looks so little and slight, being held there. Her face has gone so pale I wonder if he has already cut her. I look closely, but there's no blood.

'Dad, please, please, please stop it, please don't hurt her; she hasn't done anything wrong, please!'

I'm crying and sobbing and begging, all those things I vowed I would never do in front of him again, but I can't let him hurt my mum. Seeing her being held like this, so small and terrified, is making me sick. I start to retch and I put my

181

hand to my mouth to catch any vomit. I'm rooted to the spot. I can't move anywhere. I'll just have to throw up here. My heart is battering away inside my chest. My brain is working so hard. How can I get that knife? Or can I persuade him to put the knife down? Or should I just rush into the dining room and ring 999?

We've always been reluctant to ring the police in the past, since I once rang and asked if they could help if a drunken member of the family was hurting another. When they told me they don't get involved in domestics, I put the telephone down, all hope evaporated. Now we need all the help we can get.

My mum must have read my mind, because her next words are: 'Chris, don't!' Maybe she thinks ringing the police would force him to hurt her, or maybe he would come after me before I could get to the phone.

He holds her for a matter of minutes, but to me, it feels like years. He moves the blade slightly, then starts to taunt her again. On television 'armchair thrillers' on a Saturday night, the blade always gleams and sparkles, but this one doesn't. It's an ugly dull grey colour.

'I don't know whether to just slit your fucking throat, or chop you in two and throw you out of the window. You're just a fucking useless cunt, you are. I wish I had never met you. I should just chop your fucking head off and be done with it.'

His voice is getting angrier and angrier, and his hand shakier. His hand moves several times and the blade at my mum's throat moves up and down slightly.

'Harry,' my mum finally speaks. 'Stot dis!'

She's trying hard not to even open her mouth as she speaks. God, the blade must be really tight against her throat. She sounds full of terror. Oh my God, this is awful.

'Don't you fucking tell me what to do,' he rages, taking his hand from her chest and grabbing her hair to pull her head back.

Now, with her throat more obvious, I can see how close he has the blade. It's right up against her Adam's apple. I daren't speak any more. I don't want to risk winding him up. Without moving, I look round for something heavy I could clobber him on the head with. My body rigidly still, my eyes dart round the little kitchen. There's nothing obvious. Besides, my mum's between us, and there isn't room to get round the back of my dad. But I have to save my mum.

I think back to the night two years ago when he had the gun at my forehead. I thought that was my most terrifying moment. Now it's history. This is horrendous. Seeing my mum so little, thin and frightened is like someone putting their hands inside me and wringing out my heart, until every last ounce of happiness has gone. I love her so much and I never take my eyes off her eyelids as he holds her there. I can barely see her eyes. They're fixed on the blade.

I know at this moment that if my dad had his back to me, I would stick a knife in him without a second thought. I hate him that much. I'd be prepared to go to prison and I know it would be worth doing in return for my mum's life. These thoughts flash through my mind like one of those slide shows we have at school, there one moment, gone the next. I see myself in a prison visiting room, my mum sitting opposite, then I see myself at my mum's funeral, then I see my dad in court … fast thoughts in just a few seconds.

It's so quiet. I can hear the hum of our little fridge. After a while it gives a few little ticks, before it goes quiet, then it starts humming again. Not even the telly is on as we were reading when he sprang this early arrival home.

His hand is still shaking as he stands there, but I can see his eyes filling with tears. My one hope is he is realizing he can't do this. Is he coming to his senses, or is he crying because he knows what he is about to do? I have to try once more.

'Please, Dad, don't,' I say, embarrassed to hear my own voice, so timid and wobbly. I sound more five than 16. I know this is my last chance. Whatever is going to happen will happen within the next few seconds. It's as though there's some clock ticking somewhere and I can hear it counting down to zero.

'No, this isn't right,' he snarls, lowering the knife slightly for the first time. It's still very close to my mum's throat but not tightly up against it.

'I need time to plan this. I'm going to enjoy a few more practices yet,' he says. 'I need to get it right, the way I want it. I'm not sure if I want you to suffer, you whore, or if I want it over in one go. I might do you both at the same time, and be shot of the pair of you. What a fucking happy day that would be.'

He goes off into that ridiculous laugh, a series of high-pitched 'eee, eee, eee' sounds that always makes me want to smack him in the gob. I hate him. He calmly puts the knife down on the top of the spin dryer. I'm amazed he doesn't slam it down. Then he hurls my mum towards me, and pushes past the two of us to go upstairs.

I hug my mum. She's so frail with her tiny shoulders and I cry so loud that in the end even my mum has had enough of my heaving and howling and she whispers: 'Christine, for God's sake, pull yourself together. Don't let him hear this.'

I can barely speak.

'I can't help it, Mum. I was so scared, I thought he would kill you,' and my sobbing starts up again.

My whole body is now shaking. I feel out of control. I will my dad not to come back downstairs and see me like this, and he doesn't. After he has peed, he flops into his bed. We hear the bedsprings.

'Is your throat OK, Mum?' I ask, but she avoids eye contact. 'Did you think he would do it?' I ask nervously.

She looks at me steadily. She has already pulled herself together, as if she's just flicked a little switch in her head.

'Of course I didn't,' she says calmly. 'I was more worried his hand would slip and get me by accident,' she says. But she still isn't making any eye contact.

We sleep together in my little bed and the next day my mum wears a polo neck with a tank top on top. I never learn if she was bruised or hurt. I break all our rules and tell my Uncle Sam, my dad's brother, I can't stand to live there any more. He persuades me to stay until I've done my A levels – not that I had anywhere to go anyway.

'One day, when you have a family of your own, you'll look back on all of this and it won't matter,' he says quietly, as I sit on my bed and wonder how the hell I can stand two more years of this.

My mum doesn't talk about being held at knifepoint for at least 20 years, when we're sitting together late one night, drinking brandy and both ending up crying for ages at how awful it was that night. I'm not even sure if she ever tells my brother this happened.

◆◆◆◆◆

Jack is scissor-happy. Even the sharpness of pencils fascinates him. I regularly find him with the sharpest scissors in the house, trying to cut the top off the cardboard tube from some aluminium foil.

'Oh my God! Jack! What are you doing?' I shriek, imagining the end of his thumb in the tube.

'Don't worry, Mum,' he says, happily. 'I'm just making a chimney for my house.'

Jack may have a bedroom full of toys, but he's happiest when he's painting an old cardboard cat-food box, cutting out doors and windows and sticking chimneys on. It's fascinating to watch, because he even works out which way the windows will open. Maybe he's going to be an architect or a double-glazing salesman.

'Jack, please don't use those very sharp scissors,' I repeat. 'Can't you use the children's ones in your art box?'

'They're rubbish,' he tells me. 'I like a good blade that I know is going to cut. I like knives and things. Do you like playing with knives, Mum?'

I'm astounded he even knows the word 'blade', yet a shiver goes through me as I remember the night my dad held the knife to my mum's throat. I also hate the way Jack emphasizes the word 'cut'.

I know I'm overprotective but I always put all knives away and I hate Jack even using scissors. One lapse in concentration, which he's particularly prone to, and he could amputate a few fingers.

My one consolation is he's incredibly honest. He's too young to be sneaky yet. If I ask a question, he answers it honestly. Every night, when he's in bed, I scour the room for sharp objects. I am a truly paranoid mama.

◆◆◆◆◆

It's nearly bedtime now, so it's almost time for that nightly bedroom search. It's becoming more of a struggle to get Jack to bed, as he's expert at negotiating extra time. I think he's been on one of those communications courses which teach you how to ignore

186

what the other person is asking, and strive for what you want, no matter what.

'Bedtime, Jack,' I say, in a sharper than normal tone because I'm gearing up for a struggle.

'I need some crayons, Mum,' he replies, doing that ignoring thing I just mentioned.

There. I know now I should ignore him too and repeat the bed thing. But no, I'm too inquisitive. I've been sucked in immediately.

'What do you need crayons for?' I ask, looking round.

It isn't obvious.

'I'm making a moat to go with my castle in my bedroom, and I need a blue to colour the water in,' he says, perfectly reasonably, gathering up the things he needs to play with, long after I've read him a story and tucked him up for the night.

At least he said the word 'bedroom'. I must be more assertive myself.

'Jack, it's bedtime. I want you to get your pyjamas on, wash your face, brush your teeth and go to the toilet. Come along now.'

He knows he has to go, but he looks round the room like a burglar casing a joint for anything he's forgotten.

My attention is diverted by a phone call, so the next time I see Jack he's pottering about near the bathroom.

'Jack, have you had a wash and done your teeth?' I ask, knowing full well he hasn't.

It's summer. The sky is still blue. The sun stopped shining only an hour ago. How can you get children to bed when they know full well they could be out on their bikes? He goes to the bathroom while I scoop up another pile of laundry. Seconds later, we're both heading to his bedroom, but he's slightly in the lead.

187

'I hope you don't have any crayons or things about your person, young man,' I say.

I try to make my nagging a joke, as it depresses me to hear myself constantly carping, but Supernanny would say that's the problem. Jack probably has no idea when I'm being serious.

I see him just straightening up as though he's bent to pick something up, but there's nothing obvious in his hands and he has jumped straight into bed.

'Jack, show me your hands,' I demand.

It always strikes me as cruel that kids start to play up when you're flagging. It's like they sense that you're totally knackered, and they get a second wind. He obeys. His hands are empty, but there's guilt in those brown eyes. I just know.

'Why are you looking guilty?' I ask. 'What have you done?'

'Nothing, Mummy,' he answers, looking me straight in the eye.

'Have you brought any dangerous objects to bed?'

'No, Mummy, honestly,' he says. 'I've just brushed my teeth, front and back, so they don't fall out, and I've washed my face and checked there are no potatoes behind my ears.'

Then, quick as a flash, just as he learned on his communications degree course, he deftly changes the subject and quips: 'Let's read a nice story tonight. How about one by the Danny man.'

'The Danny man' is Roald Dahl, whose *Danny, the Champion of the World* had Jack gripped during a holiday in France. He knows I love fiction – far more than all those fact books about sharks, castles, dinosaurs and wild animals. He has almost won me over, until I suddenly remember him straightening up as I followed him into the room.

'OK, I'll get your big Roald Dahl book,' I say, but as I hop off the bed, I look underneath and I see before me our biggest, sharpest pair of scissors.

The little bugger must have ducked down and shoved them under the bed when he heard me behind him. I know he's just done it because I used these scissors about 20 minutes ago.

'Jack!' I say, mocking horror to hide a very real disappointment that my little boy has just looked me in the eye and lied – for the very first time, to my knowledge.

For once he remains quiet. Aha, so they didn't teach him how to retract lies on his How to Get Out of Doing Anything You're Asked course.

'Get out of bed!' I demand.

He's looking worried now.

'Come with me and we'll explain to Daddy exactly what you've just done.'

I march through to Ian, who's checking his e-mails, and explain that Jack has just told me a lie. Dramatically, I produce the scissors as evidence. Jack hates being told off by his dad. He knows it's bad when we take it to Daddy. If I'm Magistrate's Court, Ian is Crown Court. Once Ian has lectured him, I start doing so as we head back to bed.

'Jack, the crime in all this is the lying,' I say, as we lie side by side. 'You should never tell a lie to us, because our job is to look after you and make sure no harm comes to you.'

I know I'm repeating everything, probably not unlike the way my dad used to, but with fewer expletives and a less swaying gait.

'We can't look after you properly if we don't know all the facts.'

'But, Mummy,' says Jack, with all the confidence of a defence lawyer. 'I was only going to use the scissors to cut out a moat.'

'But what would have happened if you'd cut yourself, and you'd started bleeding, and you were lying in bed all on your own?' I ask.

'I'd shout for you,' he says, leaving the word 'stupid' hanging unspoken in the air.

Determined he won't win this one, I add desperately: 'Well, we might not have heard you and you could have bled to death.'

Instead of this scaring him, Jack's eyes open wide. All this talk of blood and gore is thrilling and definitely worth a try.

'I won't tell fibs again, Mum,' he says.

'Too right you won't,' I add, feeling like a complete bully now. 'I'm going to confiscate your *Star Wars* Top Trumps cards until you stop telling me fibs.'

There. I've played my Top Trump card. Jack loves his *Star Wars* cards. No longer does he accept numbers per se. They're always related to Luke Skywalker's Jedi Powers rating or Han Solo's Dark Side figure.

There's no story tonight, not even by that Danny fella, but I lie in bed and stroke his hair and tell him once more he mustn't lie because we love him and want to look after him.

'I love you too, Mummy,' he says.

I cuddle him closer and thank my lucky stars I have such a lovely child. I still feel betrayed by the blatant lie, but maybe this incident has been a valuable lesson and one that has brought us closer. I can't ditch him just because of one lie. If he were 35, maybe, but not five.

Then, just as I think my cherub is dozing off in my arms, he adds: 'Mummy, did you hear me when I said I love you?'

'Oh, I did, thank you, sweetie. You're a lovely boy. And I'm going to forgive you, because now you know it's bad to lie, I know you won't ever do it again.'

'I won't, Mummy,' he says quickly, too obediently for Jack. 'I'm going to sleep this minute.'

And that, I realized three hours later, after he'd spent ages pottering and moving around his room, was Lie Number Two.

CHAPTER 12

Why Do You Always Cry at Weddings?

It's the early hours of 8th April 1978, my brother Chris's wedding day. He's in the back bedroom, and his old schoolfriend Billy, who's going to be best man, is on the sunlounger alongside him. They've been out tonight and I think they've had a few pints. There was some laughing earlier when they got back in.

My mum's still up, even though it's about 2am, and I'm lying in bed waiting for my dad to come home from the pub. I'm 17 now, and waiting for him is just as scary as when I was five. Probably scarier because I now know what he's capable of.

We've never had anyone staying over at our house before, and I'm so embarrassed and scared. If my dad comes in ranting, how will we explain to Billy? He knows we have a lunatic for a father, of course. We've told him over the years how my dad has been behaving. We knew it was safe to let Billy in on the secret. It also helped that he lived at the other side of town so he wouldn't gossip and tell our neighbours by accident.

Billy's one of these guys who's in touch with his emotions. He has often gone into our kitchen and asked: 'How's things, Margaret?'

But although Billy knows the background, he's never really seen my dad in action. I think he'd be quite confused, for one. He'd be scared if he knew the array of weapons at my dad's drunken fingertips.

My mind is racing, and I'm getting hot with panic. My dad is bound to be pissed. It's too late for him to come home sober now. This really is the nearest to purgatory I've been, I think to myself. But then I remember, I've also had a gun to my head and seen a knife at my mum's throat. Now that was purgatory.

It also doesn't help that I had a bit of a crush on Billy about a year ago, and though that's worn off a bit now, I'm still really embarrassed at him seeing my dad plastered and ranting. I wonder if it would make him see us differently, or judge us, thinking we must be like my dad in some way.

◆◆◆◆◆

My mum has what she calls 'a little job'. She has started looking after two little boys, Bobby and Eddie, while their mum Julia works as a hairdresser. My mum loves these kids and they love her too. On my way home from school, I cringe when I see her whizzing round on their scooter with one of them laughing hysterically on the front. You wouldn't think she's nearly 56.

'Bobby, I can't do that!' she told the little one the other week. 'I'm getting old, you know!'

But he just replied: 'You're not old. You're Margot!'

The job is three days a week and it's at the big house at the top of our road, so it's handy for my mum.

My dad didn't like it, of course. But she leaves him all sorts of meals like stews and casseroles to warm up when he gets in. I sometimes call into Bobby and Eddie's house on my way home. My mum begs me to do this rather than going home to face my dad alone. Only if I'm feeling brave do I go home.

You'd think working would mean my mum has a bit more money and independence, but my dad has cut the housekeeping money he gives her and uses the extra on drink. So she isn't really any better off – she just gets out of the house a bit and he has more money to get pissed.

My mum isn't in bed tonight because she's so nervous about the big day. For a start, she didn't have enough money to buy a new outfit, so she's going to wear one of her old suits – a pale blue one with fur round the collar. Just as well our Chris didn't get married in July.

But the big worry for my mum is my dad. If he goes to the wedding, will he behave? And if he doesn't go, as he is threatening, will Chris be upset, and what will people think?

I think I know the answers to both questions. Chris will be upset, but it won't be the end of the world for him. He's always been far more tolerant of my dad than I have, and where I think my dad is psychotic, Chris just thinks he's eccentric. Even so, I think he would like my dad to be there.

He's also a very soft touch, and always has been. Once when my mum was trying to get a spelk out of her finger, she handed Chris a needle and asked him to get the little black thing out.

'I can't, I can't, Mum,' he apologized, dithering and hopping from one foot to another. 'I can't bring myself to hurt you.'

'Oh, give us it here,' I said, snatching the needle from him, and I shoved it into my mum's finger. Blood shot out, but so did the spelk.

'Oooh, you're a bad little bugger,' said my mum, laughing, grabbing a tissue to mop up the blood. 'But it's out, that's the main thing.'

A second later, I saw her look at Chris and smile. It must have been a small consolation in her life that her son was a sweet boy who loved his mum too much to hurt her. But he's just as soft with my dad. Maybe he just wants a peaceful life, I wonder.

Yet in other ways Chris isn't as soft as I think. The things my

194

dad has said don't seem to have affected him as much as me either. He never really seemed that heartbroken when my dad wished us all dead in a car crash, or when he called us stupid or thick. He just remained logical, and when I was crying that our dad wished us mutilated on the M62 on the way back from our holiday at Auntie Alwena's in Wales, Chris said: 'He's just pissed, ignore him. It doesn't matter what he says when he's pissed.'

Most of the guest list is family. While most of our family know what my dad is like, Eva's family don't, and they will probably think it odd a father doesn't show for his own son's wedding. I know this is what's uppermost on my mum's mind now. She's worried sick what the in-laws will think.

◆◆◆◆◆

My dad's back and he's ranted a bit, but it wasn't as bad as I thought it would be, and he drunkenly falls on his bed. Hurrah, we're going to get some sleep. I start to get excited. I'm a brides-maid in a few hours. I'll be wearing a full-length cotton dress with a small floral pattern, and lace pinafores on the front and back.

Ten minutes later, my dad is up, drunker than ever, and he's in Chris and Billy's room.

'Come and have a walk with me, Billy,' he says menacingly. 'There are some kids who hang out in these fields at night and they need sorting out. We're the two to do it.'

Oh God, I can picture him now, doing a mock fighting display, hunched over, boxing with his fists. What a bloody dickhead!

'Harry, don't be ridiculous,' my mum intervenes. 'It's almost 3 o'clock. No kids will be there now. Let these lads get some sleep.'

'Well, we'll just bloody see about that, won't we, Billy? Get up, lad.'

'Dad, look, just piss off back to bed. I'm getting married today and I want to get some sleep,' I hear my brother step in.

'No, come on, Billy, let's go,' says my dad.

He isn't all that angry, just very determined.

'Chris, don't worry, I'll go,' says Billy, in a tone that implies he's keeping the peace and is going to let the rest of the house sleep.

'You've got a screw loose, Harry,' I hear my mum say as they pass through the kitchen.

And the pair of them set off in the middle of the night. I always knew the best man had to look after the ring, organize the stag night and make a speech, but what Billy's having to do really is above and beyond the call of duty.

◆◆◆◆◆

I'm at Eva's mum and dad's house now to get ready to be a bridesmaid. I'm absolutely shattered and can't really concentrate on anything as my brain feels too dopey.

When I left home this morning, my dad was still in bed and Chris and Billy were going out to look for an earring Eva had lost last night when they were all out.

I asked my mum whether my dad was going to the wedding.

'Haven't a clue, love,' she said, shaking a head full of rollers.

I looked at her, full of pity. She must be the only mother of the bridegroom who hasn't seen a hairdresser for a good 15 years.

'But how will you get to the church if he doesn't drive you there?' I fret.

'Christine, I'll be there; now you go,' she said, pushing me out of the door.

I'm being a bridesmaid with Eva's sister Irena, who, at 15, is two years younger than me. We call her Rena for short, and the two of us get on well. We've even written to each other a bit this summer, even though we live about six miles apart and Chris and Eva see each other most days.

We leave the house in our floral dresses, holding yellow and white posies. My heavy, tired eyes make me look a knackered matron of honour, not a fresh-faced 17.

◆◆◆◆◆

The first thing I see at the church is my dad's car. A few members of our family have gathered outside the church, and my mum's wearing her suit and a little blue hat. I'll give her credit, she's done a good job with her make-up. You'd think she gets a regular 8 hours' sleep every night. She also looks very trim and shapely.

My dad's chatting to one or two people, like the Mr Nice Guy he is when he's out in public. His two brothers are there with their families, and my mum's niece Anne is there with her parents. Billy and our cousin Andrew start ushering people around, and Chris appears in his dark suit, looking about 22, not 26.

It's a cold day and we all shiver with cold and nerves as we file into the church. The others go and take their seats while Rena and I wait for Eva and her dad.

Eva's mum Sandra is Italian. Her real name is Santa but she has anglicized her name since she moved to Bradford 20-odd years ago. Her dad Stephan is from Ukraine and he calls me 'Kristin'. We're all into *Dallas* on telly so I quite like sharing the name of the woman we all suspect of shooting J R Ewing.

197

The guests on their side of the family are mostly Italian and Ukrainian, with glamorous nicknames given to them by Rena.

'That's "The Godfather" over there!' she giggles, pointing to a man in a dark suit coming into church.

Soon Eva is here, in her high-necked white dress and a long veil and carrying her yellow bouquet. The organist starts up, and as Rena and I take our place in front of Eva, the music has set off a wave of emotion I didn't know was even there.

◆◆◆◆◆

I walk down the aisle with my head down, my flowers under my chin, sobbing my eyes out. I don't know if I'm crying because of all the stress of the last few months, because I'm so tired, because I'm losing my brother and therefore our only ally in the middle of the night at home, or because I'm going to hear all about marriage and what it means, and I'll be sad I've never witnessed it at home. I've been to one other wedding, my cousin David's, so I know roughly what goes on.

As we reach Chris and Billy, Irena and I move to a little pew for the two of us. Billy is opposite us. Even though he's quite a way away, I see him gesturing at me to stop crying, but his attention just makes me cry all the more. I know I must have mascara all down my face. I must look a wreck, but I can't stop it. It's as though it's all been waiting to come out, and the organ music set it off. I wonder for a second if I'm cracking up and if I'll be carted off to a mental asylum in a bridesmaid dress.

◆◆◆◆◆

Once the service is over, people gather round me to mock my crying, which they think is sweet and very typical of the bridegroom's little sister.

'Weddings always make people cry,' one guest tells me. 'Are you sad you're losing your Chris?' asks an auntie.

My mum is less sympathetic. 'Christine, for God's sake, pull yourself together, girl,' she says sharply. 'You can't go around behaving like this.'

But I can tell she's concerned about me and she knows these aren't just frivolous wedding-day tears. About five years of misery just came out in that church.

◆◆◆◆◆

We're at the reception now. I've had some champagne and am a bit merrier. Even my dad has behaved. But the minute he has finished his dessert, he gets up and goes to my brother. It's hard to see because I'm on the same top table, a long one, but I see Chris raise his arms as though to try and get him to change his mind. But it doesn't work.

My dad leaves the hotel, leaving a very obvious empty seat next to my mum for the next round of excitement – the speeches. Later, when people start probing, my mum says: 'He had to go home, things to do and he had to go feed his horses.'

But I can tell she's very angry with him for leaving his own son's wedding reception so early to go to the pub and get completely rat-arsed.

◆◆◆◆◆

We're invited to a wedding. I look at the ivory invitation and my eyes do a double take when I see the names of the invited guests on there.

'Jack!' I say, feigning joy, but I'm speaking more loudly so Ian can hear me. 'We have an invitation. It's for Jayne's wedding. You're invited!'

Amazingly, Ian hasn't had my reaction at all.

'That's nice, isn't it, Jack?' says Ian cheerily. 'We'll all be able to see Jayne and Neil get married together.'

A hundred thoughts are whizzing through my head, but they're all centred on my cream dress that would be perfect for a spring wedding. It looks cute with its flippy skirt and neat little waistline, but with chocolate paw marks, a few dribbles of orange juice and a bit of soil from the hotel grounds all over it, it would look like the dog's dinner. Jack beams. He's already looking forward to this wedding.

◆◆◆◆◆

It's the wedding day and the three of us have checked into the hotel where both the service and reception are taking place.

'Jack! Get dressed, sweetie!' I call from the bathroom, where I have spent the last half hour doing my make-up.

'Why?' he calls.

He's busy playing with some Action Man he sneaked into the car at the last minute.

'Because we have to go downstairs to a room where the wedding is going to be held,' I say. 'Jayne's going to walk into the room with her daddy and Aidan, and she's going to take some vows and promise to love Neil for ever.'

I should have known what was coming next.

'Why?'

'Because that's what two people do when they want to show everyone and each other how much they love each other,' I explain, wondering if all my friends who are co-habiting would tut at this explanation and accuse me of filling his head with out-of-date nonsense.

'Why is she walking in with her daddy if she loves Neil so

much?' asks Jack.

'Because her daddy gives her away to Neil,' I reply.

'Doesn't her daddy love her?' Jack continues. 'That's not very nice, is it, giving someone away on their wedding day?'

'No, it's not like that, it's just tradition, Jack. Jayne's daddy loves her a lot, and she loves him. The bride's father walks her into church, then she takes her vows and walks out with her new husband.'

'But it isn't a church, Mummy. It's a hotel.'

'Ah yes, well, these days some people get married in hotels. In the olden days, people just got married in church.'

'Did you and Daddy get married in church because you got married in the olden days?'

He's now totally fascinated by weddings.

'We chose to get married in a church, Jack,' I say, wondering how the hell I'll get out of this one without making Jayne and Neil look like a pair of heathens, and me and Ian look like a couple of religious maniacs.

But I needn't worry. There are more questions.

'When you got married, did your nasty daddy give you away?' Jack asks.

'No, my daddy wasn't invited to our wedding, Jack,' I say.

Then, to cheer up the atmosphere, I add: 'Your Uncle Christopher gave me away, and everyone we saw on the way to church thought what a young-looking father I had.'

'Why didn't your dad give you away?' carries on Jack. 'He would have enjoyed that, wouldn't he? He would have given you away much earlier, wouldn't he?'

All this time I've been coaxing him into his blue-and-white patterned stripey and flowery shirt and smart blue trousers. When he looks in the mirror, he smoothes his hair down and says: 'Co-oo-oo-ol.'

'Because on your wedding day you want to be surrounded by lots of people you love. I didn't love my dad so I didn't want him to give me away,' I reply, aware the whole concept of giving away a bride is very confusing.

Jack has the last word.

'Well, it's a good job the police didn't see Uncle Christopher pretending to be your daddy when he wasn't. He could have got into a lot of trouble. You weren't even his to give away!'

◆◆◆◆◆

As we file into the room where the service is to be held, I cleverly manoeuvre it so Jack sits next to Ian, not between the two of us. A saxophonist is playing and the flower-decked room looks gorgeous. Outside the sun is shining. It's a sweltering hot May day.

The bridegroom is at the front with his family, but the heat becomes too much for him and he strides towards the window to let some air in.

'You can't make a run for it now, Neil,' quips his mum, and everyone laughs, releasing the nervous tension you get when you have a load of strangers in a room together, all trying to look and behave their very best.

Shoulders relax, little ones start to speak again, and people begin to look round instead of sitting dead straight staring in front of them. Jack edges nearer me, and perches himself in the middle of me and Ian.

'Daddy, I'd like you to give me away,' he announces.

'Really, Jack?' asks Ian. 'What do you mean?'

'When I come into church one day, and take my vows to love Mummy for the rest of my life, I would like you to give me away.

It's what daddies do.'

I've obviously not done a very good job of explaining the great British wedding ceremony, but it's too late now.

The bridegroom has swapped the music unbeknown to the bride, and as she comes through the door with her dad and Aidan, the saxophonist stops and the song *She* sung by Elvis Costello strikes up. I wipe a little tear from my eye, and Jack looks at me confused, but luckily he says nothing. We all stand and I take a slight step away from Jack to preserve my cream dress at least until they're husband and wife.

They're married now. We've stood outside in the sunshine, drinking champagne, while Jack and Aidan and Aidan's cousins have played in a little playhouse. I didn't go anywhere near them in case I got grubby marks on my dress. I'm perfectly aware of what an appalling mother I am.

Now we're at our table, with some of the bride's friends. There's another little girl on our table, so we have plenty of conversation, along the lines of 'Don't knock your drink over,' and 'Don't pull that cloth.'

We have our starters. Jack's main course is going to be chicken nuggets. We fob Jack off with bread. Better he overdoses on wheat than plays up.

I turn round and catch Jayne's eye on the top table.

'Lovely food,' I gesture.

Jayne nods back, appreciatively, just as Aidan looks over to our table and catches Jack's eye. Jayne notices this, and, being the bride, calls over, albeit in a very demure bridal way: 'Are you having a good time, Jack?'

Jack completely ignores Jayne's question, but sees the fact that she has called over the room as permission for him to do the same.

'Oi, Aidan,' he bellows across to the top table, his Yorkshire accent very pronounced when so loud. A hush comes over the room, and heads turn our way.

Aidan is more refined than Jack and raises an eyebrow to invite more conversation. We don't have a long wait, and all eyes on Jack don't seem to put him off.

'I haven't even had me chicken nuggets yet!' shouts back the hungry little Yorkshire boy, as everyone laughs.

Damn, I'm never going to be able to pretend I'm graceful and elegant with Jack around. I give him a hug and get a pat of butter right on the crotch of my otherwise spotless dress.

◆◆◆◆◆

The evening do is about to start, but word is going round there's a problem with the band. They've been taken hostage somewhere in the grounds of the hotel. I can tell by the tone of the evening guests arriving they're not being serious, but I wonder what the delay is. I decide to investigate. Jack is also missing; he went running off with Aidan and some older cousins and friends five minutes ago.

I find the band, four men and a woman, looking amused, but being refused entry through a door by Jack and Aidan who are acting out their favourite scene from *Peter Pan*.

'Say you're a codfish!' instructs Jack, holding a twig from the hotel grounds at one of the men's chests, probably because he can't reach his throat.

'Yes, Hook, say it!' orders Aidan, taking confidence from Jack's brave tone. 'Say after me, "I'm a codfish."'

'Jack! Aidan! Leave these poor people alone. They need to get set up so they can play some music for us to dance to! Come along!'

'Why are we going to dance?' asks Jack. 'I didn't think you were very happy about Jayne and Neil getting married. You can't dance if you're not happy.'

'But I am happy, Jack,' I say. 'I love weddings.'

'Well, why do you always cry at weddings, then, Mummy?'

'They're happy tears, Jack,' I say, aware Aidan is looking at me as though I'm gaga. I suspect he's doing some sort of psychological analysis and has concluded I'm a crackpot.

'When I see a bride getting married, it brings a little tear to my eye,' I explain, trying to appear normal. 'Sometimes you cry when you're happy as well as when you're sad,' I conclude.

'Well, I don't cry when I'm happy, Mum. I cry when I leave my teddy bear in airports, when I fall over and hurt my knee and when my dinner's ready in the middle of *Star Wars*. That's when I cry, nothing happy about that. Bloomin' miserable in fact.'

CHAPTER 13

Did Your Mummy and Daddy Sell Each Other?

It's my first year at university. For the first eight weeks I threw up several times every day. What was once my puppy fat has dropped off me. I may be almost 19, but I look a bit gaunt.

Most people think it's sweet.

'Is the little lass from Bradford homesick?' asks Paul, a fellow first-year who is trying to get me – and several other girls – into bed.

I just smile when Paul takes the piss out of me with his plummy accent. My new friends have no idea. They think I am missing a wonderful family life.

What they don't realize is that I'm sick with worry about my mum. Now she's on her own, who knows what my dad could do to her? While my friends' parents are away on golfing breaks in Portugal, my mum is probably fighting for her life, trying to out-wit a total psycho. In the two years since Chris got married and left home, my dad has been unbearable, often threatening getting his gun and that nasty truncheon that weighs a ton. In my diary I've regularly written: 'Am scared Harry will give me brain damage with that truncheon.'

Every night, I hover in the reception area to our college. When no one's within earshot, I phone home. It's usually about 9pm, as I need to be sure my dad's out so my mum can talk freely.

206

'Hiya, Mum, it's me,' I say as cheerfully as possible. I don't want her to know how sick I am. I love university, the work and my new friends, but I long every minute of every day to know my mum is safe.

'Are you OK, Mum?'

'Yes, I'm fine,' she says, in a voice that tells me differently. 'How are you getting on, love?'

'Yeah, good,' I say quickly. 'How's he been? Has he been going out? What's he been like?'

'He's been going out,' she says quietly.

'He's not there now, is he?' I say quickly.

I sense she isn't telling me much, and wonder if she's covering up, or if she just can't speak freely.

'Has he used anything?' I have to ask.

As I lie awake in my bed at night, I've pictured that gun and knives, and I need to know. Every night I ask her. I know a day can be a long time and a lot can change in a day when you live with my dad.

'He's threatened,' she says quietly.

Oh my God, my poor mum must wonder if she'll survive to Christmas at this rate. But she changes the subject.

'I've put you a little birthday present in the post, love,' she says. 'You break up for Christmas in a week or so now, don't you?'

I feel a surge of joy that next week I'll be with her. I'm not bothered about my birthday, just breaking up for Christmas and being able to look after my mum. At least she'll have me as an ally for a whole month. I've got a part-time job packing fruit and vegetables in a factory for two weeks. It's brilliant pay. I worked there a bit in the summer and made loads of student friends. We've kept in touch and we've all been taken back on again.

'I got taken on again at that job. I got the letter today. So we'll have a bit of money, Mum,' I gabble on. 'They're giving me a pay rise, too.'

'Oooh, that's great, Chris,' replies my mum.

For a second I picture us being able to go into town and buy things, go for coffee in posh coffee shops and maybe even get the train to Leeds.

Then I realize all my excitement will be sapped out of me the minute I walk through the door. But what's worse? Being worried sick away from home, wondering if my mum's still alive, or being in the thick of it, fighting to survive? Being there wins. At least I'll be with my mum.

◆◆◆◆◆

My dad hates the fact I have a grant and I can spend it on what I want. Having wrongly imagined I've been having sex since I was about 13, he must also torture himself with thoughts of all the hanky-panky I might be having, too. Now I'm days away from my 19th birthday, he must imagine I've shagged half the campus. I can't help grinning when I think how that thought must wind him up.

I haven't, of course. When you're stick-thin with worry about whether your mum's alive or dead, losing your virginity comes way down the list of priorities.

We're all setting off for Christmas. Some parents have arrived in cars, and are planning to take their kids for a pub lunch before they head off back to Manchester, Birmingham and West Sussex.

I've got the campus bus into Lancaster and walked to the station with the biggest suitcase in the western hemisphere. It's so heavy my left arm is at right angles with my body to try and get

208

me some leverage for the weight. I'm proudly wearing my red, grey and blue striped scarf. I want everyone on the train to know I'm a student.

I change in Leeds for the last leg to Bradford, and as we pull into Bradford Interchange, my heart is doing cartwheels with excitement. I am longing, absolutely dying, to see my mum again.

I scour the platform for her. My mum would never wait at the ticket barrier. She eeks every ounce of joy out of happy times, probably because there isn't much for her to be joyous about.

I've seen her. Fantastic, she's here. I heave my case off the train, and drag it to her. But she runs to me and I hug her and kiss her and when we finally look at each other, we're both crying and laughing at the same time.

'I've been so worried about you,' I sob, remembering the last 11 weeks, then laugh with relief we're back together, albeit for a month. But it's as though nothing else matters. We have each other. My mum might be 57 but she's game to carry my case for a bit.

'Bloody hell, Chris, have you brought a fella home in this?' she laughs.

'You must be kidding, how the hell can I bring a fella home?' I say, and we both laugh, as my mum displaces a few vital internal organs heaving my case.

We share the case to the bus stop. I chatter on and on about boys at university and who got off with whom in Intro Week.

As we're getting off the bus, I look down the leafy avenue to our home.

'He's at the pub,' says my mum, reading my thoughts. 'Went about 12. He was OK when he went out. Asked what time you'd be here.'

Like telepathy she knows what I need to know. The vital stuff, no mucking about.

◆◆◆◆◆

We don't have long to wait.

'So you're home, then?' he says, as he comes through the back door.

I'm standing in the living room, where my mum has laid a little table for him to eat his meal on. It's about 3pm, so I'm not sure if it's lunch or tea.

He hasn't seen me or spoken to me for 11 weeks. Surely he's missed me. But I don't know what to say. I can't say I'm enjoying my lectures because he'll say I'm a thick cow, and I can't say I love the bar because he'll imagine I'm getting pissed and laid every night.

I look at him carefully. In the night, when I've been lying awake, I've pictured his face glaring at my mum, and he's been bigger in my imagination. He's shorter in real life. How could that have happened in my mind in just three months?

'Yeah, do you like my scarf?' I ask.

I think I've gone for a harmless one. Surely he can't be nasty when I'm happy and enthusiastic? How wrong I am.

'Yes, how much was that?' he asks.

So far so good.

'A few quid,' I reply.

He hates us having any kind of independence, and he now hates money to be spent on anything other than beer. I can see him getting angry. He's like a pan about to boil. Oh shit, I was so stupid to brag about my scarf.

I don't know if the scarf represents my new freedom but he

suddenly flips. He picks up ornaments and smashes them against the wall. Once again his dinner, which had been left to simmer while my mum came for me, is trickling down the wall. Great big lumps of Yorkshire pudding slither down the embossed silver-and-white wallpaper in our living room. I'm shocked. I've seen him trash our dining room many times, but he's always been a bit more respectful of our living room.

'You!' he points at me. 'You go away and do that, and I'm here and I have nothing, I have nothing.'

He's almost whining. I haven't a clue what I've done. Oh please, don't let him start going on about sex. Maybe I'm over-reacting. Does he just mean I've spent a few pounds on a scarf?

'She ruined me, your mother, she held me back. I could have been something, but she didn't let me.'

He's sticking his chest out to mime how very important he might have been. He looks a complete psycho. His eyes are losing it again. Oh my God, I'm panicking. I'm out of practice. I haven't been in the thick of the action for so long now, I wonder if I can stand another minute of it.

'I'm not fucking putting up with this any more,' he starts to gather pace.

This is getting scary, like a storm brewing, ever so gradually, but you know when it hits you, you'll know about it.

'You two won't be the end of me. You won't beat me. I used to be strong, I was tough,' he says.

Now he's putting up two fists to symbolize fighting. I wonder for a second if he thinks we're so thick we don't understand the English language.

'I'd always hoped you'd be so maimed in a train crash or a car crash, you wouldn't be recognized. Your heads might come off, or your eyes fucking shoved back into your heads, but no, it

211

didn't happen. I'm going to finish you off, both of you.'

Of all the insults, this is the one that makes me retch instantly. I can never understand what makes a man wish a perfectly normal wife and daughter such a violent end, and the way he describes it in such detail is sickening.

'Harry, calm down,' says my mum.

Blimey, I can hear now in her wobbly voice just what a hard 11 weeks she's had since I've been away.

'She can take that scarf back, I'm sure.'

It sounds a ridiculous thing to say, but it seems to calm him for a minute. Maybe it was the scarf after all. I should have kept my big mouth shut.

Then he perks up again and smashes some more ornaments. Out of the corner of my eye I see my mum carefully removing some of her more treasured ones.

He opens the sideboard, and glasses clink and smash against the wall as he pathetically sobs about how his life could have been. I have the feeling that our whole lives have been building up to this day. I don't know if it's having been away from home, or just the worry of the last three months, but I know instinctively it's all going to end here today. This time tomorrow life won't be the same. I know that for certain.

'I'm going to do one of you in first while the other watches, then the other, you'll see.' He's doing that high-pitched hysterical laugh now. 'I need to work out which one first.'

With that, he staggers off to bed. My stomach is in knots. There's a loud gurgling. I'm getting nervous diarrhoea. But I can't go upstairs to the loo. I don't want this to go on a second longer. I want him to get to bed and sleep. I don't want him fishing around in his wardrobe for weapons. That gun is still loaded, as far as I know, and there's that truncheon thing. One whack with that and we'll be a goner.

The stairs creak. He's coming back.

'And when I've finished you off, I'm going to chop you up in little pieces,' he says with relish, looking me right in the eye from about a foot away.

He stoops ever so slightly, but not as much as usual as I'm wearing heels. I hold my breath for a moment to avoid the stench of beer, but I start to go dizzy and have to breathe again almost immediately.

Then, turning and focusing on my mum, he adds: 'And I'll throw you out of the window where you belong.'

Normally, she would look him in the eye, then quickly move her head, chin high, to look into the distance, just as a defiant child would. Today she cowers, a shadow of the woman she once was. This is it. She's lost all her fight. The time has come.

He heads off back upstairs, muttering to himself about bumping us off once and for all. Problem is he means it this time.

◆◆◆◆◆

'Mum, we can't live like this,' I say quietly.

I have said this before, when I have been beseeching her to come up with an answer. But this time I feel like the strong one. I really can't stand this any more. I've been away. I've seen how other families live and I can't do this any more.

She looks at me, her hazel eyes imploring me to tell her what can be done. She has hardly any money. She's scared of him. We both know he'll go berserk if she leaves him. Yet he's going berserk anyway. We both know he's getting nearer and nearer doing something nasty to us. It's all he's thought about for months, if not years now, how he's going to kill us.

I try my trump card. It isn't planned and it's a gamble. I'm not even sure I mean it.

'Mum, I've got something to tell you. I've done a lot of thinking while I've been away,' I prepare her. 'I'm not going to come home again if we have to live here, with him. We can't live like this, Mum. He will kill one or both of us soon. I believe it. He's got much worse since I went away. Why didn't you tell me? He means all this stuff now. I know it. I know he'll do it one day soon. Time is running out.'

I'm talking fast because I'm so scared, scared at the madman upstairs, scared at what I have just threatened my mum, scared that I have the power to affect my mother's life and her 28-year marriage and force her to give up on vows that meant so much to her.

'I didn't want to worry you. He's taken a knife to me a few times since you went,' she replies. There's a lifelessness in her voice. She knows this has to end.

We tiptoe around so we don't wake him. My mum picks up the broken glass and china. My dad sleeps for a couple of hours. Then, still drunk, he gets ready to go out again.

'You're fucking going to get it tonight,' he jibes, laughing. 'Oh, I am going to fucking enjoy this. I've nothing to lose now, it's gone, it's lost, it's gone. I can't fucking wait. I'm going to have a few pints, then come back and really enjoy myself with you two. I'm going to have some bloody fun, I am.'

His tone's different. He sounds sober but he moves as though he's still drunk. I'm convinced he means what he's saying.

He goes to the pub. We sit and drink tea for a while. We're both too terrified to stay. Our life at this house is about to end tonight, one way or another.

My mum and I never discuss what we do next. She's like a zombie who just needs to be told what to do. I suspect she's been a verbal punchbag for the last three months and all her fight has gone. She puts herself in my hands. It feels odd that three months ago I went away a child, leaving home for university, and I've come back an adult in charge of my mum. Our roles have reversed for ever.

I ring my brother. 'I'm home and we can't take any more. He's mental, Chris. We're really scared. Can we come and stay, just a night or two, just to get away?'

He agrees, and though my mum has always said she'll never go and stay with either of her children, she follows me round the house like a puppy. I get a black binliner and we pack up some of our most treasured belongings – my school reports, a few baby photos, some clothes, my diaries, and we heave the binliner and my enormous suitcase to the bus stop at the top of our road.

Luckily, this bus is direct. We leave the case downstairs in the luggage rack, and we sit upstairs at the back so no one will see us with our black binliner of possessions.

We're quiet. We know the enormity of what we have just done. We know my dad will go absolutely crazy when he comes home. We suspect he may come and look for us to do whatever he has planned. He must know we've gone to stay at Chris and Eva's.

The future is so scary still. He could be round any corner any time. When we lived with him, we could keep track of him. Now we'll never know where he is and how he's thinking, and it's a frightening thought.

But seeing him so determined to finish us off was chilling. We stare straight ahead on the bus. Some young lads get on and light up. To them it's just a normal night on the town, but for us it's different. We've left home. A chapter of our lives has ended tonight, and we will never go back there again.

◆◆◆◆◆

Saturday night. It's summer, it's gorgeous, it's still warm and we're going out for a meal. We decided 10 minutes ago. Jack's still playing out so we call him over to the car.

We head off to Masham, a village about 15 miles away with a particularly stunning chocolate shop, sadly closed by the time we get there. Ian fancies a wander round, while Jack and I are desperate for food, so we both go slightly sulky and trail behind.

We stroll behind our master the way some of the wives used to do in Bradford supermarkets when I was growing up. Up and down the streets we go.

It isn't even particularly scenic. We must look rather suspicious, the three of us. Ian and I are at least clean, but ragamuffin Jack looks like he could do with a good bath and some cleaner clothes. I bet people think we've hired him to get through those tight bathroom windows.

Jack and I are getting pretty fed up with this stroll.

'Hey, Crossy,' I call, 'we're starving. Let's find somewhere to eat.'

Our complaints are met with selective deafness and Jack and I carry on regardless, hand in hand and relaxed. As we saunter in the early evening sun, Jack chats.

'Mummy, you know your mum and dad?' he asks.

'Aha,' I say, trying to second-guess the next stage.

'Did they live together?' he asks.

'Yes, they lived together for nearly 30 years,' I explain. 'They were very long years for your grandma. Why, Jack?'

'But they didn't live with each other all their lives?' he asks.

'No.' I pause for a moment, then realize I need to explain.

'Sometimes mummies and daddies stop loving each other, so they decide it might be best if they don't live together,' I start.

216

'So did your daddy stop loving your mummy?' Jack continues, with terrier-like persistence.

'Yes, and in the end my mummy stopped loving him,' I say. 'So they got a thing called a divorce. That's when you go and see a judge and he or she says it's OK not to live with each other any more.'

'What did they do with each other, then?' asks Jack. 'Did your mummy and daddy sell each other?'

'No, sweetie,' I reply, quite amused at the thought.

What a novel idea. If someone were a really good spouse, but you were just fed up with them, you could take them to Sotheby's in London and get them auctioned, then go on a round-the-world cruise with the proceeds.

If they were crap, like my dad, you could take them to the dump. You wouldn't put someone like him in a charity bag because you wouldn't wish him on anyone else. My dad would have been quids in once again. He'd have got a good sum for my mum.

'You don't sell people,' I continue. 'You just go your separate ways.'

There, I've explained divorce and made it sound almost attractive. No longer will my darling be traumatized by separation and divorce.

'A bit like us and Daddy?' Jack asks.

I've been so engrossed explaining divorce, I have no idea where Ian is. We stop, we look around. There's no sign of him. He's wandered off again, expecting us to follow.

'Yes, Jack, it's true we can't see Daddy anywhere, but we can always ring his mobile. No need to worry.'

'Mum,' Jack starts up again. 'Do you think we'll ever sell Daddy?'

'I hope not, sweetie,' I answer, a shiver going through me at the number of times I have read children of divorced parents are more likely to get divorced themselves.

'We couldn't possibly sell him when he buys us such lovely meals,' I laugh, about to dial Ian's number. Just as I finish dialling, Ian appears round a corner.

'Daddy!' says Jack. I can tell he's obviously feeling insecure about this divorce lark because he's using his baby voice now.

He runs to Ian for a cuddle.

'We thought we'd lost you, Daddy,' Jack chats on. 'Mummy has been talking about divorce ever since we lost you.'

'Blimey, I just went for a walk,' replies Ian.

I chip in: 'Jack and I were discussing other people's divorces and what happens to people after divorce.' I laugh at how such an innocent conversation can be misunderstood.

'Jack wondered if you sold your ex-wife or -husband once you got divorced. The best ones would go to a posh London auction.'

I can tell from Ian's proud face that this is where he would expect to end up. He's always had the best self-esteem, my husband.

Jack knows this and is about to take great joy in deflating him. I can tell from the glint in his eye.

'Yes, Daddy, we thought we might take you to a car boot sale,' says Jack, laughing.

'Listen, let's cut a deal,' I suggest. 'Daddy takes us and buys us our supper, and we won't slap a sticker on his head when we next go to a car boot sale. How does that sound?'

'Bloody wonderful, thank you very much,' mutters Ian in a sarcastic tone which makes us all laugh again, and Jack laughs so much he starts skipping ahead of us.

CHAPTER 14

Do All Houses Have Three Bathrooms?

My mum and I stay at Chris and Eva's house for a few weeks. I'm out a lot. I'm packing vegetables by day, and I do overtime. Some evenings I go and meet student friends from the factory, but by about 8 I'm quite tired. I find factory work knackering – a bit like my old market job for being on my feet all day. My mum says I need support tights but I tell her I'm 19, not 90.

I'm getting quite good now at getting three tomatoes in one hand on the conveyor belt. My friends from university have all got secretarial jobs, or they're working in nice shops. I haven't told them much about my packing job. They wouldn't under-stand what a laugh it can be when my co-workers come to work yawning, with love bites all over their necks.

Trouble is, my mum has insisted on keeping her job over at Julia's with the two little boys. I wish she would just explain and let them find someone else. But she's being very loyal, or obstinate, or downright stupid. I'm not sure which. Every day she gets two buses over to where we lived with my dad, then two buses back. Her bus fares alone take most of her wages.

I'm living in fear my dad will wait for her one day, if he doesn't come over to my brother's house and hurt us in some way. I know he's angry we've left. He's told people he's upset we've gone. They probably think he's a sad, sensitive man who's been wronged by his wife and daughter. If he doesn't get us at

Chris's house, he'll get my mum when she's walking the oldest boy, Eddie, to school – the primary school I went to, bang on my dad's pub route.

My mum thinks he won't bother us at Chris and Eva's because he doesn't drive his car much now. That's the best she can do to reassure me.

◆◆◆◆◆

No one has told him, but my dad knows where we're staying. He's rung a few times, and ranted obscenities down the phone to Chris, who has eventually put the phone down and left it off the hook. Trouble is, that will anger my dad even more and he might just risk driving over to us.

It's usually late at night when he rings and I can't get back to sleep after. It's ironic. I couldn't sleep when we lived with him; now we don't live with him and I still can't sleep.

Chris and Eva don't have a spare bed, just their double bed. They've barely been married two years and I'm sure they don't want me and my mum loitering round, so we try our best to make ourselves scarce and we go to our bedroom about 9pm. None of us has much money. Chris and Eva are working like mad to pay off their mortgage, and my mum and I are sharing a campbed that has a thin blue mattress and steel legs at each end. If you don't get the middle legs right, you'll collapse. My mum and I take it in turns to sleep in it. The other sleeps on the floor. But my mum usually says I can have her turn, especially if I'm working the next day.

We use our early nights to chat – or whisper, as though we're in a school dorm. Now and then we laugh, but we know there's the very scary danger my dad will come and find us.

'Problem is, he knows where we are,' I say, thinking aloud.

'It's the obvious choice. Where else would we go? And what will you do when I go back to uni?'

There's always this unspoken thing between me and my mum. In the first week of January, I'll bugger off back to Lancaster and she'll be left on her tod. Well, that's how I see it. I know she would never want me to pack it all in for her. It sometimes feels like she's lived her whole life for me to go to university.

I hate the thought of leaving her again. I just want to be around to protect her. The thought of getting on the train at Bradford Interchange makes me feel nauseous. It will pull out of the station in slow motion and my mum will be crying on the platform. I like university, but I hate leaving my mum, especially when she doesn't have a real home. Still, her being at Chris's is better than being with my dad any day. I might even have some fun next term.

'Don't worry, love, I can always go to our John's,' she reassures me.

◆◆◆◆◆

Our John is my Uncle John, my mum's youngest brother, who lives in a back-to-back house across town. If you imagined a triangle on Bradford, my dad's house is at one tip, Chris and Eva's at another and Uncle John's on the third tip. They're all two bus journeys away from each other, into town and back out.

Uncle John is a bachelor and was a very good-looking one at that. He's been a bit of a recluse in recent years. He goes into town once a week to do his shopping, he comes home and labels his tins and uses his shopping in the 'right order'. I accept his eccentricities because he's always been so good to my mum and us.

My mum has read my thoughts.

'Look, I know it's not the kind of area we lived in before, Chris, but beggars can't be choosers,' she says.

'It's not the area, it's just … there's no bath and no toilet, is there?' I ask.

'Yes, there's an outside toilet,' she tells me, as though she's talking of some luxury hot tub. 'And I don't need baths. I can wash myself OK and keep myself clean.'

Now she's beginning to sound like a cat.

I feel like a spoilt brat, but surely an inside toilet and a bath aren't too much to ask for?

I secretly hope my mum will just stay at Chris and Eva's, or go and stay with one of her friends, even though I know Uncle John would share everything he has with her, and she'd feel at home with him.

◆◆◆◆◆

My dad keeps ringing Chris and Eva. They usually don't answer, but tonight the phone starts ringing at midnight.

I have no intention of answering it, but I go out and meet Chris on the landing, just so I can listen in, and be prepared.

'I'm bloody sick of him,' he says wearily, going downstairs to the phone in the hallway by the front door. 'It's OK for him. He doesn't have work tomorrow.'

'Chris, don't tell him we're here,' I say nervously.

I'm scared he'll slip up because he's so tired.

But Chris has already got the receiver and I can hear my dad from the top of the stairs.

'She's a fucking bastard, your fucking mother!' he's yelling. If I can hear him at the top of my brother's staircase, God knows what his poor neighbours are going through.

'She's fucking left me just when I was at my lowest.'

His voice is going calmer now, into his self-pitying tone. This is when he repeats everything. He really was wasted. He could have been an editor of *Roget's Thesaurus*.

'I needed help. I needed a friend,' he says, building up to another blast.

'But she abandoned me, she left me, she didn't stay with me, she packed her bags and went, she's a fucking whore.'

My brother is holding the phone away from his ear. Eva and my mum are now standing with me. We're huddled together at the top of the stairs.

'Well, she's not getting away with this,' he adds, menacingly. 'I'm going to sort her out. I know where she goes.'

My stomach lurches at the thought of my mum walking home with two little boys. What if one day my dad's there waiting for her? What will he do to her? There's the gun, knives, all sorts of disgusting things he could use. And he'd plan it, too. He'd enjoy that project. He said he'd enjoy it three weeks ago, when we left.

I feel nauseous but I stay rooted to the spot. Even though we're six miles away from him, I still need to know how he's thinking.

'Say goodbye to your mother,' he adds in an evil tone, the word 'mother' packed with hatred. 'I'm going to finish her off.'

He slams the phone down and we hear the bang from the top of the stairs. My brother replaces the receiver, and laughs when he sees my terrified face.

'He's just pissed, Chris,' he says, quite calmly. I am such a wimp. Why can't I be as calm about it as him? 'He won't do anything. He'll wake up tomorrow morning, and won't remember a thing. I'm off back to bed.'

But the thought of my mum walking home from school, on those dark January afternoons, fills my dreams. At 4am I wake up completely.

'Mum,' I say, as though it's perfectly normal to expect someone to be awake at that time.

'Yes,' she answers, a bit too quickly for someone sound asleep.

'Can you change jobs?' I ask. 'So you don't have to go anywhere near him? I'm scared of him.'

'But I love those kids,' she tells me. She has obviously considered this.

'If we go the other way from school, I don't see him at all,' she adds.

'It's not him coming to the house that worries me,' I continue, whispering. 'I'm scared he'll lie in wait for you when you're coming home. He'll have been to the pub and had a lunchtime session, then he'll wait to get you.'

I make it sound like schoolyard bullies, lying in wait. But this is much more serious.

The thought of being miles away at Lancaster knowing my mum is walking so close to my dad is sickening.

'I'll think about it,' she says. 'Let's get some sleep.'

I go back to sleep, but I wake screaming. I've seen my mum's dead body by the side of the road, with two little blond-haired boys standing nearby. Police are scouring the area for clues. Their sirens are blaring out ...

But it isn't a siren. It's my alarm and it's time to get up. I'm packing cabbages today, while I see which of my carefree colleagues has been struck by the love-bite bug in the night.

◆◆◆◆◆

I always knew my mum would go to stay with Uncle John. They were both born on the same day, September 30, but two years apart, and they're alike in a lot of ways.

'Your grandma told me our John was a present for my second birthday, and I must always look after him,' my mum once told me.

Even though my mum now officially doesn't have an inside loo, I'm happier when I go back to university. She's content with Uncle John. I picture the pair of them late at night, having a cigarette together, chatting quietly. It will be bliss for my mum.

But at the back of my mind, there's the thought of my dad turning up pissed. After Chris and Eva's, Uncle John's would be the next most obvious place. And Uncle John's a lovely, gentle man, no match at all for my dad's vicious ways and horrible obscenities.

I carry on ringing my mum every evening.

The 'what-if's run through my mind all day. What if my dad has got her? What if he has gone to Uncle John's house?

'Hiya, Mum,' I say, trying to sound upbeat, whereas my whole mood depends on her tone in the next second.

'I've got good news, Chris,' says my mum excitedly. Thank God for that. One, she's alive. Two, she's happy. Thank you, thank you, God.

'Ada's house at the front is coming vacant,' she tells me.

My mum's family own a few of the houses where Uncle John lives. The share of the low rent my mum has had from the houses over the years has helped her out when money's been tight at home with my dad. When she got an electricity bill she couldn't pay from the measly amount my dad gave her, she rang Uncle John to see if she had any rent due.

Now, it appears, the front house – not quite as dark and cut-off as Uncle John's back house – is going to be empty. She never wanted to go there before because she didn't want me to change schools.

'I'm thinking of taking it, Chris,' she says. 'I won't have much, but I'll feel safer there knowing our John's round the back. I can bang on the wall if I need anything. He doesn't go out. He'll hear me. I won't be scared any more.'

I don't want my mum to be scared. I'm pleased. But I also want her to have some kind of comfort.

'I'm going to see if I can get a grant to get a bathroom put in,' she says, once again reading my shallow little mind.

'And I might get some money out of our house. I'm going to see a solicitor to get a divorce. Your dad'll have to sell it.'

'Do you want me to come with you?' I ask, my heart completely sinking.

My dad will definitely kill her before give her any of his money, from the bank or the house. I know it's fair that she should have some money, after years and years of domestic work in our house. But does she realize how much danger she's putting herself in? I despair when I suddenly realize this terror I have is going to run and run – there's no end in sight at all. In fact, it will get worse. I know it. He'll go spare when he gets divorce papers and when he's told to sell the house and share it with my mum.

'See when it is,' she adds. 'You concentrate on your studies.'

Part of me is relieved she sounds happy, but part of me is horrified at my mum living in Ada's house without an inside toilet.

◆◆◆◆◆

I go straight to the bar, hating the part of me that resents this raw deal. I should be so grateful my mum is OK and sounds happy.

My friends are at the bar. Paul calls over: 'Hey, Chris, you

226

must come too. We're all going to my place for the weekend.'

His place is in Buckinghamshire.

'Bring your swimming gear, we've got our own pool,' he says, 'and a sauna.'

Fantastic. He has a swimming pool and sauna. My poor mum doesn't even have a toilet. She'll have to wash standing up at her kitchen sink.

I half smile and suggest I sleep on it overnight.

He nods. He really has no idea what trauma I go through every day. But I like it that way. I don't want everyone here knowing what a sad little life I have in Bradford.

I don't go to Buckinghamshire. I've too much on my mind to be frivolous in a swimming pool and sauna.

◆◆◆◆◆

We've been moving house for at least three years. It has dragged on and on so much that now whenever we say we're going to move, people say: 'Yeah, yeah, yeah.' We look at houses, even like some, but the problem is we never agree on the ones we like.

Even Jack is bored with house-hunting.

'Are you looking for houses again?' he asks.

'We are, Jack,' I answer. 'We actually saw a nice one this week and Daddy and I both liked it.'

It's true we've found a four-bedroomed house with enough space for our two offices. It also has an en-suite bathroom, a main bathroom and a downstairs loo, all very important attractive features after house-hunting with my mum all those years ago.

'So are we buying it, then?' continues Jack.

'Yes, there are just a few little problems with it,' I reply, smirking. Ian looks at me and raises his eyebrows.

'What are they, Mum?' asks my budding estate agent son.

'Well, it's quite near the railway line. We'd see all the trains whizzing by,' I venture.

'Wowee, we could wave Granny off from here,' says Jack.

Typical bloke, any excuse not to hike to the station and wave to a guest.

'It might flood if there were a lot of rain,' I continue.

'Has it been flooded already?' asks Jack excitedly.

This house sounds better by the minute. Trains whizzing by, torrents of water rushing through …

'No, but it might,' I reply.

'There's also another slight problem,' I say, thinking aloud by now.

'Yeah?' asks my interrogator.

'It's number 69!' I say, smirking while my innocent child waits for an answer.

'What's wrong with 69?' asks Jack. 'Is it unlucky, Mummy?'

'No, Jack, some people would say it's a very lucky number!' I laugh, as Ian glares at me for being so unnecessarily rude in front of an innocent child.

♦♦♦♦♦

We don't get number 69. Isn't that typical? I'm glad, really. I couldn't have gone through life, cringing every time I gave my address, nervously discussing oral sex with complete strangers.

Ian said I wouldn't have to discuss oral sex whenever I gave my address, but I said I would, because I knew everyone would be thinking: 'Nudge, nudge, 69!' And I wouldn't want them to think it hadn't crossed my mind and I was a bit slow or something.

It's now August, and we've sold our house. Our sheltered accommodation has been snapped up by a couple in the next village who actually WANT a bungalow.

We agreed we'd move out as soon as they want, and they want us out by the beginning of September. We're quite cool about this until we realize all rented places are on a six-month basis, and they don't allow pets. I look at Kitty, her green eyes and her spotless white bib.

'I'm not going anywhere without our Kit,' I say to Ian. 'We'll just have to go and stay at that caravan site on the way to Darlington.'

'Ooooh! Can we, Mum?' asks Jack, excited.

It must be ace to be a child and contemplate homelessness with such excitement.

When I don't reply he turns to Ian.

'Can we, Dad?'

'I don't think they allow children,' replies Ian.

◆◆◆◆◆

I start to get a bit panicky. We have all sorts of offers, including friends who say we can stay. It's kind but I really don't want to live as a family with anyone else. We need our own home.

It's 10pm when I have a brainwave, and remember Angela, a friend who has moved away, leaving her house empty. Her house would be ideal for Jack's school, too.

I ring her and promise we'll look after the place and it won't be for long. All she asks is I look after a piano, a family heirloom that needs a specialist removals firm. I give her my word.

◆◆◆◆◆

We've been here a few weeks now and we're settling in. I don't miss our old house at all, but it's an odd feeling not having our own place. I wonder about how my mum felt when she was homeless, and remember how grateful she was for the house at the front of the back-to-backs.

No wonder she was scared to leave my dad when we were younger. As a mum, you want to disrupt your children as little as possible. You want the best school, the best area to live in for them. I didn't realize that back then.

Jack has his own playroom, and we have a bathroom each.

'Do all houses have three bathrooms?' he asks, forgetting our last one had two.

♦♦♦♦♦

I've been to London for work. When I get back, the late afternoon sun is shining through the window. Ian and Jack are out. Kitty arches her back the way I try to do in yoga and greets me.

I look round the living room to see what Jack has been up to. There are some drawings of battles on the coffee table and a few crayons on the floor. His video game is out of its box. The plastic baseball bat and ball are in the hallway.

At that moment, a ray of sunshine hits the piano and my eyes fix on one word: Jack. The little bugger has carved his name onto Angela's family heirloom! I can't even pretend it was her own son. There's no way you can mistake 'Jack' for 'Thomas'.

I look more closely. Yup, it definitely says 'Jack'. Anger rises up from the pit of my stomach, up my chest and down my arms and legs. I am so angry with him. I promised faithfully I would look after this house.

♦♦♦♦♦

I look more closely at the piano. There's more writing that wasn't obvious before.

There, in childish scribble, is the word 'Pinw'. 'Yes, piano,'

230

I say to myself out loud and I chastise myself for never telling him not to write on furniture. But because he never has, I never saw the need.

Where would I stop? I'd say: 'Don't go round kicking dogs, Jack.' He'd say: 'I don't, Mum,' and I'd say: 'Don't anyway.' It would be pointless.

But, oh my God, I wish I'd said it now. I'm enraged he hasn't respected someone else's property. But he's five years old, damn it. Blimey, I'm glad he's not here. This is the angriest I have ever been with him. I look to the side of 'Pinw', and see in perfectly-formed letters: 'I love Mum'.

I'm angry about what I'm going to do to redeem this family heirloom. I'm ranting to myself: '200 quid, that's how much it will cost to get this put right, at least, and that's if we can even get it put right.'

Oh, I am so angry. I stomp around, cleaning up, slamming my dishcloth hard on the kitchen surfaces and scrubbing with a passion I don't usually have for housework.

◆◆◆◆◆

Later, I'm calming down. I look at those three words and I think about my mum, how much I loved her and what she would say about little Jack's declaration of love for me.

She'd say: 'You miserable bugger, Christine, your little lad has written how much he loves you, you should be grateful, not angry.'

Then she'd have a laugh and add: 'A child's love should be cherished.'

She'd be right, of course. Jack returns. He's really happy to see me, and runs to me, jumps up and we hug. But I'm still angry and I march him over to the piano. I say nothing, just point to his writing in an aloof, frosty way.

He confesses immediately. 'Yes, I wrote that, Mummy,' he says. 'I used a pencil. I wanted to see if it made the same kind of mark as this.'

He points to a mark, obviously from years ago.

'Jack, you should never write on furniture. If a policeman found out, he would be very angry. As it is, I am very angry. This isn't our piano.'

'But my letters are all the right way round,' says Jack. 'I'm sorry, Mummy. I didn't know I shouldn't do it.'

His eyes look so brown and honest.

'You must never do it again,' I say, not convinced I have got through to him. 'For a punishment, you won't watch any television or have any sweets for a week.'

His face drops. A whole week. 'Poor little bugger,' I imagine my mum's voice. 'You miserable devil, Christine.'

I wonder sadly if Jack will ever again express his love for a woman so publicly, and if I am doing psychological damage telling him off. But we struggle on with no sweets and no telly until the seven days are up.

Weeks later, a French polisher strips the piano and covers up the graffiti.

'They never write: "I love Dad",' he says wryly, moving his cloth in a figure of eight. I just smirk because I know Jack loves his dad madly.

It costs us a mere £35 and I'm quite sad it's all covered up. Once I had got over the shock and I confided to a few friends the enormous secret of my delinquent son, I was quite proud my little lad loved me and wanted to express his feelings.

If that had been our furniture, I would have treasured it. My mum's voice in my head was right. A child's love should be cherished for the rest of your days. I really, really hope she cherished mine.

CHAPTER 15

Can I Chop Your Leg Off, Mummy?

It's March 1997, and I've been staying with my mum for a couple of days. She got the bathroom in and has lived in her back-to back house alone for almost 17 years. She's been all over Britain visiting me in my various reporting jobs on newspapers, but she's probably happiest at home with her snappy West Highland Terrier, Whisky. I've been freelance for four years, so I can visit her when I like and work from her house.

My dad never did go over to 'get' her, nor did he lie in wait for her while she looked after the little boys. It took time, but gradually, over the years, my fears of what he might do to us have subsided. Now he's a lonely old man, living alone. My mum hinted there had been other women in his younger days, but since they separated I've never heard of anyone else. He's been on his own, as far as I know.

Chris sees him every now and then, but since my mum and I left home, I have seen him just the once, at my grandma's funeral when I was 22. He cried the most of any of the mourners that day, and part of me couldn't help wondering if it was fuelled by memories of shouting at her, calling her abusive names, threatening to throw her out in the middle of the night … I hardly spoke to him, and when I did, he just mocked me, so I didn't say any more. He knew, and I knew, he could still upset me.

The thing is, I'm 36 now and he can still upset me. I know

he can. Just one word and my pseudo-confidence will vanish. How can he have this hold on me after so long?

My mum's 74 now and I'm worried about a funny-looking blister on her left big toe that's making her hobble. She's always been so active it hurts me to see her in pain and unable to walk.

'I just wish I could walk our Whisky,' says my mum anxiously, looking at the dog with the face of an angel and the heart of a devil. Whisky seems to have replaced my dad in my mum's life. No matter how vicious Whisky is, there's always a place for her on my mum's knee at the end of the day. But now, because my poor Mum can barely move, Whisky hasn't been walked for ages. I shudder at the thought of all that pent-up aggression.

Ian and I have just got engaged. I've known him for 8 years and have been going out with him for 7. It hasn't been easy. I've really mistrusted men over the years, but I knew from the start he was the one for me.

From day one he's encouraged me to be myself, quirks and all. We've laughed at the differences between us. He loves Newcastle United and I love walking in the countryside. He plays squash and I love yoga. But he has that integrity I've been looking for. I love him, I want to be with him and I trust him. We're planning our wedding for seven months' time, and I'm deliriously happy and excited. I'm going to be a bride and have a husband I'm bonkers about – but first I have to get my mum's foot sorted out.

◆◆◆◆◆

She has had tests and an exploratory op, and now she has to go in for a much bigger operation to bypass the blockage in her left leg.

I'm so scared for her, but she asks me to look after her dog Whisky for her. As I promise, my voice is wobbling. I love my mum. Seeing her there on a hospital trolley, so vulnerable, makes me wish we could swap places. I walk with her as far as we can go, then I amble back to what was her bedside, before her bed was taken to theatre.

I get a shock when I next see my mum. Not just a little surprise – a proper shock that literally takes all my breath away, makes my legs feel weak and the people in front of me appear distorted. The colour has been drained from my mum's face. I think she's dead. She's in intensive care, all wired up with about four tubes leading away from various parts of her body. Tears pour down my face. I can't believe I persuaded her to have this operation. Look what I've put her through.

A nurse explains she's doing fine, but I sob and sob. After years of putting on a brave face in front of my dad, I'm usually so tough in public, but here and now I can't help it. My mum doesn't look fine. She looks like a corpse. Her face is deathly white. How will she ever recover from this?

This is when I meet her consultant for the first time. He's called David Wilkinson.

'She's doing really well,' he says, reading my mind. 'Has she said if she's in any pain?'

What? Are we talking about the same person? My mum looks as though she needs the last rites, not a chat about how she's feeling.

But he's right.

'Are you in any pain, Mum?' I ask her. I haven't spoken to her yet because I thought she couldn't hear me. I can barely get to her because of all the tubes. But she recognizes my voice and says: 'Christine,' so slowly. Then she nods, and points to her leg.

I report back to Mr Wilkinson. He ups the morphine.

◆◆◆◆◆

Two days later, my mum is back on her ward. Her leg is still aching, and when I see the operation wound I am not surprised. She's been cut from her inner thigh right down to her mid-calf. I'm expecting her to be in low spirits. I know I'll need all my energy to gee her up.

'Have you seen him?' she asks me all excitedly.

Her eyes are shining. She's propped up in bed, and the colour has come back to her face. I look round the ward, but can't see anyone she might be talking about.

'Who, Mum?' I ask. I wonder if she's having one of those mini-strokes she's had in the past – transient ischaemic attacks, which send her temporarily gaga, and have her imagining she's seeing her own dead parents.

'Who?' I ask again nervously, 'my granddad?'

'No, not your granddad, you daft bugger!' she says, quick as a flash. 'Your granddad's been dead for 30 years. Wilko! My consultant.'

Aha, so Wilko's the reason for the bright eyes.

'He's gorgeous,' she babbles on. 'He came to see me last night, and said I'm doing well. He'll be back today.'

She's in a lot of pain, heavily drugged on morphine, but she's enjoying life on the ward. By now, she knows all the nurses' problems, all their first names and the names of their children. She's still deeply interested in people and gossip, despite the pain.

Indeed, Wilko returns. He's taller than I remember from our meeting in intensive care. I was in such a state of shock there, most of the staff looked like cartoon characters. Wilko seemed about 3 feet tall.

He has dark hair, looks about 38, and I can see why my mum

likes him. He's got a very smart dark suit on, and his shirt and tie match. She likes her men smart, if nothing else.

We observe him from across the ward. He walks from bed to bed with a team of doctors and nurses alongside him. He's businesslike and looks like he takes no nonsense. Oh please, oh please, don't let us go through some embarrassing morphine-induced chatting-up of Wilko, I pray silently.

She's well-behaved as she looks into his eyes and answers his questions. Yes, her leg hurts. Yes, she has tried to walk a little. Yes, she knows the op has worked. She's polite and she thanks him, smiling.

There, she has behaved impeccably. Then, just as the team turns to go, it's as though she just has to say something for the hell of it.

'Hey, Wilko!' she says. Mr Wilkinson obviously recognizes his nickname and turns, astonished.

'I like your tie!' she quips, nodding and raising an eyebrow flirtatiously, to the amusement of the whole team.

She is such a tinker, but she brightens everyone's morning and from that day Wilko has quite a soft spot for my mum. Inside that old body, all sewn up and in pain, is still the flirt she was at 25.

◆◆◆◆◆

The op is a success and my mum goes home. I persuade her to have a day out and come along to see my wedding dress.

She can just about walk up the steps to the changing area of the bridal shop. I'm nervous going out for what will be the most honest opinion of my wedding dress I will ever receive.

At first she can't speak. I automatically think she hates it.

Then I see tears.

'It's lovely,' she sobs. 'It's beautiful, you look lovely.'

We walk back downstairs and to my car. It's probably the last time my mum ever walks outside the house. A week later we discover her bypass has blocked. I'm not sure you can bypass a bypass. I try to bypass even thinking about what this all means. It can't be good.

◆◆◆◆◆

A month later and my mum's toe is now turning a very odd colour. It's been red and inflamed. Now it's going purple. It started at the tip, but now it's spreading down to the toe joint. Ironically, the rest of her foot is going the colour her toe once was, as if a stage behind.

She's in excruciating pain. She's been on the hospital ward a week now. Wilko's on holiday. But his colleague comes every day, looks at my mum's foot and says he'll keep an eye on it. I'm spending my days by her bedside, wondering what the answer is. I say not knowing is worse than knowing. But I'm not sure which is best.

She's losing her mind, too. I don't know if it's the poison from her toe that's doing it, or the morphine she's on to relieve her pain. When she's told she might need another operation, she says: 'I can't have an operation, love. I've got a little boy. He's only five. He can't manage without me.'

My brother is in fact now 45, so she's only 40 years out, but even so I'm scared at the change in her. If she thinks Chris is five, she must wonder who the hell I am.

Day after day, doctors come round, look at her toe and shake their heads. One tells her she has 'dead tissue' on her toe. Everyone is avoiding the eventual explanation. I'm not even ready to go there yet, but I know her time is running out and I have to get my act together quickly.

A ward sister eventually plucks up the courage and takes me, my brother and Eva into a small room. I can't even remember her words, just my fear when she mentions the word 'amputation'. But I tell myself, amputation of the toe is OK. We can all lose a big toe and still enjoy life.

I must have known where the amputation would be from. I knew where the blockage was. The logical side of me knows there's no point amputating from beneath the blockage. That wouldn't solve anything.

But when it's spelled out to me it sounds horrifying. She probably has about three weeks to live if she doesn't have her leg amputated from the knee. What's worse is my mum can't even make the decision herself. She's out of it on drugs, yet the doctors say it has to be her decision.

I spend days talking to her. Sometimes she calls me Mum. Other times she remembers I'm getting married in nine weeks' time. We talk about the dead tissue but it doesn't seem to mean anything to her.

I'm passing the nurses' station one day when I ask: 'Can you tell me, is this dead tissue we're talking about gangrene?'

The answer's yes, so I go back to my mum, and say the word that everyone has avoided. But I see an immediate reaction. Having lived through the Second World War, 'gangrene' means far more to her than 'dead tissue'.

'Oh, bloody hell,' she says with a look of horror on her face.

It's the first sensible reaction I've had from her in days.

I hate doing it, but I mention taking it off. Somehow, putting it like that sounds less barbaric than getting a saw and chopping it off. I think she hears me, but she's dozed off again and I never get an answer.

◆◆◆◆◆

239

Time is definitely running out. If she doesn't sign the consent papers for this operation, she'll die. I selfishly imagine my wedding without my mum there. Weeks ago, during a mini-stroke, she told me she wouldn't be at my wedding. Then, her own mother had sent her back, she said. It wasn't time for her to go yet.

I wonder if now is her time. But there are so many things I still want to tell her. I have always told her I love her, she knows that. I want her to be at our wedding. Ian's the only boyfriend I've had she's ever approved of. We've laughed this day would never come, and now it's almost here, she might not be. She calls him 'Crossy' in a matey sort of way; she loves him. They even love the same footballer – Alan Shearer.

Every time the doctors do their rounds, they have consent papers for a limb amputation, but she won't sign them.

Nurses ask her sympathetically: 'Margaret, would you like us to take your leg off?'

She always shakes her head. Of course she wouldn't.

'Oh, I give up,' I say under my breath, in despair at the nurses' persuasion skills.

No one is ever going to say: 'Ooooh, what a fantastic idea, I would absolutely love my leg to be chopped off. Thanks for suggesting it. I can't wait to spend the rest of my days in a wheel-chair.'

My brother and I are so desperate we ask if we might sign them on her behalf. We're told she's considered still capable of making a decision. When we're told that, we look at her to see if we're just imagining how barmy she is. Maybe we're the ones who have lost the plot.

'Isn't it lovely here on this beach?' she asks, as though to confirm our thoughts. 'It's so warm and I can hear the sea.'

Bradford is about as far from the beach as you can get in

Britain. We shake our heads in misery, sadness and frustration. Ian comes in and has a word with her. She's more lucid and she says she knows they will have to chop her leg off. We think we've cracked it, until she refuses to sign the consent forms again, and we're back to square one.

I have one last go. A junior doctor is doing his rounds.

'Mum, this is almost your last chance now. If you don't sign this form, you're going to die. I'm sorry, but if you have your leg off, it will save your life.'

Hard, but that's how I feel. It had to be said, and amazingly, she takes the pen and signs the form in her maiden name, a name she hasn't used for 46 years. Apparently that'll do, it's legal, and the doctor rushes off to get her on the operating list for the next day.

◆◆◆◆◆

I spend the evening at my mum's house alone. I am sobbing hysterically. Great big massive hysterical sobs – never before nor since have I sobbed like this. I know the enormity of what I've done. I have persuaded my mum to have her leg amputated, almost bullied her to sign the consent forms. She's always been an active woman, she will hate her life from this moment on, and I know it. I wonder if I should have let her die. At least she would have gone thinking she was on a beach.

I feel a burning resentment for my dad, who's still able to walk to the pub and back every day. I know he does, because Chris has kept in touch with him, and he reports back. Where's the justice in him keeping his legs to go to the pub, yet my mum who leads a clean, healthy life loses one of hers? I feel the anger rising in me that he has never had to go through this, yet my mum has this, on top of all the misery he gave her. I sob that it isn't fair, the way four-year-olds sob when they can't play longer or have sweets.

But then my mind switches to artificial limbs. There's still hope for my mum. She's a determined woman when she puts her mind to something. She could learn to walk on an artificial leg. I can't think about wheelchairs. She would hate to be disabled and dependent on others.

But that night I lie in bed, and imagine hacksaws and bins of amputated body parts. I see the leg that ran with me as a child being sawn off. My mum was always so proud of her shapely legs. Now one is to be chopped off and rendered useless.

The leg that has hoofed it round the shops with me and come to stations to wave me off on trips is about to be chucked into some bin somewhere, discarded for ever. The leg that's walked miles with me when we had no money to get a bus, but we've chatted and had such a laugh money didn't matter. If we had enough, we've had fish and chips and walked along eating them, chatting.

It's drama-queen-meets-sentimental-rubbish but it's a rough night. I am a hysterical mess. Having had little sleep, and what I had tormented, I'm there the next day as my mum is seen by an anaesthetist. I'm aware this could be goodbye anyway. She's weak, she's frail and she's been heavily drugged now for several weeks. I imagine this will be the biggest operation she'll ever have.

We say our goodbyes as usual. My brother tries to hide his tears when my mum says: 'You'll never see me again.'

I try to be strong for us both.

'Oh, she's a bugger, she's having you on,' I say, knowing full well he could be reassuring me in a minute.

But I too wonder if this really is goodbye to a woman who has been a fantastic mum for almost 40 years. Somehow this operation seems the biggest of all – yet it's scheduled for less time than the bypass surgery.

It's amazing what drivel you remember about crucial times of your life. This is August 14th and the papers are full of the new football season. I sit and learn the names of all the Premiership grounds. I remember Mary Archer revealed she'd learned poetry by heart during Jeffrey's trial. The second one hadn't taken place then. Isn't that typical? Fragrant Mary Archer gets the poetry. Scruffy old me, who stinks of hospital freezer meals, hasn't eaten for weeks, needs her hair washing, gets the Premiership football grounds. I go back to my mum's house and make a cup of tea. I look around and wonder if she will ever come back here. Several hours go by, but I sit and stare.

♦♦♦♦♦

There's a cowardly part of me that is glad I am not there when my mum comes round. I'm scared she'll reach down and discover part of her leg isn't there. I'm almost too terrified to face her, but I know it has to be done. I got her into this. I need to go and see her and take the blame.

The ward sister stops me on my way in to explain. The surgeon tried to take off the leg from below the knee but it didn't work. He ended up taking more off – from her mid thigh.

A sick feeling comes over me. That's virtually the whole of her leg. She's going to come round from the morphine and wonder what the hell has happened. She thought she could rely on me and I've just gone and let this happen to her. I even persuaded her to sign the consent papers.

My mum's conscious when my brother and I get there, but she doesn't seem aware of what's happened. We ask her how she's feeling. She looks a whole lot better though, as though her body is rid of poison that was killing her. Her face is bright and she looks younger, but none of that is going to mean anything when she discovers the horrendous truth.

◆◆◆◆◆

Over the next few days the truth dawns on my mum.

'Chris, what's happened to my leg?' she asks. 'Why did they do it?'

Tears are streaming down her face – and soon mine too. I've let her down badly, and now I need to explain.

'Mum, you were dying,' I say, and I can see she's visibly shocked. 'They had to take your leg off or it would have killed you.'

There. I've said it. Part of me hopes she will now accept the op and get on and learn to walk on an artificial leg. But I know there's a long way to go yet.

'I would rather have died,' she says flatly. 'I'm no use with one leg. I can't walk. I can't do anything. What is the point of keeping me alive?'

I wonder. My brother wonders. For a long time the pair of us wonder if we did the wrong thing. There didn't seem any choice for us at the time. We were completely ruled by our hearts, and maybe our selfishness, because we wanted to keep her alive for us, no matter what state she was in. We thought that was what she would have wanted, but it was, in fact, what we wanted.

◆◆◆◆◆

Jack is going to be a doctor, I'm sure. He loved his doctor's plastic case, with its stethoscope, syringe and auroscope. Unfortunately, some of the items from his old Bob the Builder kit have crept into the doctor's equipment, which has graduated from a case to a medical trolley on wheels. Most of them don't bother me, but there's a saw in there that sends shivers through me. It's quite an innocent-looking thing – a purple blade with a red handle – but the serrated plastic edge gives me nightmares.

'Mum, lie down and let me examine you,' says Dr Jack, with his stethoscope round his neck.

I look into his lovely eyes and wonder if he has any idea at all how many hours I have spent in hospitals over the years. What is a game for him contains horrible memories for me. Then I start to wonder if Jack will have to make decisions about my health in the future. God, I hope not. He loves blood. Any excuse and he'll amputate. Just hope I don't get many headaches or it'll be, 'Off with her head!'

He listens to my heart. That's fine. He checks my throat with a utensil that has never been washed. I'll need a proper doctor five days from now when I go down with a strange tropical throat infection, unheard of in North Yorkshire. I'll be on the front of *The Northern Echo* and the nationals will follow up the story on their health pages.

'You're very well, Miss Fieldhouse,' Dr Jack informs me solemnly. 'I'll just check your arms and legs.'

My arms are 'just fine', he says, pressing the part just above my elbows, though 'not as cuddly' as his granny's. But when he looks at my legs he starts to frown. My right leg is given the all-clear. It would have to be my left leg, wouldn't it? Is that Sod's Law or what? I've never told Jack that my mum was an amputee, though I think he knows she spent her last years in a wheelchair. I hate him to think of her as anything other than active. I know she would hate to be remembered as inactive.

'I'm so sorry, Mummy. I'm going to have to chop your leg off. It's poorly, you see,' says the little doc.

I'm quiet for a second. I know I shouldn't let what happened

245

to my mum affect a little boy's role-play. I take a deep breath and lie this one out. I am truly amazed when he places the little saw at exactly the point on my thigh where my mum's leg was amputated.

'I can't do this, Jack. I'm sorry, I know you're only playing, but I'm frightened,' I gasp, jumping up from the sofa.

'Mum, you're just no fun any more,' he says despairingly, removing the Bob saw. 'Please can I chop your leg off, Mummy?'

Then he focuses his dark brown eyes on me, sees me shaking my head still, and asks: 'Is there a reason why?'

'Yes,' I tell him. 'I really, really like my legs. I need them to walk around and play with you. I don't like the thought of having them chopped off.'

Jack sighs with relief as though he's uncovered one of my deepest fears and he knows he can make everything all right.

Shaking his head slowly in disbelief, he says: 'Mummy, it's only pretend! I'm not really going to chop your leg off.'

He even has his hands wide and his palms up. His body language is saying: 'Believe me.'

Then, lowering his voice conspiratorially, he adds: 'This saw is a toy, it can't really cut!'

There, he thinks, he's explained it and I'll be pretty chilled next time he gets the old hacksaw out. But I reckon it'll take a good few years before I willingly offer up my limbs for amputation, pretend or not. Some memories fade with time. This one hasn't and whenever I see someone in a wheelchair, I look to see if they have one leg, two, or none. And I feel tremendous pain for them, and for the person pushing them along.

CHAPTER 16

I've Seen Heaven in Real Life

Because my mum is in a wheelchair and needs lifting in and out, we don't have her to stay with us until Jack's four months old. My Caesarian scar has healed. It's August 2000, we have a Bank Holiday weekend coming up and I'm longing to have my mum in the same house as our baby.

I just know she's going to love all those everyday things about Baby Jack that can already seem boring to me – all the spooning of baby rice, the rocking to sleep, those lovely baths, and that constant squawking for attention that sometimes drives me nuts. I can't wait for some entertaining adult company. Maybe she will even sit with Jack and play while I do something really adventurous, like have a cup of tea. There are endless possibilities. I could even make a phone call.

I know it isn't going to be easy. My mum will need looking after as well, but she can get into the en-suite bathroom OK and she's mentally back to normal. I wonder for a moment if fate put me in this bungalow for this time in my life – so my mum could come and stay.

It's a sunny Friday evening when Chris and Eva drop my mum off. Ian and I have had Whisky with us since my mum's leg amputation three years ago, so she's ecstatic to see her dog again, even though I take Whisky to visit her at least once a week.

But my mum secretly loves our laid-back house, where we're

always happy to crack open a bottle of wine and sit around and chat for hours. I think she sees us as a bunch of easy-going scruffs who occasionally do a bit of work, while between us Ian and I work pretty damn hard. She also loves being around Ian. I think she appreciates the way he's so tolerant and kind, and she always pretends to stick up for him, saying he shouldn't have to do any housework or cook any meals. It's fun seeing the pair of them together.

We settle her in, then I bath Jack and hand my mum the clean-smelling baby wrapped in a fluffy towel. I watch the two make eye contact, and see the love on her face, and think her leg amputation was worth it for this moment alone. I'm always trying to justify it. It's such a huge burden of guilt for me to carry. My mum isn't like me. I read a paper while I feed Jack. I actually look for diversions. My mum doesn't need a diversion. This is what she does best. Bringing up babies. Now and then it feels like what I do worst.

◆◆◆◆◆

It's Saturday. My mum, Jack and I have a lovely day at home. My mum loves doing all the things she can't do since she gave up trying to be independent and went to a nursing home nine months ago. She relishes folding up clothes, moving laundry from the washing machine to the dryer, washing up and drying dishes.

But best of all, she loves playing with Jack. He lies on his back under his baby gym, and my mum sits in her chair, telling him what a gorgeous boy he is. He grins at her and she coos time and time again. I get that cup of tea in total peace and think about employing my mum as an au pair.

That night, my mum and I sit and leaf through a catalogue.

She places her order – birthday presents for her friends – and we just sit at the dining room table and chat. Ian's back and is watching the football match he's just been to on TV in the living room. My mum wheels herself between the two of us. There's a peace about our house on this lovely summer evening.

◆◆◆◆◆

The next day, we're all ready to do our regular Sunday walk. We have to stay on the roads because of the foot-and-mouth outbreak, but we have a sturdy pram and we love our four-mile walks to a pub with a garden, where we have lunch, then have a leisurely walk home.

I'm to push Jack and Ian's to push my mum. Whisky is to walk alongside us and can hitch a lift on Mum's knee.

'Where are we off to, Crossy?' asks my mum.

'The Wishing Well,' he tells her.

'What? At Knaresborough? Bloody hell. You're gonna be knackered pushing me all that way, Crossy.'

There is a wishing well at Knaresborough, about 30 miles away, but we're walking to the Wishing Well pub, four miles away.

My mum's full of mischief today.

'What do we do when we get there, Chris?' she asks me.

'Well, we have some lunch. They do very nice sandwiches, with home-made bread,' I tell her. 'And we have a drink or two.'

'Come on,' she urges me. 'Let's have the truth. Why do you lot walk four miles to a pub? What do you drink when you get there?'

'Well, I have a brandy or two,' I laugh.

'How many?'

'Three sometimes!'

'And what do you have, Crossy?' asks my mum, excited now this walk has hidden depths.

'About three pints, Pud,' he says, using the nickname I gave her as a teenager when all she talked about was housework.

'Three pints!' she exclaims. 'And you think you're going to push me home, do you? I hope there are no hills! You'd better not let go of me.'

We have our sandwiches and I have my brandy. But for once my mum opts for a pint of beer with Ian. She says she's thirsty and needs a long drink. I'm amazed. I've never seen her drink beer. Like me, she's always hated the stuff.

Sure enough, Whisky hitches a lift on the way home, and we look even more like the Beverly Hillbillies with the dog riding on the wheelchair, too. But we turn up home, some five hours later, laughing, happy and slightly tipsy.

That night, after another peaceful night in, I pack my mum off to bed.

'All mothers and babies have to be asleep by 10,' I say, helping her get undressed and into bed.

She kisses me good night and tells me she's had a lovely day. I know she has. It's been one of those magical days that you only get a few of in a lifetime, where everyone has been happy, the sun has shone and you've had fun.

An hour or so later, I check on Jack, sleeping happily in his cot in the back bedroom. My mum's also asleep, in the front bedroom, but she's talking. She has always talked in her sleep, and gave us such laughs when we were kids.

'I've had a real time,' she's saying. 'It's been lovely, real.'

I rush in to Ian.

'My mum's saying she's had a real time,' I say excitedly. 'She's talking in her sleep.'

We both giggle, but we're also happy she's had so much fun she's even acknowledging it in her sleep.

'She's had a good day,' says Ian. 'We all have. We'll have to get her to come up more. She'll enjoy our walks.'

◆◆◆◆◆

The next morning, the Bank Holiday Monday, I'm excited. We're taking my mum and Jack to Ian's parents for tea. It's his mum's birthday, and a very special one – her first as a grandma. Baby Jack will be all toothless grins, no doubt. My mum will enjoy sitting in the garden, eating sandwiches and cakes and chatting – normal things she doesn't do any more.

My mum's always been an early riser. I swear she was the person who tuned in first in Britain on the day Princess Diana and Prince Charles got married. 'Chris!' she'd shouted up the stairs. 'Di's hairdresser's just arrived!'

But I haven't heard her stir yet. I pop my head round her door and she's awake. She's looking at me and smiling. Her lips are moving, but no sound is coming out. At first I think she's messing about, exaggerating being quiet because of Jack, but then I see her bed is wet. She's tried to get up to the bathroom, but hasn't managed.

I look closely at her face. She looks exhilarated and wildly happy. She's really pleased to see me. But she's frustrated she can't make me understand her. I ask her if she's OK and she smiles.

From the way she's trying to manoeuvre herself, it looks as though she can move some of her body. She has had mini-strokes in the past, where her arm has been affected for a few days, but she's soon gone back to normal. She's never lost her speech, though. My heart starts to thud. I rush to Ian in our bedroom.

'I think my mum's had a stroke,' I say to Ian. 'She can't speak.'

Part of me wants to cry with fear, but I know I have to hold it together. I need to get organized, get my mum cared for properly, and make sure Jack is OK.

In the past I've rung emergency doctors, but even if they have come out, they haven't done much for mini-strokes. This time it feels more serious. I dial 999.

'I need help with my mum,' I tell the operator. 'I think she's had a stroke.'

The ambulance is here quickly and my mum is secured in a chair and taken away. She smiles at the ambulance men with gratitude, probably embarrassed she can't speak to them. She's a great thanker and would have said 'Thank you' 50 times before she'd even got in the ambulance. She always feels like she's putting people out.

I follow in the car and when I get to hospital my mum is sitting up in a bed. I answer all their questions about her health. As we wait for a doctor to see her, I look around me. We're in accident and emergency. Four months ago I was in this hospital to give birth. Now here I am hoping for a miracle for my mum.

◆◆◆◆◆

A doctor comes to the bedside and examines her. She's able to nod and shake her head. She understands his questions. Then he shakes his head and turns to me.

'This can go three ways,' he explains. 'Your mum has had a stroke. The next 24 hours are crucial. Her speech could return and she could go back to normal. She may stay like this, or she may have another stroke that will kill her.'

I nod as if on automatic pilot. Within about an hour, we've

gone from a trip to my in-laws for a pleasant Monday in their garden to a death-bed scenario in hospital. It may only be 8.30am on a Bank Holiday but I know I need my brother to get here fast. He sounds sleepy when I call. Although the doctor put the worst-case scenario last, there was something in his voice that makes me think that is the option he'd put his money on if he were a betting man.

I sit with my mum but I barely speak to her. It's as though I'm waiting for her speech to return so we can catch up. I hold her hand. I tell her the doctors will help her and she'll be OK, but the two of us know I'm not entirely convinced myself. That doctor must have seen hundreds of stroke victims. He must know the chances of recovery.

Chris and Eva arrive just before my mum is transferred to a ward. She seems the same. Chris holds her hand, asks how she is, as though that's a perfectly normal question. We follow her to ward 12, where more doctors come and ask questions.

I feel almost drunk. I'm in a bit of a daze. Adrenaline kept me going before when I was on my own with my mum, but now my brother's here I'm not quite with it. I have no memory of whether she is given any kind of drug. I just sit there, hold her hand and talk to Chris and Eva.

There are six beds in the bay and we pull the curtains round ours. It's not that we are unsociable. We just want some privacy. We hear people coming and going, visitors arrive to see their loved ones before they set off on days out. It's another beautiful sunny day out there. Jack will have had his breakfast. He's just trying new purees. So far we've tried apple and banana. The books all say we need to introduce new fruits carefully in case they hurt his tummy or they disagree with him.

I ring Ian.

'What's Jack had for breakfast?' I ask, the controller in me emerging once more.

'Raspberry puree.'

I expect he'll be moving on to the next course of bacon, eggs, sausages and fried bread. But in the scheme of things, it doesn't really matter as long as he's OK.

It's about 2.30pm when Ian and Jack arrive. My mum recognizes them both immediately. She smiles at Ian, then her whole face melts when she sees smiling Jack. He gives her a toothless grin that lights up his eyes and she smiles back. It's a moment of no words, but many, many words, as a look of love flashes from a grandma to her grandson.

If she could, she would now say 'Isn't he gorgeous?' about 50 times. She would cuddle him and hold him, and offer him a chocolate (which would annoy me). But she just reaches for his hand and he giggles. Good old Baby Jack. He may whinge all day for me when we're on our own, but this one time in hospital, he's Perfect Baby. He smiles, he gurgles, he laughs, all on cue.

They don't stay long, setting off to see Ian's mum. None of us says it, but we're all thinking the same: this is no place for a baby. Besides, I don't want Jack here. As they go, I wonder if Ian realizes this may be the last time he sees my mum alive. But then I wonder if I am being too pessimistic. I thought she was dead three years ago when she was in intensive care. Am I just living in fear of the moment I dread, the day I lose my mum?

They're gone just a few seconds when my mum starts trembling all over. She's gripping my brother's hand. We ring the emergency bell. A nurse comes, then she alerts the doctors. They examine her, and confirm she has had another stroke and is probably now in a coma.

I kick myself. All this time I've been waiting for my mum to come round so we could chat. Now she's gone a stage deeper. Her eyes are closed. There's barely any movement. She's still breathing, though, and she looks peaceful.

◆◆◆◆◆

The next few hours are pure pain. My brother leaves me with my mum so I can have a few quiet minutes with her. I hold her thin, veiny hand in mine and start to talk. I begin to say how much I love her, but I pause. She knows this. I've always told her how deeply I love her, and she has told me several times a day how much she loves me. We've signed letters 'All My Love', and meant it, for as long as I could write.

But I thank her for being such a fantastic mum, for giving me the sense of humour and strength that have got me through the hard times. I laugh and tell her how she has infuriated me at times with her stubbornness, and I know I have driven her to distraction at times. I'm not pretending we've had a perfect relationship. It's had its faults but it's also had fun and love and all the things that matter.

I'm talking in almost a monotone voice. I think I'm in shock. I tell her she'll always be in my heart and I'll never stop loving her. I realize I'm letting her go. There's no longer talk of fighting the strokes and the illnesses and holding on and the things we have to look forward to. I'm saying goodbye and I know my life will never be the same again without this wonderful woman.

◆◆◆◆◆

My brother returns and has a few minutes with my mum while Eva and I go for a cup of tea. I look around the bleak grey dining

255

area. It seems lifeless. I feel lifeless. All my hope has been drained from me today. Yesterday was sunshine and flowers. Today it's bleak and hopeless. Yesterday was about families and fun and drinking three brandies and staggering home. Today is about pain and heartache and not caring about anything ever again.

◆◆◆◆◆

We're by my mum's bedside as she jerks suddenly. For a minute hope returns and we breathe a long sigh and smile. We think she may be coming round. But it's the beginning of the 'death rattle'. Her chest starts to rattle, then she settles peacefully. The lines on the monitors stop their highs and lows. They're straight now. It's the end of a hard life and I'm not quite sure how I will ever cope.

I ring Ian from a phone booth inside the hospital.

'She's dead,' I say bleakly. I can't bring myself to say: 'My mum's dead.' Those three words encompass one of my greatest fears.

He sounds shocked. I suppose he must have been through so many scares he thought my mum would probably pull through again.

'You're a tough old boot, Pud,' he used to say, using her nick-name.

'Hey, cheeky bugger, less of the old,' she'd quip.

'I'm on my way in,' he says.

He arrives, carrying Jack in his baby car seat. It seems such a contrast. A lively baby gurgling away, and my poor dead mum lying in bed.

◆◆◆◆◆

That night, Ian, Jack and I sleep in the back bedroom. The front one is as we left it. My mum's wheelchair is at the bottom of her bed.

I've been numb until now. I've just gone through the motions but, unable to sleep, I get up and walk around, switching on lights, afraid of the dark. I feel my mum's with me everywhere I go.

Back in bed, I try to sleep. I doze off, then I let out a piercing scream. Afraid of terrifying Jack, I get up and walk around again. I don't know how I will ever cope with this.

How will our marriage survive this misery? How will I be a good mum to Jack when I'm so sad inside? How will I ever care again what we have for dinner? How will I ever have the patience to play with my baby when all I want is my mum?

◆◆◆◆◆

We're driving home from town, Jack and I. He's in the front seat, chatting away about life.

'Mummy, but how old will you be when I'm 70?' he asks.

'I'll be 109,' I say, the certainty in my voice disguising the fear I'll be long gone by then and Jack will have to make his own cup of tea with two sugars in a morning.

I've always tried to appear happy in front of Jack, even during those months after my mum died. I never let him see my pain. Instead I waited for him to close his eyes and sleep, and then the tears from a whole day's repressed sadness flowed. I cried because my mum didn't see Jack's first tooth or witness him crawling for the first time.

After the first anniversary of my mum's death, I stopped crying every night, but I still cried she didn't see him take his first steps or hear him say 'Mama' and 'Dada'. A month later, Ian and I went out for a meal, and I felt guilty for feeling happy again. But my mum would have wanted me to be happy. She loved us to laugh.

I've always chatted to Jack about my mum, and he has talked about her as though he remembers her.

'Hey, wow, look, Mum!' cries Jack suddenly. 'Look up there. Isn't it lovely?'

'Where am I looking, Jack?' I ask, afraid of taking my eyes off this road. Although it's a country road it's busy and bendy, and boy racers are overtaking all the time. But I manage a quick peek upwards, and it's true there are white lines running parallel, like a fountain, in the sky.

'Wow, what's caused that? It isn't a cloud, is it? Maybe an aeroplane has gone by, or several planes from the RAF base,' I suggest.

'It's not a plane, Mummy,' Jack informs me with total confidence. 'That's Heaven up there. That's where Grandma Pud is.'

'Ah Jack, how lovely that you can see Heaven,' I say, fascinated. 'But how do you know it's Heaven?'

'Because I sometimes see it at night when I'm asleep in my bed. Grandma Pud steps out of there and comes to see me.'

He knows he has my undivided attention. I'm always desperate to know my mum's OK.

'How does she look, Jack?' I ask.

I've never told Jack my mum was an amputee as I couldn't bear him to make childish fun of having one leg. In my dreams since her death she always has two legs again, and I've found this reassuring.

'She's really happy,' he tells me. 'She's back with her mummy and her daddy, and she can walk again. She looks younger, a bit like you now.'

'What does she do when she comes to see you?' I ask.

'She just sits and looks at me, and smiles at me, then she flies off back to Heaven,' he chats on. 'I'm not frightened at all.

It's a bit like having my own angel, you know.'

'Wow, that's so special, Jack,' I say.

'Does she ever ask about me or come and see me?' I continue selfishly.

'Sometimes she pops her head round your door. She sees you sleeping. She nods,' laughs Jack.

I cringe when he laughs. Is he really taking the piss out of me? Is he thinking, my mother's barking mad, let's humour her for a while?

'But at the end of the day Grandma Pud knows you're happy if I'm OK, so she often doesn't have to check on you at all, just me,' he informs me.

Then he sits back in his booster seat, contented.

'I'm really, really glad I've seen Heaven in real life now,' he adds, as though that's another major thing to tick off his list, along with 'Meet Mickey Mouse', 'Watch *Star Wars* 500 times' and 'Abolish School'.

We've seen 'Heaven' a few times since. It's above the A684 between Northallerton and Bedale, in case you're wondering. If you dare take your eyes off the road, it's quite a comforting place. But don't look too long. The way those cars fly along there, you could end up in Heaven sooner than you want.

CHAPTER 17

I Don't Want You to See That Nasty Man

I'm in bed with a cold and I have woken up from a feverish sleep with some even more feverish thoughts.

'How are you doing, sweetie?' asks Ian, who's working from home.

I check the paracetamol packet to see I haven't taken any A-class drugs with hallucinatory effects. Nope. The packet says paracetamol.

I lie flat on my back, staring up at the ceiling. The two things my instinct has told me throughout my sweaty afternoon are to get Jack christened – and go and see my dad.

Now, getting Jack christened I can handle. We'd tried a few years ago and the dates had never quite worked out. I think it would be nice and then, when he's older, he can make his own choices about religion.

But see my dad? It's been 22 years. I'm still scared of him. I still see those clear grey eyes looking maliciously at me, crazed with drink. I still hear his foul mouth, spouting obscenities. I can still feel the shame that our neighbours can hear him and the fear of what he will do to us. And worst of all, the way he makes me feel – ugly, worthless, hopeless, depressed.

I mull it over in my mind. If I go and see him, will he say something nasty, and will I start all my self-doubt all over again? Will one visit put me in therapy for years? Will he try some-

260

thing? Will he hurt me physically? Yet I know now I have made this decision, NOT going to see him will be more painful. I'll feel cowardly and I will always wonder how he would have been with me.

Later in the evening, when I make it to the living room, I break the news to Ian.

'Yes, sweetie, whatever you think, it would be nice,' he says of the christening, hardly taking his eyes off some Norwich versus Bolton game.

'And I'm going to see my dad.'

There, it's out, I have to do it now. Derr, derr, drum roll, Ian looks away from the television.

'What's brought this on?' he asks, obviously expecting some logical explanation.

'I must have had some fever this afternoon,' I say, trying not to sound like a total crackpot in need of immediate medication.

'I woke up wanting to see him, to put my mind at ease. He's ill. He's in hospital. I want to tell him I've forgiven him as much as I ever will. I want to face him, for my sake. I want closure.'

I pause, then add: 'Now I have Jack, I've realized that what happened in the past doesn't matter any more.'

I hear a cheer for a goal, but Ian still doesn't look at the screen. We've known each other 15 years. Ian has never met my dad. I don't think he has even seen a picture of him. I have never once mentioned wanting to see my father. I've once or twice expressed sadness when someone else's father has died, sadness they lost a decent father when mine was still prowling the streets.

'When will you go?' Ian asks. 'Do you want me to come with you?'

A shiver from age 14 goes down my spine. I don't ever want

my husband to meet my father. I am so desperately ashamed of my dad, of his small-mindedness, his cruel tongue, his weird mind. I almost panic and invent lies so they don't have to meet, before I realize I don't have to pretend any more.

'No, I need to do this alone, thanks. I'm going to go as soon as I'm better,' I say. 'If I go while he's in hospital I'll be able to visit him unawares, and he won't be able to prepare any torture instruments.

'It will be neutral territory,' I add, picturing the alternative – a visit to his home. Who knows what he might do after he's let me in? Lock the door, hurt me? Now, that would be just too scary.

'I'm not going to tell anyone else,' I plan. 'I don't want him tipping off.'

Within a few days, I feel better and I start to prepare for the visit. I do my research. After years of no interest whatsoever, I ask my brother which ward my dad is on, which hospital he's in and the visiting times, without him even suspecting a thing.

I know I won't make the morning session, but I could make it for 2, and be away by 4 when my brother gets there after work.

My dad's on a ward I know very well. It's where my mum was for some of her time in hospital. I spent months by my mum's bedside, hardly eating, pale and worried, hoping against hope a guardian angel would come and save her life. The staff all thought me a totally devoted daughter.

Now I'm about to re-enter that ward, the total opposite of the person those doctors and nurses knew. They may have all changed jobs. They might not remember me. What do I say if they ask who I am? Do I say daughter, friend, foe? I can't bring myself to call him Dad, even.

I start to think it all through, planning my journey there. I'll drop Jack off at his gran's and pick him up on the way back. It's constantly on my mind, like an exam or job interview that's looming. I vow I won't mention it to Jack. I don't want him to start asking questions. Telling Jack would be a very bad idea.

'Jack,' I say five minutes after I've made my mind up. 'You know that nasty man I told you about, who was my daddy? Well, I'm going to see him later this week.'

A look of panic comes over Jack's face.

'He's poorly in hospital, he won't be able to hurt me now and I need to see him so I'm not frightened any more,' I tell him.

He looks confused that I'm actually going to see someone I was once so frightened of.

'OK Mum, but I don't want you to see that nasty man,' he says. 'He was horrid to you when you were a little girl. I don't like anyone who's horrid to my mummy.'

It's a sweet opinion but I know I have to go. I always thought I would have to face him at a family funeral. It would be embarrassing with people looking on and emotions running high. At least this way, I'm in control. He's going to be taken by surprise and he can't plan anything nasty. I know from Chris he's on all sorts of machines. For a moment, I wonder if seeing me will finish him off. Amazingly, I don't feel a surge of joy at the thought. I really seem to have lost most of my bitterness since I had Jack. Could it be true what my Uncle Sam, my dad's older brother, told me all those years ago? Am I really thinking differently now I have a child of my own?

◆◆◆◆◆

I ring Ian from the hospital car park, as though I'm an undercover agent on a dangerous mission.

'I'm about to go in,' I say, picking up my bag as though it's a hand grenade.

'Good luck, sweetie, and take care,' he tells me.

This must seem so odd for him, with his nice normal family.

I go to ward 20, looking at the noticeboard as though I know exactly where I'm going. I don't want anyone to ask me questions. I don't want to have to say his name, or his relationship to me, or anything. I don't want some well-meaning nurse leading me into the ward, saying loudly: 'Harry, your daughter's here.'

I finally ask a nurse where he is.

She looks at her clipboard. 'Next bay, last bed on the left.'

Great, there's no chance she's going to escort me in there.

I see him. He's sleeping. The face that once terrified me looks calm, but it still has the remnants of the features that scared the life out of me. The eyebrows are still quite bushy. His nose looks bigger now his face is so thin. Luckily, the scariest of all – those cold clear eyes - are closed.

I tiptoe over to get a chair and I move it to the other side of his bed, so I can sit with my back to the rest of the ward. I want to sit and look at him for a while. I want to be the one there when he wakes up this time, just as he used to do to me when I was a kid. Admittedly I don't have a 12-bore shotgun to his forehead. I don't even wish I had, now. I don't even want him to go through that fear now. Blimey, I am mellowing.

I look around the bed. There are tubes leading from him into various machines. I recognize a heart monitor. It will be interesting to see how that reacts when he sees me. Or maybe he'll think he's died and he's in Heaven. Even that thought doesn't make me laugh. This is too serious for that.

I sit for a moment longer and he starts to stir. Now it's not so much his heart I'm bothered about as my own. My chest starts to thump, but I take deep breaths. I am not going to mess this one up with nerves. I must have disturbed him when I moved the chair. From the back, I must look like a normal visitor. No one can see my terror.

He opens his eyes. Yes, they're still grey, still pale, still bloody terrifying. I hold his look. As a child I was too scared to look him in the eye most of the time. I hated not being able to do it, but the minute I made eye contact with him, I was sometimes physically sick with fear. This time, I'm going to meet him eye to eye and hold it for as long as it takes.

I don't know much about his health, except he had bowel cancer and has had a colostomy. He's in hospital with stomach problems now. But I wonder if he has cataracts because he looks at me as a baby does, trying to make out features he recognizes. His eyes seem to travel round my face, then my hair, then down to my shoulders and over my shirt.

'Who are you?' he asks.

There it is, the voice that once dished out insult after insult, threat after threat, and the cruellest of words. 'Whoever you are, you're a grand lass.'

I realize then he's referring to the way I look. It's his way of saying I'm not that bad-looking. An anger rises in me. Inside I'm screaming: 'You told me as a kid how ugly I was, now as a 40-odd-year-old woman you tell me I'm not. Why couldn't it have been the other way round? How much pain and self-doubt could that have prevented?' But my anger is for the child I once was, not for me now.

He looks for a second or two longer and I remain totally silent. I'm almost goading him now, the look on my face is saying: 'Come on, then, smartarse, who am I?'

Then the penny drops.

265

'Bloody hell,' he says, drawing out the 'bloody' in shock. 'Christine.'

He says no more, his eyes are filling with tears. God knows what's going on in his mind, but mine is with my mother and all the pain he put her through. Just thinking about her miserable life with him brings tears to my eyes.

'Don't you cry for me,' he says. 'Have you come because you want some money?'

Great. That's done it. My tears stop. I'm tough again.

'Money,' I sneer. 'I don't want your money. Do I look as though I need your money? And I'm not crying for you.'

I take the venom out of my voice now. I'm not here to cause him pain, add to his distress. It isn't payback time. If it were I'd just unplug the machines and walk away.

'I'm crying because of my mum. She was a good wife to you and you didn't treat her well.'

I temper my language, trying hard not to sound accusing.

'But I'm not here to talk about that,' I say, keeping my voice steady. I know I have to say what I came to say, in case I don't get the time or opportunity. It's like writing a news story. I have to get the important things in the intro.

'That's in the past. I'm here to tell you that what happened doesn't matter any more,' I say. 'I don't want you thinking I'm still bitter or frightened of you. I'm as near forgiveness as I'll ever be. I have my own life now, and you should just concentrate on your health.

'I've got a husband and a little lad and I'm really happy. I've got over all of that.'

There, I've said it. I wonder if he realizes what I mean by 'all of that'. Maybe the way he treated us was no big deal to him and he doesn't understand what I am trying to say.

266

But he nods. Then his voice gets back that nasty tone of old.

'So you're saying I can die now, is that it?' he asks accusingly.

I'm not going to fall for that one. He wants me to throw myself at his bedside, swoon and cry out, 'Oh Dad, please don't die! Let's start all over again.'

Well, bugger that for a game of soldiers.

'You can do whatever you want,' I say, realizing there's no feeling in my voice. There's neither love nor hate, just indifference.

'Live or die, it's up to you, but I wanted to come and see you and tell you the past is over. I'm more interested in the present and the future now.'

He starts to talk.

'I've been so ill, you know. I've been poorly,' he tells me, with tears once more.

There follows a list of complaints he's had over the years, from his bowel cancer to a pair of false teeth that didn't fit properly. I steer him away from teeth. He was always less than complimentary about my own crooked collection. I just don't want to go there any more.

Then he cries about my mum.

'She was a lovely lass, and you were good kids. I've been a bloody idiot. I got in with the wrong crowd. I thought women, cars and drinking were important and they weren't. I have suffered, Chris.'

While he wallows in self-pity and regret, I relax enough to picture my own child, little chubby-cheeked Jack, and I wonder what it would be like if I behaved so badly I didn't see him for more than 20 years. I feel as though the pain would kill me.

My dad continues to talk to me as though I'm a normal everyday visitor.

'They've been good to me here, Chris,' he starts. 'But this pain in my stomach, they don't know what this is.'

I realize I'm bored. When my mum was here, I sat for hours with her, chatting, and trying to sort out every possible discomfort. Sometimes it felt like I suffered every ache and pain with her. Today's so different.

I've been here 30 minutes. My dad knows the basics about my life from my brother. He's seen my newspaper cuttings, apparently. He's seen photos of Jack. I feel as though there's no more conversation we can have. I've said what I came to say.

I look at my watch and say I have to go. I deliberately mention Jack and say I have to pick him up from his gran's on my way home. But he doesn't ask me anything about Jack. I obviously didn't get my journalistic skills from this gene pool, then.

I put the chair back, dreading him asking if I'll come and see him again. I would have to be honest and say I don't know. I don't want a relationship with him. I don't want to visit him at weekends, take his washing home and send him a card on Father's Day. Worse still, I don't want to introduce him to Jack. Women protect kids from men like my dad. They don't introduce them to them and encourage them to spend time together.

'I'll see you,' I say, avoiding adding the word 'later'.

'Bye,' he says. His voice sounds cold, but tears are streaming down his face. I wonder what emotions he's going through – regret, sadness, anger, bitterness?

Outside in the car park, I breathe in the fresh air and feel almost blinded by the sun. I feel as though a load has lifted from my shoulders. I'm ecstatically happy. In the car, I sit in the driver's seat and call Ian.

'I'm OK,' I say, relieved. 'I survived. Oh, and I don't think he thinks I'm ugly any more. I'll see you later.'

268

◆◆◆◆◆

I call at my in-laws on the way back, where Jack has been baking cherry buns. He runs to greet me in front of his gran, but when we're alone in the living room, he whispers, 'Mum, did you see the nasty man?'

His mind obviously hasn't been on his culinary practice with Granny.

'Yes, I saw him, sweetie, and you know, I'm not frightened of him any more,' I tell him.

I feel a real sense of freedom when I say those words. This is better than any therapy. I wonder if I'll start to look younger every morning now this huge weight is off my mind. God, I hope so.

I can see my words sinking into Jack's mind slowly, the way people react to translation. I see worry lifting from his face. It almost seems that he's no longer frightened for me, either.

'Oh, great, Mummy!' he exclaims.

I expect some Jack philosophy on healing parent-child rifts, but no. I look at him and realize this is what matters in my life now – a bright-eyed boy full of excitement and happiness, not things that happened in another lifetime 30 years ago.

'Have a cherry bun,' says Jack, his anxious face now bright and cheerful again. 'Me and Granny have baked them, and I didn't pick my nose once. I even washed my hands, too. They're quite nice, apart from the cherries!'

CHAPTER 18

Is Your Daddy Going to Heaven or Helen?

The whole of Britain is gearing up to vote. It's May 2005. Tony Blair has panda eyes. The stress is taking its toll. I look at him and think back to the days when my female colleagues and I fancied Blair, one of our local MPs. Now he looks as knackered as the rest of us.

I'm in our village shop looking at Blair's photo on the front of the papers. There's a story about him having sex five times a night. 'He must mean five times a year, mustn't he?' I say to Pauline in the shop.

'You can't have that many kids and all his stress and still perform five times a night, can you?'

We're still laughing when my mobile vibrates with a text message from my brother.

My dad is in a very bad way in a nursing home. His cancer seems to have returned, but no one is saying where. He can't get out of bed, he has lost a lot of weight, and it isn't looking good. I haven't seen him since my visit to hospital almost a year ago, but Chris is visiting him most days.

If Chris were a friend whose father was dying, I would be supportive. I know I would. I try my hardest to leave my own indifferent feelings aside. I hate to hear him so down. It must be hard for him.

'H no beta,' comes the text.

Over the last few years we've never known what to call our dad to each other. Do we say 'My dad', 'Your dad' or 'our dad'? In the end we've settled for Harry, or H, seeing as we usually converse by text.

'Doc c-ing him l8r.'

'R u ok?' I reply.

'Yup,' he replies.

Deep down I have this fantasy that I'll go to my dad's bedside and we'll laugh. Last time I saw him there were so many recriminations and there was so much sadness. I want us to talk, and laugh, and put all that heavy stuff behind us.

I carry on working, collect Jack from school and supervise about 20 children in our garden when my mobile rings. It's my brother. I swallow hard. If he's ringing, this must be it. He's died. I never got that chance to laugh with him.

'Chris,' says my brother. 'Harry's here. He wants a word with you. I'm going to put the phone to his ear. He wants to say something.'

I haven't spoken to my dad on the phone since I was at university and he rang me there to ask my mum to go back to him, but these are probably going to be his last words to me. I say hello.

All I can hear is deep agonized breathing. He's trying to say something, but I can't understand. It seems such a contrast to the lively children in our garden.

'Hello, how are you?' I say loudly.

I'm being ridiculous. He can't speak, he can't breathe and I'm asking how he is. He's hardly going to say: 'I've never felt better.' But what can I say?

'Mum, who's that on the phone?' Jack has come in and seen my worried, troubled face.

I shoo him back to the garden.

'Did you get that?' asks my brother.

'No,' I reply. 'Did you?'

'No,' he says.

We hang up and I check how many children have been injured in our garden in the two minutes since I left them.

Then something comes over me. It's a strong desire to find out exactly what my dad was trying to say. I need to know. It will probably be the last thing he ever says to me. It might help. It might hinder. But I need to know.

I abandon the garden of kids to Ian, and drive down to the nursing home. It's a 90-minute drive, much of it on country roads, and it's dark when I arrive. The staff are with my dad. We have to wait to go in to see him.

On the bedroom door there's a photo of a thin man smiling. I assume it was the man who had this room last and the staff haven't got round to changing it.

'That's Harry,' says my brother.

'It's not,' I retort. 'It's nothing like him.'

I look beyond my brother and Eva. My dad is lying in bed, but he doesn't look anything like the man I saw a year ago in hospital, who still looked like the man I knew 25 years earlier. He looks like a skeleton covered in skin. He must weigh three stones. He's so thin his jaw looks as though it's receded into his throat.

I go right up to him. Imagine, a year ago I was still terrified of facing this man. Now he can't even sit up in bed. He can't even speak to me.

I stand above him and he focuses on my brown eyes. Then I see his own eyes start to water. He's recognized me. He knows

272

I'm here. We have barely anything in common, me and this man in a bed, but I think back to what made him happy. I dredge up all the animals he loved.

'Do you remember Rosie?' I venture, remembering the Welsh Mountain pony he bought when I was two. There's a spark of interest. He tries to nod. Then he attempts a smile.

'And Prince?'

He nods his head about a centimetre, the most he can probably move. I remember how we both cried when Prince died. Blimey, that was a bad choice. What do I say now?

'Touch him when you speak to him,' says Chris.

I tentatively put my hand on my dad's arm, but anyone watching will see how repugnant I find touching him, not because he's ill and looks so terrible, but because of the way I have felt about him all these years. Oh my God, I hope no one asks me to kiss him.

'Do you remember trying to ride Beauty when you'd been to the pub and you fell off? I didn't half laugh.'

My Bradford accent is getting stronger with every word. I just want him to understand me. I suddenly think how horrendous it would be if you were desperate for pain relief when someone's talking gibberish about animals from 30 years ago.

'Are you in any pain?' I ask.

He doesn't move. I cut to the chase. His reactions are slowing down.

'What were you trying to say on the phone, Harry?'

He opens his mouth a bit more. It sounds like an 'S' sound, but it's hard to understand.

'Are you trying to say you're sorry?' I ask, in a mocking tone to hide my embarrassment in case he shakes his head and he isn't at all sorry.

273

He nods.

'Look, it's OK,' I say quietly. 'That's all in the past now. Don't give it a second thought. Don't you worry about all that now.'

I imply he has far more things to think about. After all, who knows what happens next? None of us does if the truth be told.

It's now midnight. I'm glad I've been to see him, but I just want to get home. I'm extra tired because of the stress.

'I'm going to stay,' says Chris. 'I just don't want him to be on his own.'

'Well, I can come back tomorrow and sit with him while you sleep if you like,' I offer in the same tone I used when I took over from people on stakeouts at work.

I ask: 'Do you know how long he might be like this?'

'The doctor said it could be minutes, hours or days; they don't know.'

'Well, the offer's there. I'll come tomorrow. You could go home and sleep while I'm here,' I urge.

Driving home, I think of all the confusions within a family. I haven't seen my dad all these years, yet I have just offered to sit with him while he dies.

And what was my dad trying to say? Shut up? S'hot in here? Or sorry? Did I put the word into his mouth, or was it already on his lips, waiting to come out? I prefer to think he was volunteering an apology, but I shall never ever know.

◆◆◆◆◆

The next day, I explain all to Jack.

'Jack, you know Mummy's daddy in Bradford?' I ask, testing the water.

274

'Well, he's very poorly,' I continue. 'I went to see him last night.'

'Yeah, I know. He's dying, isn't he?' asks Jack, happily swinging on his dining chair, while cereal goes all over the dining room carpet.

'Yes, he is going to die,' I say.

'That's good, isn't it, Mum?' Jack looks bright-eyed and unperturbed.

I realize I've spent so long telling this child how bad my father was to me, I can't take it all back now and pretend he was a good man.

'Well, it's always sad when someone dies, Jack,' I explain. 'Uncle Chris is going to be very sad.'

'But you won't be, will you?'

Aha, the million-dollar question. I wonder.

'I'll be sad about what happened in the past and the fact we couldn't be friends,' I say. 'I'll be sad at the waste of a life. But no, Jack, it's not going to be anything like when my mum died. I probably won't cry for a whole year.'

'Mum?' asks Jack. 'I have a question. Will your daddy go to Heaven or Helen?'

For a moment I want to hug him. I have two friends called Helen, and though I've sometimes shortened them to Hel, I've never thought of them as Hell. Jack obviously has.

'Mum, you don't get to see Jesus if you've been a naughty boy, you know. Jesus and God only see good boys,' he informs me. 'Good boys go to Heaven, but bad boys go to Helen.'

'I'm not sure what will happen to my dad,' I answer. 'I think he said sorry last night so maybe now he'll get into Heaven after all.'

'Right,' says Jack, trying to understand. Then he looks as though he's struck gold.

'So we can be as naughty as we like, but if we say sorry right at the very end of our lives, Jesus will forgive us? Right?'

Oh hell. He now thinks it's OK to misbehave as long as he says sorry. Hell, hell, hell. Or should that be Helen?

◆◆◆◆◆

Later that morning, text messages keep me up to speed.

I'm interviewing Sally Gunnell by telephone about Olympic medals, health, fitness and her three young sons. Every five seconds my landline phone starts crackling. Another text message to say my dad is still alive.

I can't explain to Sally my dad is dying. I sound quite normal. We've even had a laugh about melted chocolate. You can't go from guffawing about chocolate to: 'Hey, by the way, Sally, my dad's dying. Any minute during this interview I'll get a text or a call to say he's gone.'

Around mid-afternoon, several hours after the interview, my mobile rings and it's my brother. His voice is wobbly. This is it.

'My dad died this afternoon,' he tells me. 'I got a call to go back to the home, but he had died. I wasn't there for him.'

I feel tears pricking at my eyes and I'm not sure whether they're for my dad or for my brother's regrets and grief. Or for the news that it's all over, all so over.

'He probably didn't want you to be there,' I blub. 'He was a bit like that, wasn't he?'

I'm amazed I'm crying so easily and I'm not sure whether I'm crying for my dad or my brother or both.

We arrange to phone each other later. I toy with the idea of going to see my brother and then I sit at the dining table and cry. I cry for 82 years of my dad's life that were thrown away, a whole lifetime chucked down the drain. I cry for the misery we all went through. I cry for my brother's pain.

I cry for the child I once was, so frightened and so quiet, because of my dad. I cry in amazement he could treat a child like that. I cry because I'm sorry for myself because I'm now an orphan, and then I cry some more because for the first time in five years, I'm not crying about my mum.

◆◆◆◆◆

I've often wondered if I would even go to my dad's funeral, but now the time is here it feels right to go. I was his daughter. I want to say goodbye. I want to sit there, look at his coffin and see how I feel, because at the moment I'm not sure how I feel.

Do I want to say thanks, I wonder. Thanks for his life. I think back to my childhood when we went on walks together. I have always been grateful he paid for an eye operation for me after I had measles. I had horses to ride. He sent me for riding lessons when I was five, the age Jack is now. That's already more than a lot of kids have.

There were happy moments, but they were wiped out almost immediately with the next drunken rant.

I talk about him a lot to Ian. He's beginning to sound a bit of a charmer, a loveable rogue.

'I didn't know he liked classical music,' says Ian, amazed that the man I have described as a psycho actually had some taste.

'Yes, and he always polished his shoes before he went out,' I add. I'm now trying to make him seem respectable. It's as though in death all is forgotten.

'My mum and dad used to be members of the Yorkshire Driving Club and go out in landaus and drive,' I say. It's sounding more *Brideshead Revisited* by the minute. I can tell Ian's

277

beginning to wish he'd met this fine upstanding member of the community.

◆◆◆◆◆

The funeral's 50 miles away, at 10am. After dropping Jack at school, we head down the A1, listening to tracks on CDs, as my job has been to choose the music. The clarity of Dusty Springfield fills the car. My dad loved Dusty. He got his records out every Sunday teatime and played them. Dusty, Lulu and Petula Clark were his favourites, though he quite liked The Carpenters in the early seventies.

'I just don't know what to do with myself ...,' sings Dusty, as we hit traffic jam after traffic jam. It's ironic he loved songs about everlasting love, yet his own life was so loveless.

We're late, of course. I thrust the classical CD into the undertaker's hand and rush inside. There are about 25 people there, mostly my dad's family, and a couple of his friends. I'm embarrassed. I wonder if anyone will bawl me out for never going to see him. I'm also not sure where to sit. Do I sit at the front with Chris and Eva? Or behind them, seeing as I was estranged? And what about Ian? Can you sit on the front row at a funeral when you've never even met the person who died?

It's soon all immaterial. I sit next to Chris and Eva, Ian sits next to me. I take one look at the coffin and cry. I've wished my dad dead on so many occasions; now he is. I'm not crying with grief. I hardly knew him. I'm crying because it's the end of an era. It's all over now.

In that coffin is the man who reduced me to a nervous wreck, made our lives hell and gave my mother more heartbreak that any human being can take. I'm sad because it wasn't different, because we weren't a happy family, because I didn't have one of those fantastic father–daughter relationships.

The vicar does a good cosmetic job. He talks of a man who loved animals, classical music, the outdoors ... there's no mention of loving his wife or his children. I cringe at the mention of him being a granddad. He refers to my mum and dad's divorce, how my dad and I drifted apart, and the wonderful care Chris and Eva gave him throughout his life.

I'm quiet on the way home. We're racing to get back for Jack after school. Ian tries to make me laugh with impressions of an uncle at the funeral who hummed and tapped his feet when the *Blue Danube* struck up during the service.

Jack comes bounding out of school and I want to hug him.

'Gerroff, Mum, what's up with yer?' Jack asks me, embarrassed.

I just want to pick him up and kiss him and then sit and look at him for ages. I've been through so many emotions today. I just want to consolidate for a minute and appreciate what I have. I want to look into his eyes and tell him how much I love him.

'Jack, I really love you,' I whisper.

'Oh, for goodness sake, Mum, not here, please! Mummy, please don't let my friends hear you!' he says, shocked, as boys come up and ask if he wants a quick game of football, while the mummies chat.

'Can I, Mum?' he asks, eyes shining.

Truth is, I'd much rather not hang around today. It's obvious I've been crying, but I can't refuse him a quick kickabout. I stand and watch as he tackles one boy, gets the ball and passes it, then calls for it to be passed back. He's beginning to look like a proper little boy now, not just a toddler growing up.

◆◆◆◆◆

He comes over to chat about the funeral.

'Did you go to say goodbye to your daddy?' asks Jack.

'Yes, Daddy and I went. Uncle Chris and Auntie Eva were there, too. They send their love,' I say.

'Did your daddy say goodbye to you?' asks Jack.

'No, sweetie, not today, he couldn't speak today,' I explain. 'He died last week, remember? When you die, you can't speak.'

'Well, you can, but not until you get to Heaven,' explains Jack earnestly. 'Problem is, we're not sure where your daddy is going, are we? Maybe you can't speak as often as you like in hell. Maybe you lose your tongue when you get to hell.'

It's at that moment I realize that if there is an afterlife, I don't wish my dad to end up in hell any more. I don't want payback for him any more.

I want him to rest in peace in the afterlife because he didn't seem to have much inner peace throughout his own life. I just hope that my forgiveness got him a place in Heaven, that by going to see him I made it clear that the past really didn't matter any more.

'Mummy, I've been thinking about your daddy today,' Jack informs me. 'He wasn't a good daddy to you, but my daddy's a good daddy to me, isn't he?'

'Ye-e-es?' I query, wondering what is coming next.

God, I hope it isn't a message from the other side already. I've always dreaded my dad dying and coming back to haunt me regularly.

'I'm going to be the best-ever daddy when I have a little boy of my own,' says Jack.

'How will you be a good dad, Jack?' I ask, intrigued.

'Well, for a start, Mum, I'll let my little boy have sweets

280

whenever he wants them, even for breakfast, and he can sit and eat them in front of the television.'

I fake horror.

'What? Sweets for breakfast?!' I exclaim. 'Surely he won't watch telly before school?' I ask.

As one who isn't allowed TV before school, Jack nods enthusiastically.

'Well, that's the next thing. If my little boy wants to stay at home instead of going to school, that will be OK,' he giggles, aware he's being very controversial.

'Little boys need to be allowed to do what they want, not always have their mummies and daddies tell them what to do. I'm going to be the best dad ever, and my boy will watch *Star Wars* all night and all day long. That's the kind of daddy I will be,' he adds, thrusting his jacket, book bag and drinking flask into my hand so he can go and take a corner.

◆◆◆◆◆

It's a daft conversation, but it puts everything into perspective. I look over at my champion footballer. He may be a dad one day. God, what kind of grandma will I make? Can't bake, can't sew, can't knit.

I feel tears welling as I hope Jack will be a dad. I hope he knows the love and joy of having a child of your own. The past is gone now. It made me who I am, for better or worse, but it's the present and the future that count now.

Titles of Related Interest

Saving Samantha,
by Samantha Weaver

Left To Tell,
by Immaculée Ilibagiza

You Can Have What You Want,
by Michael Neill

Ask and It Is Given,
by Esther and Jerry Hicks

Dr Lucy Atcheson's Guide to Perfect Relationships,
by Lucy Atcheson

Love Yourself … and It Doesn't Matter Who You Marry,
by Eva-Maria Zurhorst

Everything I've Ever Done That Worked,
by Lesley Garner